CW00662765

THE 19th CENTURY
UNDERWORLD

Underworld n. 1. the part of society comprising those who live by organised crime and immorality. 2. the mythical abode of the dead under the earth.

Oxford English Dictionary

THE 19TH CENTURY UNDERWORLD

Crime, Controversy and Corruption

Stephen Carver

PEN & SWORD HISTORY

AN IMPRINT OF PEN & SWORD BOOKS LTD.
YORKSHIRE – PHILADELPHIA

First published in Great Britain in 2018 by
PEN AND SWORD HISTORY
an imprint of
Pen & Sword Books Ltd
Yorkshire - Philadelphia

Copyright © Stephen Carver, 2018

HB ISBN 978 1 52670 754 3
PB ISBN 978 1 52675 167 6

The right of Stephen Carver to be identified as
Author of this work has been asserted by him in accordance
with the Copyright, Designs and Patents Act 1988

A CIP catalogue record for this book is available from the British Library.
All rights reserved. No part of this book may be reproduced or
transmitted in any form or by any means, electronic or
mechanical including photocopying, recording or
by any information storage and retrieval system, without
permission from the Publisher in writing.

Typeset in Times New Roman 11/13.5 by
Aura Technology and Software Services, India

Printed and bound in the UK by TJ International Ltd,
Padstow, Cornwall

Pen & Sword Books Limited incorporates the imprints of Atlas,
Archaeology, Aviation, Discovery, Family History, Fiction, History, Maritime,
Military, Military Classics, Politics, Select, Transport, True Crime, Air World,
Frontline Publishing, Leo Cooper, Remember When, Seaforth Publishing,
The Praetorian Press, Wharncliffe Local History, Wharncliffe Transport,
Wharncliffe True Crime and White Owl.

For a complete list of Pen & Sword titles please contact
PEN & SWORD BOOKS LIMITED
47 Church Street, Barnsley, South Yorkshire, S70 2AS, England
E-mail: enquiries@pen-and-sword.co.uk
Website: www.pen-and-sword.co.uk

or

PEN AND SWORD BOOKS
1950 Lawrence Rd, Havertown, PA 19083, USA
E-mail: uspen-and-sword@casematepublishers.com
Website: www.penandswordbooks.com

For Professor Roger Sales

Contents

Acknowledgements

Special thanks to Jonathan Wright and Laura Hirst at Pen & Sword for commissioning this project and their help and guidance, and to my amazing editor, Linne Matthews. I'd also like to thank the historians Jessica Cale and Geri Walton for sharing some of my research on their influential blogs, Dr George MacLennan for tracking down the Charles Hirsch reference, and Professor Roger Sales for his continued interest in my work and for getting me into much of this material in the first place. (I am basically your fault.) Finally, my heartfelt thanks to my wife and son, Rachael and Vincent, for your steadfast patience and support. I couldn't do any of this without you.

Table of Illustrations

Fig. 11. Robert Seymour, 'Burke Murdering Margery Campbell', Anon, *The Murderers of the Close: A Tragedy of Real life*, Cowie & Strange, London, 1829.

Fig. 12. 'Phiz' (Hablot Knight Browne), 'Resurrectionists', Camden Pelham, *The Chronicles of Crime; or, The new Newgate calendar*, Thomas Tegg, London, 1841.

Fig. 13. J.S. Agar, engraved from a drawing by A. Wivell, 'Sir Astley Paston Cooper, 1st Baronet', George Lawford, London, 1825.

Fig. 14. H. Anelay & E. Hooper, 'The Kinchin-Ken', G.W.M. Reynolds, *The Mysteries of the Court of London*, Vol. I, John Dicks, London, 1850.

Fig. 15. John Thomas Smith, 'Vendor of Matches', *Vagabondiana: Or, Anecdotes of Mendicant Wanderers through the Streets of London*, William P. Nimmo, Edinburgh, 1883 (original work published 1817).

Fig. 16. Anon, broadside, 'Ikey Solomon as printed from a drawing by the Lambeth Police', June 1830.

Fig. 17. Walter Thornbury, 'Field Lane about 1840', *Old and New London: A Narrative of Its History, Its People, and Its Places*, Vol. II, Cassell, Petter & Galpin, London, 1873.

Fig. 18. Anon, 'Flora Tristan', Messieurs de Balzac, Roger de Beauvoir, and Raymond Brucker, *Les Belles Femmes de Paris et de la Province*, Au Bureau, Paris, 1839–40.

Fig. 19. W.T. Stead, photographed by E.H. Mills, London, 1905.

Fig. 20. Anon, 'The Royal Saxe Coburg Saloon', *The New Swell's Night Guide to the Bowers of Venus*, J. Paul, London, c. 1847, British Library.

Fig. 21. S. Loudan, lithograph from a daguerreotype by Richard Beard, 'A Night House – Kate Hamilton's', Henry Mayhew, *London Labour and the London Poor*, Vol. IV, Griffin Bohn & Company, London, 1862.

Fig. 22. Edward Sellon, self-portrait, from *The Ups and Downs of Life*, Dugdale, London, 1867.

Fig. 23. Anon, daguerreotype, c. 1855. Anon, *Risque Collection*, 2005, Disc III (8) 'Early Risque, 1850–1900'.

Fig. 24. Anon, 'He sits in a beautiful parlour...' Henry Spencer Ashbee (as 'Pisamus Fraxi'), *Catena Librorum Tacendorum*, privately printed, London, 1885.

TABLE OF ILLUSTRATIONS

Chapter 1

Various Crimes and Misdemeanours

The concept of an urban 'underworld' triggers a specific set of associations. It is another world, deep beneath our own, like the mythical abode of the dead – a dark, distorted reflection of civilised society and all its institutions. Although essentially metaphorical, the underworld is universally represented as a black economy based around poverty, criminality and vice. It is also perceived as a physical space, an alien world of sex and violence often only a stone's throw from the prosperous parts of town.

Nowadays, the nineteenth-century underworld is almost entirely the product of popular culture. It is a simulation of historical reality, a gothic period drama in the tradition of the Hammer film and the police procedural. Usually Victorian London, the dark urban labyrinths are strangely familiar. Even if you've never read Dickens, you know what his world looked like. Infernal rookeries full of gin spinners, sneaksmen and Covent Garden nuns yawn out of the fog like the ruined bones of some ancient, primitive animal, while wraithlike urchins scatter with the rats as footsteps echo on the glistening cobbles. There is murder here, poverty, and immorality of every kind, all available for the price of a measure of gin, and if there is law here at all it is the brutal Darwinism of the human jungle. We've all seen *Ripper Street*, after all.

Our nineteenth-century ancestors were just as fascinated by the dark side of the street, but for different reasons. This was not history to them, but an attempt to make sense of the massive social upheaval of the world's first industrial nation and its growing urban underclass, particularly in the capital, 'the pariahs of the body social', according to the Reverend Thomas Beames, 'a distinct caste, yet not bound together otherwise than by common wants'.[1] And beyond this tone of earnest social investigation, there was always the sensational language of the penny blood. As the Chartist G.W.M. Reynolds wrote of Smithfield in the 1830s in his epic serial *The Mysteries of London*:

> hundreds of families each live and sleep in one room. When
> a member of one of these families happens to die, the corpse

is kept in the close room where the rest still continue to live and sleep. Poverty frequently compels the unhappy relatives to keep the body for days – aye, and weeks. Rapid decomposition takes place; – animal life generates quickly; and in four-and-twenty hours myriads of loathsome animalculae are seen crawling about.[2]

To Reynolds, London was defined by contrasts: 'With Civilisation does Vice go hand-in-hand,' he thundered. 'There are but two words known in the moral alphabet of this great city, for all virtues are summed up in the one, and all vices in the other: and those words are WEALTH. POVERTY.'[3]

This Shocking Catalogue of Human Depravity

London's population had grown at a phenomenal rate. At the time of the first census in 1801 it was 1,011,157, representing 13 per cent of the entire population of England. The irregular enclaves of eighteenth-century urban sprawl were falling to unfettered development, beginning along the main roads into the centre. In the East End, Thames-side land gave way to St Katherine's Dock, the East and West India Docks, the New Docks at Wapping and the Commercial Docks at Rotherhithe – all feeding international commerce and creating new communities of dockers, chandlers and seamen, as well as the mudlarks, rat catchers and scuffle-hunters who quietly relieved the ships of the odd bit of cargo, and the publicans and prostitutes that served the sailors. In the West End, the great chase to the south of Primrose Hill became Regent's Park, Trafalgar Square was cut out of the last open space, and John Nash re-imagined London as a classical city under the patronage of the Prince Regent.

But just as the gambling, womanising Prince George led a notorious double life, the proud stucco façades of Regent Street were also designed to conceal sprawling inner-city slums; districts like Whitechapel, a dark hinterland close to the docks but only a few streets over from the Square Mile, the Devil's Acre in Westminster, Jacob's Island in Bermondsey, and the rookeries of St Giles and the Seven Dials. One need not walk far from the prosperous clubs of Pall Mall, for example, to enter a maze of filthy courts and allies packed with desperate humanity and teeming with crime and disease. As Reynolds later wrote, 'The most unbounded wealth is the neighbour of the most hideous poverty; the most gorgeous pomp is placed in strong relief by the most deplorable squalor; the most seducing luxury is only separated by a narrow wall from the most appalling misery.'[4]

Crime, like the population, was also rising. It was impossible to walk any crowded street in broad daylight without running the risk of having one's pockets expertly picked by kids trained by felonious parents, while shops and market stalls were routinely robbed, the perpetrators well skilled in losing themselves in rat runs and back alleys if spotted. Organised criminal gangs were rife, and housebreaking so common that no dwelling left unattended was safe. Forgery, gambling and prostitution were epidemic, and careless associations frequently led to blackmail, assault and theft, if not murder. More than half the wheat sold in London markets, meanwhile, was converted into alcohol, and gin shops and flash houses abounded. The streets were teeming with beggars, vagrants and paupers. What social control there was had not moved with the times, and outside London's two ancient citadels, Westminster and the City, a patchwork of uncoordinated parishes and county boards, many of which still operated under medieval statutes, could not contain the avalanche.

In the second half of the eighteenth century, Henry Fielding's Bow Street office in Westminster set the standard by which all other law enforcement efforts should have been measured. But even after the Gordon Riots of 1780, no government dared to challenge perceived notions of individual 'freedom' by seriously considering a coordinated policing system. William Pitt's Solicitor General, Sir Archibald Macdonald, tried it in 1785, but such was the level of political outrage that Pitt was forced to abandon the proposed London and Westminster Police Bill. Instead, the City relied on one thousand watchmen – known as 'Charleys', having been originally raised during the reign of Charles II – who patrolled during the hours of darkness with a rattle, a stick and a lamp, loudly proclaiming their presence and thus warning any lawbreakers of it well in advance of their arrival. Regular patrols operated only in the City, which accounted for no more than about a tenth of the population, while most of the notorious rookeries and thieves' kitchens into which felons effortlessly escaped were close to but outside City boundaries.

Crime continued to rise. It was as if Pitt's failed bill had provoked the gangs to step up their assault on property. The Bow Street Runners and a newly formed armed street patrol were pushed to breaking point, while politicians became increasingly concerned that the alarming levels of urban theft and violence might augur a coming revolution like the one in France. The government response was a private member's bill that became, after moderate opposition, the Middlesex Justices Act of 1792. The Act set up seven new Public Offices, in addition to Bow Street, to which three stipendiary magistrates were attached, with six constables appointed to each office, all under the brief of the Home Secretary. The offices were strategically placed, with one in Southwark, two in Westminster, and four established in Holborn, Finsbury, Whitechapel and Shadwell. The City remained exempted and the Charleys endured. Over a generation before Reynolds described 'the city of fearful contrasts', one of the newly created magistrates at the Worship Street office in Finsbury Square set about exploring the 'present state of the morals of the Metropolis'.[5] Patrick Colquhoun, Scottish merchant, statistician, magistrate and twice Lord Provost of Glasgow, was about to launch a war on crime.

While Colquhoun's fellow magistrates were largely content to keep to their office hours and to take the £400 salary, Colquhoun hit the ground running. Using the spare time between his morning and evening shifts, he began researching the relationship between poverty and crime, establishing soup kitchens for the needy and compiling a register of known receivers of stolen goods. He also liaised with the philosopher and social reformer Jeremy Bentham, the founder of modern Utilitarianism, and in 1796 he published the study for which he is probably best known, *A Treatise on the Police of the Metropolis*. The book's lengthy subtitle explains its purpose: *Containing a Detail of the Various Crimes and Misdemeanours By which the Public and Private Property and Security are, at present, injured and endangered: And Suggesting Remedies for their Prevention*. Using his years of experience, the data he had gathered, and his applied knowledge of Benthamite social theory, Colquhoun made a persuasive argument for a centrally organised police force in the capital, backed up by a detailed and cross-referenced analysis of street level poverty and crime employing some startling statistics. What made this treatise particularly impressive for its time was its author's focus on public protection and the prevention of crime, rather than simply thief-taking and punishment; being essentially a product of the European Enlightenment, Colquhoun called this a 'New Science'. In an age in which it was generally believed that the freedom of the individual would be compromised by any such state intervention, this was a highly contentious argument. One anonymous pamphleteer, in fact, spoke for many of Colquhoun's critics when he denounced the proposed police force as 'an engine of despotism and inquisition'.[6]

It was not just Colquhoun's theories that were electric, but his evidence. Much of the book is an itemised demographic analysis of the London underworld, at that point the most thorough study ever undertaken. This investigation immediately seized the public imagination, as well as defining the parameters of social exploration throughout the next century. Colquhoun could also write, and he knew the value of a powerful opening statement. Before going into detail, therefore, he began with a summary of his primary categories, 'the various classes of individuals who live idly and support themselves by pursuits that are either criminal, illegal, dissolute, vicious, or depraved', including the estimated numbers. To late Georgian Londoners, these were nothing short of incredible:

ESTIMATE

Of Persons who are supposed to support themselves in and near the Metropolis by pursuits either criminal – illegal – or immoral.

1. Professed Thieves, Burglars, Highway Robbers, Pick-pockets, and River Pirates, who are completely proselyted; – many of whom have finished their education in the Hulks, and some at Botany-Bay. – N.B. There will be a considerable increase of this class on the return of Peace, now estimated at about – 2,000

2. Professed and known Receivers of Stolen Goods, of whom eight or ten are opulent – 60

3. Coiners, Colourers, Dealers, Venders, Buyers, and Utterers of base money, including counterfeit Foreign and East India Coin; 3,000

4. Thieves, Pilferers, and Embezzlers who live partly by depredation, and partly by their own occasional labour: 8,000

5. River Pilferers, viz, Fraudulent Lumpers, Scuffle-hunters, Mud-larks, Lightermen, Riggers, Artificers and Labourers in the Docks and Arsenals: 2,500

6. Itinerant Jews, wandering from street to street, holding out temptations to pilfer and steal, and Jew Boys crying Bad shillings, who purchase articles stolen by Servants, Stable Boys, &c. &c. generally paying in base Money – 2,000

7. Receivers of Stolen Goods, from petty Pilferers, at Old Iron Shops, Store Shops, Rag and Thrum Shops, and Shops for second-hand Apparel, including some fraudulent Hostlers, small Butchers and Pawnbrokers – 4,000

8. A class of suspicious Characters, who live partly by pilfering and passing Base Money – ostensibly Costard mongers, ass drivers, Dustmen, Chimney sweepers, Rabbit sellers, Fish and

Fruit sellers, Flash Coachmen, Bear baiters, Dog keepers, (but in fact, Dog Stealers), &c. &c. – 1,000

9. Persons in the character of menial Servants, Journeymen, Warehouse Porters, and under Clerks, who are entrusted with property, and who defraud their employers in a little way, under circumstances where they generally elude detection – estimated at about 3,500

10. A class of Swindlers, Cheats, and low Gamblers, composed of idle and dissolute Characters, who have abandoned every honest pursuit, and live chiefly by fraudulent transactions in the Lottery; as Morocco Men, Ruffians, Bludgeon Men, Clerks, and Assistants during the season; who at other times assume the trade of Duffers, Hawkers and Pedlars, Horse Dealers, Gamblers with E O Tables at Fairs, Utterers of Base Money, Horse Stealers, &c. &c. – 7,440

11. Various other classes of Cheats not included in the above – 1,000

12. Fraudulent and dissolute Publicans who are connected with Criminal People, and who, to accommodate their companions in iniquity, allow their houses to be rendezvous for Thieves, Swindlers, and Dealers in Base Money – 1,000

13. A class of inferior Officers belonging to the Customs and Excise, including what are called Supernumeraries and Glutmen; many of whom connive at pillage as well as frauds committed on the Revenue, and share in the plunder to a very considerable extent: principally from their inability to support themselves on the pittance allowed them in the name of salary: estimated at about 1,000

14. A numerous class of Persons who keep Chandler's Shops for the sale of provisions, tea, and other necessities, to the poor. – The total number is estimated at ten thousand in the metropolis, a certain proportion of whom, as well as small Butchers and others, are known to cheat their customers (especially those to whom they give a little credit) by false weights, for which, excepting in the parish of Mary-le-bone, there is no proper check: 3,500

15. Servants, male and female, Porters, Hostlers, Stable Boys, and Post Boys. &c. out of place principally from ill behaviour and loss of character, whose means of living must excite suspicion – at all times about 10,000

16. Persons called Black Legs, and others proselyted to the passion of Gaming, or pursuing it as a Trade, who are in the constant habit of frequenting houses opened for the express purpose of play, of

which there are at least forty in Westminster, where Pharo Banks are kept, or where Hazard, Rouge et Noir, &c. are introduced. Of these, five are kept in the houses of Ladies of Fashion, who are said to receive £50 each rout, besides one eighth of the profits: seven are Subscription houses; five have customers particularly attached to them; and thirteen admit foreigners and every idle and dissolute character, who are either introduced or known to belong to the fraternity of Gamblers; where a supper and wines are always provided by the proprietors of the house for the entertainment of their customers: 2,000

17. Spendthrifts – Rakes – Giddy Young Men inexperienced and in the pursuit of criminal pleasures – Profligate, loose, and dissolute Characters, vitiated themselves and in the daily practice of seducing others to intemperance, lewdness, debauchery, gambling, and excess; estimated at 3,000

18. Foreigners who live chiefly by Gambling 500

19. Bawds who keep Houses of ill fame, Brothels, Lodging-Houses for Prostitutes: 2000

20. Unfortunate Females of all descriptions, who support themselves chiefly or wholly by prostitution: 50,000

21. Strangers out of work who have wandered up to London in search of employment, and without recommendation, generally in consequence of some misdemeanour committed in the Country; at all times above – 1000

22. Strolling Minstrels, Ballad Singers, Show Men, Trumpeters, and Gipsies – 1,500

23. Grubbers, Gin-drinking dissolute Women, and destitute Boys and Girls, wandering and prowling about in the streets and by-places after Chips, Nails, Old Metals, Broken Glass, Paper, Twine, &c. &c. who are constantly on the watch to pilfer when an opportunity offers – 2,000

24. Common Beggars and Vagrants asking alms, supposing one to every two streets – 3,000

Total 115,000.[7]

Furthermore, the author of 'this shocking catalogue of human depravity' also estimated the cost of these thefts, from pockets picked to ships and dockyards raided, at £2 million a year in London alone. But the Government paid little serious attention to Colquhoun's call for a unified 'Police Board', while some Tory MPs dismissed him as dishonest and, because the treatise had been translated into French, unpatriotic. He was therefore snubbed when the coveted post of Chief Magistrate at Bow Street came up, the job going to Richard Ford. The private sector, however, was all ears.

As Colquhoun had noted in the fifth point of his 'Estimate', the Thames had its own pirates. As the biggest trading port in the world, thousands of commercial ships competed for moorings on woefully outdated quays along the river, offering numerous opportunities for petty larceny. 'Lumpers' were the men who unloaded cargo, some of which found its way into the poacher's pockets of the loose clothes they wore, ostensibly to keep them cool during all that heavy lifting, while the lightermen who transferred goods between ships and shore usually left something in the barge. 'Scuffle-hunters' hung around the wharves and warehouses under the pretence of finding labouring work to take advantage of the general chaos of ships unloading. They would pinch or pick up the contents of burst sacks and broken crates that had either been dropped or intentionally thrown over the side by lumpers to the scavenging 'mudlarks' wading in the moorings below. The anonymous author of *The Criminal Recorder* ascribes this colourful epithet – which Colquhoun also uses – to 'the disputes and scuffles arising about who should secure most plunder from broken packages'.[8] Rat-catchers, meanwhile, would raid the holds they were supposed to be clearing of vermin. This level of individually small-scale thieving was considered by the perpetrators to be an essentially victimless crime, but what they viewed as a drop in the ocean of trade passing through the Port of London amounted annually to £500,000.

John Harriot, a retired seafarer and adventurer who had fought for the East India Company and once lived among Native Americans, contacted Colquhoun and Bentham for help with the problem, having been ignored by the Lord Mayor of London. Colquhoun persuaded the West India Planters Committees and the West India Merchants to fund a Thames Marine Police headquarters with fifty officers at Wapping New Stairs in 1798 – sweetened with a modicum of public money – himself acting as Superintending Magistrate and Harriot as Resident Magistrate. The swashbuckling Harriot was a natural self-publicist, and used any success on the water to remind journalists and politicians that his 'River Police' was the first organised police force in England. The Thames River Police Act followed in 1800, largely because of the lobbying of Colquhoun and Bentham backed up by Harriot's showmanship, the private venture becoming a public concern. Its high profile also contributed to Ford's foundation of the Bow Street Horse Patrol in 1805, a team of sixty riders protecting the travellers on the principle roads into the capital that finally rid Hounslow Heath of highwaymen.

Just as the Chartists would later fail to achieve basic democratic rights that we nowadays take for granted, politicians and members of the public remained largely resistant to the kind of centralised police force we rely on today. The common criticism was that it would destroy the freedom of the individual that reformers like Colquhoun and Bentham argued it would protect, the latter position made more unpalatable by Colquhoun's enthusiasm for the French style of law and order. The national predilection for *laissez-faire* therefore endured, leading to select, private sector policing, which, while demonstrating to a certain extent the efficacy of Colquhoun's 'New Science' of criminology, was there to protect vested interests. That this also increased the protection of ordinary Londoners was essentially a fortunate coincidence.

But the more things change, the more they stay the same. Although the Horse Patrol finally brought the era of the English highwayman to an end and the River Police secured the docks, crime elsewhere in the metropolis continued unabated, still with no tactical means to bring it under control. Riverside districts like Bermondsey and Wapping were particularly lawless. Prostitution was rife, and savage disputes between drunken seamen were common, while the success of the River Police in scuppering the traditional livelihood of the scuffle-hunters and their brethren fostered a passionate hatred of authority among the locals. As long as this rage was contained within its own community, Londoners paid it no mind, while tacitly accepting that these were not areas you walked through at night. This relative indifference, however, was shortly to be challenged.

The City's Sacred Victim

The Ratcliffe Highway was an ancient road running east out of the City to Limehouse, dating back to at least Roman times, close to the new London Docks and forming the unofficial Wapping boundary. Cutting its way through Tower Hamlets in the heart of the East End, the road had long held a bad reputation, being close to the old Execution Dock in Wapping where pirates were left hanging to rot. It is listed in Stow's 1598 *Survey of London* as 'a continual street, or filthy strait passage, with alleys of small tenements, or cottages ... inhabited by sailors' victuallers, along by the river'[9] – 'a most dangerous quarter' according to Thomas De Quincey.[10] Just before midnight on Saturday, 7 December 1811, Timothy Marr shut up the family draper's shop at number twenty-nine while his wife nursed their baby, having just sent the maid, Margaret Jewell, out for oysters. Margaret had gone from shop to shop trying to find shellfish, and returned later than intended to a locked and darkened house. Hearing footsteps behind her, she panicked and hammered on the door with such violence that the watchman and the Marrs' neighbour, the pawnbroker John Murray, both came to her aid. Murray noticed that the back door in the adjoining yard was hanging open and went to investigate. What he found was a scene of hellish slaughter. The entire family and their apprentice had been murdered, their throats cut, and their heads beaten with such savagery that, he told the examining magistrate at Shadwell police office, brains were 'knocked out, and actually dashed, by the force of the murderous blow, across the ceiling'.[11] Nothing appeared to have been stolen; there was cash in the till and £152 untouched in a bedroom drawer. The River Police were summoned, and the first officer on the scene, Charles Horton, found a heavy maul – a long-handled shipwright's hammer – leaning against a chair, covered in blood and hair. There were two sets of bloody footprints at the back of the shop. The trail went cold at Pennington Street, which ran parallel to the Highway off Wapping Lane. The family were known to be quiet, well liked and honest, and the crime felt all the more horrific for the lack of obvious motive.

The shock of the brutal crime travelled far beyond the East End, stoked by lurid reports in the penny press. As De Quincey later wrote, 'It would be absolutely impossible adequately to describe the frenzy of feelings which, throughout the next fortnight, mastered the popular heart, the mere delirium of indignant horror in some, the mere delirium of panic in others.'[12] Then, twelve days later, on Thursday, 19 December, the killer or killers struck again, bludgeoning and cutting the throats of John and Elizabeth Williamson, the landlord and landlady of the King's Arms in New Gravel Lane, and their servant, Bridget Harrington. Witnesses claimed to have seen two men running up Ratcliffe Highway, one with a limp. Again, the reason for the attack was unclear. John Williamson was robbed of a watch, but that could hardly have been the motive for such brutality.

The age of the modern serial killer was dawning with the new century. There were questions in the House, while sensational accounts of the murders circulated widely through balladmongers, chapbooks and broadsides. Not since the days of the plague and the fire had Londoners felt so vulnerable. The watchmen of Shadwell were all sacked and replaced with younger men, sales of rattles went through the roof, and local parishes offered rewards of between fifty and a hundred guineas for information. Not only did the murder grip the public imagination to an extent not seen again until the 'autumn of terror' in 1888, it exposed the desperate need for a proper police force, a cause quickly picked up by the *Morning Chronicle*. Responding to the mood of the times, a Parliamentary Select Committee was established to examine the 'State of the Watch'. Although the Government failed to act on its damning findings, the 1812 Committee became another significant step on the long and winding road that led inexorably to Robert Peel's 1829 Metropolitan Police Act, a turning point that prefaces the Victorian age as much as the Great Reform Act of 1832.

There was one survivor of the King's Arms massacre – the lodger John Turner, who had escaped from an upstairs window and raised the alarm. His testimony suggested more than one assailant was involved, and he got a decent look at one of them. 'I went downstairs, and I saw one of the villains cutting Mrs. Williamson's throat, and rifling her pockets,' he told the Shadwell magistrates, describing the man as 'about 6 feet in height, dressed in a genteel style, with a long dark loose coat on'.[13] Although he did not fit this description, nor could Turner positively identify him, suspicion fell on John Williams, a lodger at the Pear Tree public house on Cinnamon Street. Williams was a regular in the King's Arms and also connected with Timothy Marr, both men having served together on the East India Company ship *Dover Castle.* The evidence was largely circumstantial. The original murder weapon – the maul – had been traced to the sea chest of a sailor called John Petersen, who had left it at the Pear Tree while away at sea, and Williams was deemed to have had access to it. He was also reported as having money after the attacks but not before (although he had pawned some clothes and had a ticket to prove this), and his washerwoman claimed to have received torn and bloodstained shirts that Williams ascribed to a brawl after a card game. Despite his protestations of innocence, he was remanded to Clerkenwell Gaol, where he apparently committed suicide on 28 December, the night before he was to again appear before the Shadwell magistrates, by hanging himself with his scarf. The hearing proceeded without him, and clearly eager for a swift resolution, the court declared Williams the sole perpetrator of both crimes, taking his suicide as an admission of guilt. Followed by great crowds, his body, along with the recovered murder weapons – the maul, a ripping chisel and an iron crowbar – was drawn by cart along the Highway, past the scene of both murders, to the crossroads of Back Lane and Cannon Street Road. There, as De Quincey described, 'in obedience to the law as it then stood, he was buried in the centre of a guadrivium, or conflux of four roads (in this case four streets), with a stake driven through his heart. And over him drives for ever the uproar of unresting London!'[14]

The profane burial – which has notable parallels with vampire folklore – was medieval. Suicide was deemed an affront against the laws of God and man, and the self-murderer could not thus be buried in consecrated ground. Crossroads were intended to confuse the unquiet spirit, which would be unable to choose a path, while the stake served to both desecrate the corpse and prevent its soul from rising on Judgement Day. But as De Quincey understood, the ritual meant more than that. As Peter Ackroyd explained, 'Williams became part of London; having marked a track through a specific locality, his name was buried in the urban mythology surrounding "the Ratcliffe Highway murders". He became instead the city's sacred victim, to be interred in a formalised and ritualistic manner.'[15] Just as the Metropolitan Police Act seems to herald the coming of the Victorians, the end of the Regency and the tone of the century to come, so does the Ratcliffe Highway murderer, although as P.D. James and T.A. Critchley have demonstrably argued, Williams almost certainly didn't act alone, if he acted at all.

'As the story developed,' they wrote, 'it became clear that the system of 1811 had done no more than pronounce a confident, convenient and ghoulish judgement on a corpse, while leaving the core of the Ratcliffe Highway murders wrapped in continuing mystery.'[16] There are two other notable persons of interest. Cornelius Hart, who knew Williams (though he denied it), had done some carpentry work for Marr on the day of the murders, and claimed to have lost a chisel. Margaret Jewell confirmed that her master had searched the shop at Hart's request that night but had not found it, although John Harriot spotted it at the scene in the morning and logged it as evidence. Hart was concerned enough about Williams's arrest to enquire about it at the Pear Tree, although whether this was the act of a concerned friend or a worried accomplice remains a mystery. Evidence and eyewitness accounts also suggested there were two perpetrators, and James and Critchley believed that one of them was very probably a seaman called William Ablass, who had sailed with Williams on the *Roxburgh Castle*, another East India ship, and was briefly detained as a suspect. Both had been implicated in a failed mutiny, and as Marr, Williams and Ablass had all sailed together at various times, it has been suggested that there was some bad blood; Ablass was also known to be a violent man. Ablass and Williams were drinking together at the King's Arms on the night of the second murder, and Ablass fit Turner's description of the killer much more than Williams. He also walked with a limp, thus fitting the description of one of the men seen running along the Highway after the Marrs were slaughtered, and had no alibi for either murder.

Either way, for Londoners, the nineteenth century began in earnest not with victory at Waterloo but in another orgy of blood and horror, just as it would close.

Chapter 2

A Corinthian's Guide to the Metropolis

On 11 December 1821, an estimated 22,000 people gathered on Hungerford Common to watch a bare-knuckle fight between Tom Hickman, the 'Gaslight Man', and the 'Bristol Butcher', Bill Neate. Hickman was the son of a Dudley blacksmith who had made his name in the London 'Fancy' (the Prize Ring); they called him the 'Gas' or 'Gaslight' Man because he punched out lights. 'This is the grave-digger,' he was apt to declare when intoxicated, brandishing his right fist: 'this will send many of them to their long homes.'[1]

Neate really was a butcher from Bristol, a gentle giant whose temper was as measured as Hickman's was brash and cocky. He was trained by Tom Belcher, one of the greats, whose 'elegance of attitude, and scientific precision,' wrote Pierce Egan in his *Boxiana*, 'stands unrivalled.'[2] Belcher, like his mentee, was a Bristol man, as was the legendary Tom Cribb, the retired world champion, who was also in the crowd. Because of its famous sons – Tom Belcher's late brother Jem had been equally, if not more successful in his day – the Bristol Fancy was seen as a great rival by the London set, and this was something of a grudge match. Tension was further ramped up by the Gas Man who, like Muhammad Ali, liked to wind up his opponents. 'What, are you Bill Neate?' said he, when first clapping eyes on the West Country slugger. 'I'll knock more blood out of that great carcase of thine, this day fortnight, than you ever knock'd out of a bullock's!'[3] The writer and philosopher William Hazlitt, who attended the fight – his first – and famously contributed an account of it entitled 'The Fight' to the *New Monthly Magazine*, was appalled at such impertinence. 'Even a highwayman, in the way of trade,' he wrote, 'may blow out your brains, but if he uses foul language at the same time, I should say he was no gentleman.'[4]

The Fight

This was long before gloves, Queensbury Rules, and the foundation of the Amateur Athletic Association made boxing respectable. Although prize fighting was very much the national sport, crossing boundaries of class and race, and taken to symbolise the most noble virtues of the English spirit (during the Napoleonic wars it was a vital part of anti-French propaganda), it was at this point illegal. The law was, admittedly, vague, with indictments split between charges of assault, illicit bookmaking, and riotous and unlawful assembly. But even though the Prince Regent himself was a notable patron of the sport, the official view was encapsulated by the Tory MP and judge Sir Edward Hyde East, who argued strongly against legalisation. Such bouts, he said, 'are exhibited for the sake of lucre, and are calculated to draw together a number of idle and disorderly people … such meetings have a strong tendency on their nature to a breach of the peace.'[5] Contrived disqualification, cheating and match-fixing was not uncommon, while the absence of much formal organisation meant that blatant mismatches often resulted in fatalities. Promising fighter Sandy McKay, for example, was beaten to death by Simon Byrne in 1830, while Owen Swift killed three men in the ring, the last, William 'Brighton Bill' Phelps, having also once sent an opponent to his grave. When the two killers met on Melbourne Heath in Essex in 1838, bets were placed, reported *The Annual Register*, 'that neither of the combatants would survive'.[6] The fight lasted eighty-five rounds, and Swift was subsequently convicted of manslaughter after Brighton Bill died of his injuries.

The timing and location of fights was therefore a closely guarded secret, and Hazlitt's account begins with him hanging around outside the Hole in the Wall in Holborn hoping to catch some inside information. This is followed by a mad dash on the coach box of the Bath Mail, meeting up with other pilgrims along the way, including the notorious John Thurtell (named as 'Tom Turtle' in the text), a promoter of fights between not just men but dogs, cocks, bears and badgers, who claimed to have seen the result of the contest in a dream. After a missed night's sleep by the fire in a tavern – there were no rooms to be had at any price – Hazlitt walked the last 9 miles to the designated spot, as hundreds of gigs, carts and carriages flew by and locals flooded in on Shanks's pony.

The ring itself was not raised, merely a square of clean grass within the ropes. At close to one o'clock the fighters arrived with their seconds and bottle holders, and Neate threw his hat into the ring. The umpire then called the men to the scales. Neate had a 2 stone advantage over his opponent; he was taller, too, but the odds still favoured the Gas Man and an estimated £200,000 was wagered upon the outcome, a staggering amount equivalent to almost £8.5 million today. The umpire then read the 'Articles', the seven rules laid down in 1743 by Jack Broughton, the 'Captain of Boxers', originally written to better regulate bouts conducted at his amphitheatre in Hanway Road:

1. That a square of a yard be chalked in the middle of the stage; and every fresh set-to after a fall, or being parted from the rails, each second is to bring his man to the square and place him opposite to the other; and till they are fairly set-to at the lines, it shall not be lawful for one to strike the other.
2. That in order to prevent any disputes as to the time a man lies after a fall, if the second does not bring his man to the side of the square within the space of half a minute he shall be deemed a beaten man.
3. That, in every main battle, no person whatever shall be upon the stage, except the principals and their seconds; the same rule to be observed in the bye-battles, except that in the latter Mr. Broughton is allowed to be upon the stage to keep decorum, and to assist gentlemen in getting to their places; provided always he does not interfere in the battle; and whoever presumes to infringe these rules to be turned immediately out of the house.[7] Everybody is to quit the stage as soon as the champions are stripped, before they set-to.
4. That no champion be deemed beaten, unless he falls coming up to the line in the limited time; or that his own second declares him beaten. No second is to be allowed to ask his man's adversary any questions or advise him to give out.
5. That in the bye-battles, the winning man to have two-thirds of the money given, which shall be publicly divided upon the stage, notwithstanding any private agreement to the contrary.
6. That to prevent disputes, in every main battle, the principals shall, on the coming on the stage, choose from among the gentlemen present two umpires, who shall absolutely decide all disputes that may arise about the battle; and if the two umpires cannot agree, the said umpires to choose a third, who is to determine it.
7. That no person is to hit his adversary when he is down, or seize him by the ham, the breeches, or any part below the waist; a man on his knees to be reckoned down.[8]

These rules were subsequently updated after Owen Swift's prosecution as the first 'London Prize Ring Rules'. Hickman won the toss for the sun. The men shook hands, then the umpire cried 'Set to!' and the fight began.

There were no gloves. Fights could last for dozens of irregularly timed rounds, until one combatant could no longer continue, both collapsed from exhaustion (in which case the umpire often declared a winner based on which group of supporters was least likely to turn on him), one became so disorientated that he committed a disqualifiable foul, such as punching below the belt, or a 'maw-worm' – a magistrate – broke up the gathering. Despite Hickman's skill in that department, knockouts were not popular, and unless the fallen man was completely incapacitated it was likely to only decide the winner of the round. Spectators wanted protracted exhibitions of skill, stamina, bravery and bloodshed, and expected the seconds to keep their men on their feet until they were beaten so badly they were physically incapable of continuing. (It was said of Hickman, for example, that if his hands were cut off he would still fight on with the stumps.) Head-butting, tripping (but not kicking), wrestling, throwing and holding were all generally permissible, as was hair pulling, hence it was common for fighters to keep their hair close cropped or to shave their heads completely. Rounds could go on up to a quarter of an hour, usually ending when one of the boxers was knocked down or simply collapsed, or in a clinch and a fall, whoever landed on top being adjudged to have won the round. The fighters would then take a thirty-second break in their corner before 'coming to scratch', the line in the middle of the ring, to indicate their willingness to carry on.

Hickman put Neate down in the first round and many a Cockney who had seen the Gas Man turn out a light declared it was all over bar the shouting. But Neate was not so easily cowed, although he was notably cautious in the second round, keeping his guard high. Hickman could not get past it until they struck together and both fell, neither having the advantage. This was repeated in the next round, but in the fourth Hickman misjudged a right hook and left himself open to a devastating left that 'made a red ruin of that side of his face'. Hickman went down, his right eye already swelling and closing. He rallied after a couple more rounds and both men slogged each other to the ground repeatedly, 'smeared with gore' and 'stunned, senseless, the breath beaten out of their bodies', but always coming once more to the scratch, until Neate taught Hickman humility in the twelfth round, with a punch that sent him flying. 'I never saw any thing more terrific than his aspect just before he fell,' wrote Hazlitt. 'All traces of life, of natural expression, were gone from him. His face was like a human skull, a death's head, spouting blood.' Remarkably, the fight continued for another six rounds, until the Gas Man was 'so stunned' that 'his senses forsook him, and he could not come to time' and Neate was declared the winner.[9]

Coming around, the dazed Gas Man asked, 'Where am I?' Bill Neate shook him cordially by the hand, as carrier pigeons were released bearing news of his victory to his wife and commiserations to Mrs Hickman. Tom

Cribb, not a man to gush, was heard to remark that the Bristol Butcher had done 'pretty well'.

The Gas Man did not do so well after that. For him, the fight marked the beginning of the end. He had never lost a bout before, and he bitterly resented losing this one. Reports circulated that he had died from his injuries, but he in fact retired to Dudley, becoming landlord of the Adam and Eve and turning even more to the drink. On 10 December 1822, almost a year to the day after his fateful encounter with Neate, he turned his chaise over trying to overtake a coal waggon. He was returning from a fight between Josh Hudson and Tom Shelton with his friend and fellow pugilist Joe Rowe. Hickman and his passenger were both thrown under the wheels and killed instantly.

Hazlitt's travelling companion, 'Tom Turtle', fared no better. When 'The Fight' was written, John Thurtell's name – thinly disguised for legal purposes – was one to drop as a mover and shaker from the Fancy. By the time George Borrow claimed to have met him in his memoir *Lavengro* (1851), it had much darker connotations. An ex-Marine and the son of a former mayor of Norwich, Thurtell was typical of the Fancy, a dandy with a rough edge, making a living by ducking and diving – a bit of training, fight promotion and gambling. He was a 'blackleg' in the vulgar tongue, a gamer and a sharper who made his living off the turf, the cockpit and the prize ring, so called because of their preference for high boots, and for game cocks, whose legs were always black. But a couple of years after Hazlitt met him, business was not going well. Gambling debts were mounting, and when the family bombazine warehouse burned down under suspicious circumstances the insurers were not disposed to meet the claim. Thurtell therefore moved from the low-level criminal activity that went necessarily with illegal boxing matches to robbery and murder.

Thurtell set his sights on one William Weare, a solicitor at Lyon's Inn, a dodgy Inn of Chancery inhabited by lawyers fallen very low or struck off the rolls altogether, whose principle income came from a more successful career as a gamester, a billiard shark and a bent promoter. Enlisting the help of two bankrupts well known in the Fancy – Joseph Hunt, a failed publican, and William Probert, a disgraced spirit merchant who'd graduated from debtor's prison to hard time in Brixton – Thurtell lured Weare out of London to spend a weekend playing cards at Probert's cottage at Gill's Hill in Radlett. It was assumed that Weare would be carrying a large stake, as he was known to do, and the plan was to relieve him of it. On Friday, 24 October 1823, Thurtell and Weare left London by gig, with Hunt secretly despatched to a prearranged spot to waylay the carriage. Unfortunately, Hunt missed the rendezvous and Thurtell was forced to do the job himself. He shot Weare in the face with a cheap brace of pawnshop 'muff pistols' (derringers), but the wound was not fatal and Weare made a run for it. Thurtell chased him down and used a pistol for a club, cutting his throat with a penknife for good measure. The accomplices met at Probert's cottage and divided up Weare's money and possessions (fifteen quid, a gold watch and a few coins), dumping the body in a pond on the property.

Realising that he'd dropped the murder weapons at the scene, Thurtell returned to the fatal spot with Hunt the next day, encountering a road mender. He claimed that he'd turned his gig the night before and lost some personal items. He did not find them, but the road mender did, and five days later the trio were arrested. Probert turned King's evidence and got off (he was later hanged for horse theft), Hunt was transported as an accessory, and Thurtell went to the gallows, being afterwards dissected. It was a popular murder, and the trial was covered in detail by the press, much of the interest generated not only by the sheer brutality of the crime but by the revelation of the murky sporting underworld from which the main players came. Thomas De Quincey cites Thurtell in his satiric treatise of 1827, 'On Murder Considered as One of the Fine Arts', Pierce Egan interviewed him in prison and subsequently wrote two broadsheet accounts, and children sang an eerie little rhyme on the subject that went:

> His throat they cut from ear to ear
> His brains they punched in;
> His name was Mr. William Weare,
> Wot lived in Lyon's Inn.

So pervasive was the killing, that Thurtell's wax effigy was displayed in Madame Tussaud's 'Chamber of Horrors' well into the twentieth century.

Life in London

It was in every way appropriate that the writer that twice interviewed Thurtell at Hertford Gaol was Pierce Egan. When the two men met,

Thurtell said in greeting, 'I have often read many of your sporting accounts with great pleasure,' although he denied killing anybody.[10] Egan was the greatest sporting journalist of his generation, and even if he and Thurtell had not previously met in person, they definitely moved in the same circles. In 'The Fight', in fact, with the classical allusion, the immediacy of the account, and the energetic celebration of masculinity and national character, Hazlitt was emulating Egan's established style as a ringside reporter.

Egan was the son of a road mender. Details of his birth are obscure, but it seems likely that he was born in or near Dublin in 1774, moving to London with his family as a young child and growing up in Holborn. He received little formal education, becoming a printer's apprentice in 1786, when his name first appears, listed in the Record of Apprentices at Stationer's Hall.[11] Later, in *The Life of an Actor* (1825), Egan wrote about a printer's apprentice called Peregrine Proteus who acquired his love and knowledge of literature by reading everything that came through the shop. This was almost certainly an autobiographical portrait, and the literate young Irishman rose through the ranks in the shifty world of the publisher/booksellers of Seven Dials, compositing, proofreading and contributing to chapbooks and broadsides – a jobbing hack in the age of Austen, unconnected with fashionable literary society. But it was not until his forties that he made his name writing about the Prize Ring, the Turf and the Chase for James Harmer's *Weekly Despatch*. His hugely popular series of articles, collectively entitled *Boxiana, or, Sketches of ancient and modern pugilism; from the days of the renowned Broughton and Slack, to the heroes of the present milling æra!* 'By One of the Fancy' ran from 1812 to 1820, comprising a history of the sport, portraits of famous fighters, and detailed coverage of individual bouts. Having mastered the then rare skill of shorthand, his round-by-round accounts have a sense of visceral vitality that still strikes the reader today, and like Dickens after him, he also used this ability to write fast and accurately to gain some extra income as a Parliamentary reporter. And when he saw a dodgy fight, he knew how to improvise – for example when covering the somewhat disappointing mill just outside Banbury in 1813 between the 'Lancashire Hero' Jack Carter and the American ex-slave Tom Molineaux, the 'Black Ajax', who had once given Tom Cribb a run for his money but was now tragically going to seed. When Molineaux was 'completely told out' reported Egan, instead of winning the battle his 'drooping antagonist *swooned away* in all the style of a modern fine lady'. Having no climax to report, Egan instead describes the seconds flapping about in a doomed attempt to get their man back on his feet:

> Poor BOB GREGSON, agitated beyond description, at seeing Lancashire thus trampled on, with disgrace went up to CARTER, exclaiming, 'Jack, Jack, what be'est thee at, get up and fight man!' But BOB might as well have sung psalms to a dead horse! CARTER some little time afterwards raised up his head, feebly observing – *stop a bit! stop a bit!!* And whether by ACCIDENT, *design*, or with an intent to conclude this *farce* in style, we are not in the secret to unfold – but a disciple of Æsculapius stepped up, and in the twinkling of an eye, pulled out his *lancet*, and bled CARTER, to the great astonishment of his friends and the spectators in general.

But it was to no avail, and Egan concluded that the 'man of distinction' who had offered to keep Carter's clothes neatly in his carriage 'ordered them to be thrown out with disdain and contempt'.[12]

The extravagant typographical flourishes were not typical of the period, and were something of a textual trademark, as was the journalist's enthusiastic use of 'Flash', the linguistically deviant slang anti-language of the street folk and the criminal underworld. Egan was by all accounts well liked as a down-to-earth journalist and boxing aficionado, and by hanging around with the clientele – churls, moon men, swells, half-swells, plungers, blowens and bunters, blacklegs, buzgloaks, bucks and bloods – he gained a privileged knowledge of their ways and words that would serve him well on the streets and as a writer.[13] In Egan's world, one might even spy the Prince Regent ringside, and as for the canting crew, they were not a collectively menacing underclass so much as characters to be cultivated, and with whom one might have a bit of a spree.

Egan went beyond the Prize Ring with the brothers Cruikshank with the launch of their epic illustrated serial, *Life in London or The Day and Night Scenes of Jerry Hawthorn, ESQ. and his elegant friend Corinthian Tom in their Rambles and Sprees through the Metropolis*. The project was originally envisioned as a collaborative set of prints depicting London street life by Isaac Robert Cruikshank and his elder brother, George (Dickens's future artist, then making his name in the illustrative tradition of James Gillray). Egan, with his unparalleled knowledge of the sporting set and the underworld, was recruited to provide the commentary. The series appeared in 1820 in twenty parts at a shilling each and in book form in 1821. It adopts the familiar form of the uninitiated provincial tourist following the sophisticated guide, and chronicles the urban adventures of Corinthian Tom, his country cousin Jerry Hawthorne, and Bob Logic, a middle-aged scholar with a taste for wine and women. It is an exuberant Gonzo safari of participant observation with little attempt to conceal that the worldly-wise rake Tom was George Cruikshank (before he signed the pledge), Jerry his brother, and Bob Logic, Egan.

There are obvious parallels with the 'New Journalism' of the 1960s. Anticipating Tom Wolfe and Hunter S. Thompson, Egan blended the thoroughness of journalism with the cunning of a novelist, treating himself as a character in the story while also offering scholarly opinions and essayistic asides, including copious footnotes, as well as cataloguing a journey of debauchery and excess. Egan was immensely proud that he talked the talk and walked the walk. He understood immediately that both were related, and he was highly respected for doing so by a criminal underclass that had denounced one of their own, the transported convict James Hardy Vaux, for appending a 'Vocabulary of the Flash Language' to his *Memoirs*, published in 1819. But while Vaux was accused of blowing the gaff by fellow criminals, what Egan demonstrated was admiration.

Being neither fully an outsider nor a respectable man of letters, Egan was uniquely placed to mediate between the urban underclass and his fundamentally bourgeois readership, who experience the underworld voyeuristically, without ever leaving the drawing room. 'The author, in consequence, has chosen for his readers a Camera Obscura View of London,' he explains in his introductory remarks, 'not only from its safety, but because it is so snug, and also possessing the invaluable advantage of SEEING and not being seen.'[14] But although he wanted to share his privileged knowledge, Egan, as a social explorer, preferred the company of whores and bad guys to the honest poor and the artisan labourers. He does, nonetheless, argue his corner as a social realist, based upon his unique linguistic verisimilitude and commitment to widening participation. In replying to the accusation that he uses 'a little too much of the slang' he explains that 'I am anxious to render myself perfectly intelligible to all parties. Half of the world are up to it; and it is my intention to make the other half down to it. LIFE IN LONDON demands this sort of demonstration,' because 'A kind of cant phraseology is current from one end of the Metropolis to the other.' In fact, he uses what he calls 'the (strong) language of real Life' himself because his intention is to report, without embellishment, 'living manners as they rise'.[15] This he backed up by 'revising and correcting' a new edition of Francis Grose's *Classical Dictionary of the Vulgar Tongue* (originally published in 1785).

Like Grose before him, Egan goes beyond the exclusive and obscure *argot* of the criminal underworld as decoded by James Vaux, making 'Flash' interchangeable with demotic London street slang, the evolving language of the Cockneys. This can be observed in the following episode, which is accompanied by an illustration entitled '*Taking "BLUE RUIN" at the "SLUICERY" after the "SPELL is broke up"*'[16]:

This is a fine sketch of real life ... TOM is *sluicing* the *ivory*[17] of some of the unfortunate heroines with *blue ruin* ... JERRY is in *Tip Street*[18] upon this occasion, and the *Mollishers*[19] are all *nutty*[20] upon him, putting it about, one to another, that he is a *well-breeched Swell*.[21] The left-hand side of the Bar is a 'rich bit' of LOW LIFE; and also points out the depravity of human nature. *Gateway* PEG[22] has just entered for her *ninth* glass. This '*lady-bird*,'[23] who has not only disposed of many an *unruly customer*[24] in her time, but *buzzed*[25] them into the bargain, is taking her drops of *jackey*[26] with OLD MOTHER BRIMSTONE, who has also *toddled*[27] in to have a *flash of lightning*[28] before she goes to *roost*. Both these fair ones[29] (who are as *leaky*[30] as sieves, from turning their money as fast as they get it into liquor) are *chaffing*[31] at 'FAT BET,' in consequence of the pretended *squeamishness* of the latter to TOM, that she had a great objection to every sort of *ruin*, no matter how it was *coloured*,[32] since she had been once *queered*[33] upon that suit ... Mother BRIMSTONE, an old *cadger*,[34] and a *morning-sneak* COVESS,[35] who is pouring some *blue ruin* down the baby's throat to stop its crying, has borrowed the *kid*,[36] in order to assist her in exciting charity from the passing stranger in the street ... The *Cove* and *Covess*[37] of the *Sluicery*, with faces full of *gammon*,[38] and who are pocketing the *blunt*[39] almost as fast as they can count it, have just been complaining of the *wickedness* of the times, and the difficulty of '*paying their way*'. SWIPY BILL, *a translator of Soles*,[40] who has been out for a day's *fuddle*,[41] for fear his money should become too troublesome to him, has just called in at the *gin Spinners*[42] to get rid of his last *duce*[43] by way of a *finish*, and to have another drop of *blue ruin* ... *Kit Blarney*, who has just got rid of her *sprats*,[44] which had been 'up all night' and rather the *stronger*[45] for the day or two she had had them in her possession, though she had assured her customers all the day they were as fresh as a *nosegay*, as she had just got them from Billingsgate, has dropped in for the purpose of lighting her short pipe, to get a *drap of the* CRATURE,[46] and to get rid of the *smell* of the fish, which remained about her olfactory nerves! The above scene may be nightly witnessed after the SPELL is dissolved, but in much more depraved colours than is here presented. It is, however, LIFE IN LONDON.[47]

'Seeing Life' is Egan's clarion call, life in all its social aspects, from the aristocratic exclusivity of the assembly rooms in St James's to the gin palaces of the East End, London characteristically doubled in nature and defined by contrasts. This is presented as a suitable sport for the young gentleman, and the city is laid out as a vast text containing all human knowledge available to those who are willing to learn how to decipher it. 'Indeed, The Metropolis is a complete CYCLOPÆDIA,' he wrote, 'where every man of the most religious or moral habits, attached to any sect, may find something to please his palate, regulate his taste, suit his pocket, enlarge his mind, and make him happy and comfortable ... In fact, every SQUARE in the Metropolis is a sort of map well worthy of exploring, if riches and titles operate as a source of curiosity to the visitor. There is not a street also in London, but what may be compared to a large or small volume of intelligence, abounding with anecdote, incident, and peculiarities.'[48] The image most often adopted is one of a colourful theatrical performance, in which 'the scene changed as often as pantomime'.[49]

In *Life in London*, the underworld is never represented by Egan as the menacing, gothic space it became to the Victorians. If he does wander somewhere scary, he does not hang around. This is particularly apparent in the inevitable Newgate Prison episode. Egan knows his audience will not let him avoid the place, but he is clearly torn between his essentially upbeat approach to the sport of seeing and his own basic humanity when confronted with an execution. First words fail him, which does not happen very often. 'It is a truly afflicting scene,' he confesses, 'and neither the PEN nor the PENCIL, however directed by talent, can do it adequate justice.' He then cuts and runs: 'Our heroes were offered a complete view of the prison from the top of it; but this offer was declined, in consequence of TOM'S urging the want of time, on account of having some business to transact in the City. The TRIO hastily quitted the gloomy falls of Newgate, once more to join the busy hum and life of society.'[50]

By denying nasty realities like the so-called 'Bloody Code', with almost 200 capital crimes in the statute books, while similarly caring little about the honest poor, Egan advances the belief that it is the underclass of society that has all the fun. 'It is, I am quite satisfied in my mind, the LOWER ORDERS of society who really ENJOY themselves,' says Bob to Tom in the 'All-Max' in East Smithfield, a flash ken – probably the Coach and Horses on Nightingale Street – that Egan juxtaposes with Almack's of St James's, which Jerry finds less interesting and Bob Logic avoids altogether. The appeal is in the social freedom; gender, race and class are meaningless, being all part of the same merry dance. 'The parties paired off according to fancy; the eye was pleased in the choice, and nothing thought of about birth and distinction,' writes Egan. 'All was happiness, every body free and easy, and freedom of expression allowed to the very echo … Lascars, blacks, jack tars, coal-heavers, dustmen, women of colour, old and young, and a sprinkling of the remnants of once fine girls, &c., were all jigging together.'

Class exclusivity surfaces only briefly. When Egan's trio enters the All-Max the music stops like a scene from an Italian Western (they are assumed to be 'beaks'), until a young tart reassures the clientele (in Flash, naturally), that 'the gemmen had only dropped in for to have a bit of a spree'.[51] This subculture remains, most importantly, exotic, particularly sexually. Playing MacHeath, Bob Logic has a woman on each arm (Flashy Nance and African Sall), and is crossing all the social boundaries with his polygamous dalliance outside his own class and racial group, before finally surrendering to the place completely and disappearing into the kaleidoscopic background. When Tom and Jerry decide enough is enough, Logic is nowhere to be found, a sailor 'about three sheets in the wind' explaining that 'if it was the gentleman in the green barnacles their honours wanted, as it was very likely he had taken a voyage to Africa, in the Sally, or else he was out on a cruise with the Flashy Nance.'[52]

The lower classes are presented as individuals in *Life in London*, a very different approach to its Victorian descendants. In Egan's underworld, everyone has a name and a history, one as colourful as the other, and it is an exuberant, unrestrained, ultimately unclassifiable social space where *beau monde* meets *demi monde*. In Egan, to be 'down-and-out' can be 'down-and-in', and the bare-knuckle fighter and the daring criminal are people with whom to be seen. This risqué sense of underworld *chic* was not carried over into the discourse of the Victorian social explorers. To them, the *demi monde* became the simply demographic. There was rarely, if ever, room for the individual in the rhetoric of the earnest Victorian select committees, journalists, novelists, sociologists and moral crusaders, intent as they were on recording and solving societal problems, transforming the chaotic city into a social text that, unlike Egan's, was not to be celebrated in its diversity but quantified and ordered.

Life in London became the seismic literary event of the 1820s – its influence can clearly be felt in Dickens's *Pickwick Papers* – and its crazy language was further disseminated through dozens of knock-offs, unlicensed theatrical adaptations and novelty souvenirs such as mugs, prints and handkerchiefs. What Egan had done was to make Flash fashionable, and thus common cultural currency well beyond its original social boundaries. In his *Roundabout Paper* 'De Juventute', even William Makepeace Thackeray admits to receiving a clip round the ear from a schoolmaster for reading *Life in London* while pretending to study his Greek dictionary, although he rejects the text (though not the pictures by his friend Cruikshank) as an adult and Victorian, as a vulgar part of a more primitive age, 'London in the ancient times, more curious than amusing.'[53]

By the end of the decade, Egan seemed to have calmed down. In his 1828 sequel to *Life in London*, entitled *The Finish to the Adventures of Tom, Jerry and Logic, in Their Pursuits through Life in and out of London*, he breaks Tom's neck in a riding accident, while his mistress, Corinthian Kate, dies of the drink. Logic similarly succumbs to his excesses, while Jerry settles down to a quiet life in the country. It is unclear whether Egan understood early that times, and values, were changing, or was just reclaiming his earlier text from the plagiarists and taking it in an unexpected direction; he does note in *The Finish* that there were at least sixty-five counterfeit editions of the original in print. Tom and Jerry moved to the New York stage and had a lethal cocktail named after them, which Hanna and Barbera appropriated for their *Tom and Jerry* cartoons, keeping, in some small way, the playful anarchy of Egan's colourful Regency romp alive to this day.

Chapter 3

Bad Books for Bad People

From 1833 to 1836, a few years after the *Life in London* craze had run its course, another series of articles 'representing living manners as they rise' appeared in the *Morning* and *Evening Chronicle*, the *Monthly Magazine*, the *Carlton Chronicle* and *Bell's Life in London*. Dickens's *Sketches by Boz* were subtitled 'Illustrative of Every-day Life and Every-day People', and in his preface to the first collected edition of 1836, the young author explained that 'His object has been to present little pictures of life and manners as they really are; and should they be approved of, he hopes to repeat his experiment with increased confidence, and on a more extensive scale.'[1] He did, of course, go on to repeat and refine the experiment for the rest of his life.

In common with Egan, a popular writer of the preceding age who was well worth emulating, Dickens's *Sketches* were also about 'seeing life'. Dickens, however, was already signalling a level of social realism that was largely absent from *Life in London*, with the exception of Egan's lexicography. Contemporary commentary on the *Sketches* tends to repeatedly focus upon Dickens's range and realism as something very original. 'Things are painted literally as they are,' wrote John Forster, 'it was a picture of everyday London at its best and worst,'[2] while Walter Bagehot called Dickens 'a special correspondent for posterity'.[3] An indication that Dickens was, indeed, a very new broom, can be seen in his depiction of Newgate Prison in the *Sketches*, a place upon which Egan, as previously noted, could not bear to look. In his description of a condemned man's last night on earth, Dickens did not flinch:

> The deep bell of St Paul's strikes – one! He heard it; it has roused him. Seven hours left! He paces the narrow limits of his cell with rapid strides, cold drops of terror starting on his forehead, and every muscle of his frame quivering with agony. Seven hours! He falls upon his knees and clasps his

hands to pray. Hush! what sound was that? He starts upon his feet. It cannot be two yet. Hark! Two quarters have struck; – the third – the fourth. It is! Six hours left ¼ A period of unconsciousness succeeds. He wakes, cold and wretched … He is the condemned felon again, guilty and despairing; and in two hours more he will be dead.[4]

In a piece that anticipates 'Fagin's last night alive', Dickens may already have *Oliver Twist* in view. Similarly, prototypes of Sikes and Nancy are present in 'The Hospital Patient' (in which a fallen woman beaten almost to death repents of her sins but refuses to incriminate the lover that has assaulted her); the voice of the Artful Dodger can be heard in 'Criminal Courts', and the character of Mr Bumble is already forming in 'The Election for Beadle'.

This new realism did not, however, extend to linguistic anthropology. Dickens does, on occasion, represent an accent. 'S'elp me God, gen'lm'n, I never vos in trouble afore – indeed, my Lord, I never vos,' prates the pickpocket in 'Criminal Courts' for example, but apart from the single usage of the term 'prigging', this prototype for the Artful Dodger doesn't use any Flash.[5] And as for the doomed 'Hospital Patient', she speaks Standard English. Reviewing Dickens's next project, *The Posthumous Papers of the Pickwick Club*, the playwright John Poole did suggest in the *Athenaeum* that it contained more than a 'dash of grammatical Pierce Egan', but he just meant Sam Weller's Cockney accent.[6] Dickens did not, at that point, appear to have any particular public objections to Flash, but neither was he a dedicated follower of fashion.

Nix My Doll Pals, Fake Away

The next author to seriously engage with Flash creatively was the 'Lancashire Novelist' William Harrison Ainsworth, in his breakout novel *Rookwood* (1834). This was a zesty gothic romance enlivened by the inclusion of the Georgian highwayman Dick Turpin as a supporting character, along with a crew of intemperate gypsies, which established many of the common Turpin legends, including the famous 'Ride to York'. *Rookwood* was not, however, the first significant romanticisation of the now extinct highwaymen. The politician and bestselling novelist Edward Bulwer-Lytton had got there first with *Paul Clifford* in 1830. This was a politically charged novel that was short on adventure but notable for its protagonist's bold summation of the radical philosophy of William Godwin's *Enquiry Concerning Political Justice* (1793), spoken from the dock against the Bloody Code and social deprivation: 'I come into the world friendless and poor – I find a body of laws hostile to the friendless to the poor! To those laws hostile to me, then, I acknowledge hostility in my turn. Between us are the conditions of war.'[7]

Ainsworth's Dick Turpin is no more historically accurate than Lytton's romantic hero, of course, other than in his dialogue. This verbal authenticity stemmed from a desire to use Flash poetically. In his preface to the 1849 edition of *Rookwood*, Ainsworth explained his original project:

> It is somewhat curious, with a dialect so racy, idiomatic, and plastic as our own cant, that its metrical capabilities should have been so little essayed. The French have numerous *chansons d'argot* ... We, on the contrary, have scarcely any slang songs of merit. With a race of deprecators so melodious and convivial as our highwaymen, this is the more to be wondered at. Had they no bards amongst their bands? ... The barrenness, I have shown, is not attributable to the poverty of the soil, but to the want of due cultivation.[8]

The only recent and, indeed, decent 'genuine canting-song' was to be found, he wrote, in the 'effusions of the illustrious Pierce Egan'. Ainsworth thus set out to fulfil this need, packing *Rookwood* with thirty original songs, being particularly proud of 'Jerry Juniper's Chant', 'a purely flash song, of which the great and peculiar merit consists in its being utterly incomprehensible to the uninformed understanding'.[9] The first verse goes like this:

> In a box of the stone jug I was born,
> Of a hempen widow the kid forlorn,
> *Fake away.*
> And my father, as I've heard say,
> *Fake away.*
> Was a merchant of capers gay,
> Who cut his last fling with great applause,
> *Nix my doll pals, fake away.*[10]

This can be translated as:

> I was born in a prison cell,
> The neglected child of a hanged man's widow,
> *Carry on stealing.*
> And my father, as I've been told,
> *Carry on stealing.*
> Was an excellent dancer,
> Whose last dance was bravely done from the end of a rope,
> *Never mind, my friends, carry on stealing.*

Unlike Egan, however, the Mancunian Ainsworth's connection to the underworld was strictly academic. In an interview given to the *World* magazine in 1878, he answered the question 'Did you interview thieves and Gypsies to gain authentic knowledge of "flash patter"?' by admitting:

> Not at all. Never had anything to do with the scoundrels in my life. I got my slang in a much easier way. I picked up the Memoirs of James Hardy Vaux — a returned transport. The book was full of adventures, and had at the end a kind of slang dictionary. Out of this I got all my 'patter'.[11]

Authentically acquired Flash or not, critics lined up to praise the revelation that was *Rookwood*. Ainsworth's songs were quoted at length in *Fraser's Magazine* and hailed as the most original feature of the book, towering in standard over *Paul Clifford* because Lytton had 'no sense of humour'.[12] The sincerest form of flattery followed, with numerous imitations rushed to print, inspiring a run of highwayman penny dreadfuls that flourished well into the 1860s.

Such critical accolades were not quite unanimous. Dickens's friend and later biographer John Forster, reviewing for the *Examiner*, found the slang 'loathsome', continuing:

> Turpin, whom the writer is pleased with loving familiarity to call Dick, is the hero of the tale. Doubtless we shall soon see Thurtell presented in sublime guise, and the drive to Gad's Hill described with all pomp and circumstance. There are people who may like this sort of thing, but we are not of that number.

> The author has, we suspect, been misled by the example and success of 'Paul Clifford', but in 'Paul Clifford' the thieves and their dialect serve for illustration, while in 'Rookwood' the highwayman and his slang are presented as if in themselves they had some claim to admiration.[13]

This was really the crucial point. Just as Egan had before him, Ainsworth *liked* the criminal classes, as least in concept. 'Turpin was the hero of my boyhood,' he confessed, while also admitting that he wrote with 'an eye rather to the reader's amusement than his edification'.[14] Once again, Flash was simply fun, and *Rookwood* was close enough to the days of Tom and Jerry to still catch their wave. This was not so when Ainsworth returned to the Newgate Calendars five years later, serialising the exploits of the Georgian criminal Jack Sheppard, briefly famous in the days of Defoe for several daring prison escapes, before being finally hanged in 1724 at the ripe old age of twenty-two.

The Newgate Controversy

Jack Sheppard began its serial run in *Bentley's Miscellany* in January 1839. Dickens's serial *Oliver Twist* was at that point coming to a conclusion in the same magazine, and for four months they appeared concurrently. As both stories were illustrated by George Cruikshank and concerned young boys being drawn in to the criminal underworld, they became implicitly connected in the minds of their original and massive audience, as well as many of their critics, most notably Thackeray. Ainsworth's serial was a tremendous success, and by the autumn there were eight theatrical versions of *Jack Sheppard* running concurrently in London. At the Adelphi, the actor and playwright J.B. Buckstone had astutely included many of the Flash songs from *Rookwood*, each performance concluding with a raucous encore of *Nix My Dolly, Pals* by the full cast and audience. Sir Theodore Martin ('Bon Gaultier') later wrote of this period:

> Nix My Dolly travelled everywhere, and made the patter of thieves and burglars 'familiar in our mouths as household words.' It deafened us in the streets, where it was as popular with the organ-grinders and German bands as Sullivan's brightest melodies ever were in later days. It clanged at midday

from the steeple of St. Giles ... it was whistled by every dirty
guttersnipe, and chanted in drawing-rooms by fair lips, little
knowing the meaning of the words they sang.[15]

Once more, the Flash was the fashion. But times and tastes and morals had
changed since *Rookwood*, and Egan had now also fallen from grace, dismissed
as obscene according to the new early Victorian taboos of representation.
John Forster, for instance, in a damning review of *Jack Sheppard*, suggested
that public decency had not been so threatened 'since *Tom and Jerry* crowded
the theatres with thieves and the streets with brawlers'.[16]

Thackeray struck early with his satirical 'anti-Newgate' novel
Catherine, A Story in *Fraser's* credited to the pen of 'Ikey Solomons,
Esq., Jr.' (the pseudonym playing on the name of an infamous Regency
criminal). *Catherine* was the story of Catherine Hayes, taken from one of
the nastiest of the original Newgate Calendars, *The Malefactor's Bloody
Register*, in which the wife of a London tradesman plotted his murder with
her lover and her illegitimate son. After getting Mr Hayes very drunk, the
two men killed him with an axe and dismembered the body, disposing
of it in a pond in Marylebone Fields, except for the head, which they
threw in the Thames in the hope of making identification impossible. The
head turned up however, and was placed on display; first on a pole in a
churchyard, and later preserved in a glass of spirits in the hope someone
might recognise it. Catherine Hayes claimed her husband was in Portugal,
but his friends were suspicious. Eventually, her accomplices confessed,
and the trio were executed. The two men were hanged in chains and Hayes
was burned at the stake at Tyburn in May 1726, as a wife killing her
husband was petty treason under law. In a particularly unpleasant twist
of fate, the flames caught so quickly that the executioner was not able to
strangle the condemned as was customary, and the unfortunate woman
was burned alive.

Thackeray's purpose was not to sensationalise, however, but to horrify
and shame the whole of the so-called 'Newgate school' (in which he
included Dickens) and their audience. 'The public will hear of nothing but
rogues,' he lamented, stopping the story in the third chapter to rant about the
state of popular literature and the social implications, considering Lytton,
Ainsworth and Dickens to be equally guilty of romanticising crime:

> the only way in which poor authors, who must live, can act
> honestly by the public and themselves, is to paint such thieves

as they are: not dandy, poetical, rosewater thieves; but real downright scoundrels, leading scroundrelly lives, drunken, profligate, dissolute, low; as scoundrels will be.[17]

When *Jack Sheppard* was released as a novel in October, the *Athenaeum* published a long article on 'those literary peculiarities, which we consider to be signs of the times' under the heading of a review of Ainsworth's novel, arguing that a decline in national standards of taste, intellect and morality was distressingly apparent: 'should an ambassador from some far distant country arrive on our shores for the purpose of overreaching us in a convention, we know not where he could find a better clue to the infirmities of the national character, than in the columns of our book advertisements.'

The anxiety was that literature no longer set the standard, but merely reacted to the popular market. 'In the present age,' the anonymous reviewer continued, echoing Thackeray's point about public taste in *Catherine*, 'writers take their tone from the readers, instead of giving it; and in which more pains are taken to write down to the mediocrity of the purchasing multitude … *Jack Sheppard*, then, is a bad book, and what is worse, it is a class of bad books, got up for a bad public.'[18] Henry Fielding and John Gay were then invoked as examples of the morally and aesthetically appropriate way to use criminal biography in a work of literature, although the general reader was assumed to be too dense to appreciate the difference between these and something from Egan or Ainsworth:

> without a prompt and exercised intelligence in the reader, without a familiarity with the noble and the beautiful, the irony is lost, the spirit is overlooked, the *Beggar's Opera* becomes a mere *Tom and Jerry*, and *Jonathan Wild* another *Jack Sheppard*.[19]

Oliver Twist was exempted from the Newgate school, but concern was expressed as to whether it might be popular for the wrong reasons, Dickens's readers excited by his 'strong flavour' rather than his 'undercurrent of philosophy'. The article ended with a lengthy quotation of Flash dialogue easily extracted from *Jack Sheppard*, beginning, '"Jigger closed!" shouted a hoarse voice in reply. "All's bowman, my covey. Fear nothing. We'll be upon the bandogs before they can shake their trotters!"'[20] 'Such is the "elegant and polite literature" which leads authors on their way to fortune and to fame in this the middle of the nineteenth century,' concluded the anonymous reviewer.[21]

Forster's review in the *Examiner* went a step further, moving the argument from one of taste and literary merit to what we would now recognise as the 'effects theory' of popular culture, concern being expressed that unlicensed theatrical adaptations could be disseminating moral corruption amongst the working classes, inciting copycat juvenile delinquency. 'Poisonous work is done by means of more cunning doses,' wrote Forster, 'nor are the ways of licentiousness, for those classes into whose hands such a book was in that case likely to fall, paved with such broad stones.'[22]

All hell finally broke loose the following year when the former Member of Parliament for Surrey, the legendarily eccentric Lord William Russell, had his throat cut while he slept by his valet, François Courvoisier. His Lordship had caught his man stealing the plate, and demanded his immediate resignation. Rather than give up his position without a reference, Courvoisier had murdered his master and inexpertly staged a robbery. He was caught after the stolen money was found poorly concealed in the house, but, it was alleged in the press, he had claimed he set upon the plan after reading *Jack Sheppard*. Although the story was never substantiated, the *Examiner* returned to Forster's original review, which foretold such a disaster, and ran a smug editorial denouncing *Jack Sheppard* as 'calculated to familiarize the mind with cruelties and to serve as the cut-throat's manual', and concluding that 'If ever there was a publication that deserved to be burnt by the common hangman it is "Jack Sheppard".'[23] You couldn't buy publicity like that. The book continued to sell, while the so-called 'Newgate Controversy' raged like thunder and its author became a literary pariah, black-balled at the Trinity Club and forced to withdraw from candidacy for the Athenaeum Club because of the certainty of defeat and further public humiliation. Although the two men had been close, Dickens distanced himself from Ainsworth, who never wrote another Newgate novel, though his preface to the 1849 edition of *Rookwood* did not exactly indicate repentance.

It was Thackeray's voice that was most prominent in the formulation of a new Victorian literary theory of morality and representation. In his article in *Fraser's Magazine* about the execution of Courvoisier, 'Going to see a man hanged', he sent Dickens a message concerning *Oliver Twist*:

> Boz, who knows life well, knows that his Miss Nancy is the most unreal fantastical personage possible; no more like a thief's mistress than one of Gessner's shepherdesses resembles

a real country wench. He dare not tell the truth concerning such young ladies ... not being able to paint the whole portrait, he has no right to present one or two favourable points as characterising the whole: and therefore, in fact, had better leave the picture alone altogether.[24]

When the drop fell, Thackeray, of course, turned away. He developed this argument the following month in *The Times* in a review of a new edition of the works of Henry Fielding:

The world does not tolerate now such satire as that of Hogarth and Fielding, and the world no doubt is right in a great part of its squeamishness; for it is good to pretend to the virtue of chastity even though we do not possess it ... It is wise that the public modesty should be as prudish as it is; that writers should be forced to chasten their humour, and when it would play with points of life and character which are essentially immoral, that they should be compelled, by the general outcry of incensed public propriety, to be silent altogether.[25]

Ainsworth was again judged and found wanting. 'Vice is never to be mistaken for virtue in Fielding's honest downright books,' Thackeray had continued, whereas, in *Jack Sheppard*, 'Ainsworth dared not paint his hero as the scoundrel he knew him to be; he must keep his brutalities in the background, else the public morals will be outraged, and so he produces a book quite absurd and unreal, and infinitely more immoral than anything Fielding ever wrote. Jack Sheppard is immoral actually because it is decorous.'[26] This was an impossible proposition, apparently calling for a literary realism denuded first of any subject that might cause offence to the public morals.

Dickens's champions, such as the formidable critic R.H. Horne, argued that only their man had actually performed such a representational miracle. In his influential collection of essays on contemporary writers, *The New Spirit of the Age*, published in 1844, Horne explained Dickens's originality:

Mr. Dickens is one of those happily constituted individuals who can 'touch pitch without soiling his fingers'; the peculiarity, in his case, being that he can do so without gloves; and, grasping its clinging blackness with both hands, shall yet retain no soil, no ugly memory. That he is at home in a wood – in green lanes and all sweet pastoral scenes – who can doubt it that has ever

34

dwelt among them? But he has also been through the back slums of many a St. Giles's.[27]

On the matter of any superficial similarity between Dickens the moralist and satirist and the author of a 'flash Newgate Calendar hero', Horne patiently explained that Dickens's 'secret' was 'grievously misunderstood, except in the matter of dialect, by Mr. Ainsworth in his "Jack Sheppard", which was full of unredeemed crimes'.[28] This secret, according to Horne, was to depict human violence and depravity realistically when needs must, unflinchingly in fact, but always only for an illustrative, moral purpose. In comparison, his only positive nod in Ainsworth's direction was an acknowledgement of his linguistic realism.

Dickens, himself, went further in his public response to his critics. This appeared in the preface to the third edition of *Oliver Twist* in 1841, and emphatically rejected romantic depictions of 'canterings upon moonlit heaths' (a clear reference to Ainsworth's highwaymen) in favour of the 'every-day existence of a Thief'.[29] *Oliver Twist* was therefore absolutely not the Newgate romance that Thackeray never tired of accusing it to be, but instead Dickens's 'humble attempt' to 'dim the false glitter surrounding something which really did exist, by shewing it in its unattractive and repulsive truth'. His attitude to Flash slang, which had been irrevocably yoked to the unrealistic portrayal of criminality in popular fiction, was now very much part of his rejection of the criminal romance. The linguistic accuracy of the Newgate novel had to be divorced from the realistic depiction and investigation of the criminal class in what he calls its 'miserable reality', therefore, he explained:

> No less consulting my own taste, than the manners of the age, I endeavoured, while I painted it in all its fallen and degraded aspects, to banish from the lips of the lowest character I introduced, any expression that could possibly offend; and rather to lead to the unavoidable inference that its existence was of the most debased and vicious kind, than to prove it elaborately by words and deeds. In the case of the girl, in particular, I kept this constantly in view.[30]

Dickens described Nancy as a 'prostitute' in this preface, but he never called her that in the main text. She also, he admitted, had to be particularly well-spoken. In fact, all the underworld dialogue was suitably tidied up. When Bill Sikes is introduced, for example, 'He then, in cant terms, with which his whole conversation was plentifully besprinkled, but which would be quite unintelligible if they were recorded here, demanded a glass of liquor.'[31]

This is not to say there is no slang, but, as in the *Sketches*, there is little or no Flash. When underworld argot is (sparingly) used, it is largely the invention of the author, such as the piratical oaths of Bill Sikes like 'Wolves tear your throats!' and 'Cut my limbs off one by one!'

But this was not because of the self-censorship advocated by Thackeray. Quite the reverse. Dickens didn't use Flash when describing the dark side of contemporary London, because in his view this rather trivial language was a distraction from the real issues of urban poverty and crime with which he wanted his audience to intellectually engage and to bear witness. Equally, the fad for Flash instigated first by Egan, then revived by Ainsworth, had become central to the Newgate novel debate and forever associated with romantic eulogies to prostitutes, thieves and murderers. Although Egan significantly contributed to the development of nineteenth-century social investigation, especially his understanding of the language of the streets, Ainsworth's nostalgic anti-heroes notionally contributed very little culturally, other than stimulating the debate Dickens was about to win. That said, Ainsworth's essentially romantic approach to historical villains can still be seen in film and fiction – Captain Jack Sparrow, for example, is Dick Turpin by other means – but that's another story. Thackeray's apparent condemnation of all depictions of the underworld, whether too romantic or too realistic, a third way as it were, was ultimately of even less value in this context. Dickens, however, refused to look away. Instead, he twisted the heads of his bourgeois audience towards the squalor and depravation that surrounded them, demanding that they look, and if at all possible, that they try to do something to alleviate all that bloody misery.

Dickens knew he was walking a tightrope – literary reputations, notably Ainsworth's, had already been destroyed – nonetheless, 'Truth' remained the keyword in his preface to *Oliver Twist*. Capitalised and multiply repeated in the final paragraph, Dickens positively bellowed the word at his audience and critics, frustrated at having to explain what had been so obvious to him his whole life, and hammering his realism home through his justification of the depiction of Nancy:

> It is useless to discuss whether the conduct and character of the girl seems natural or unnatural, probable or improbable, right or wrong. IT IS TRUE. Every man who has watched these melancholy shades of life knows it to be so. Suggested to my mind long ago – long before I dealt in fiction – by what I often saw and read of, in actual life around me, I have, for years, tracked it through many profligate and noisome ways,

and found it still the same. From the first introduction of that poor wretch, to her laying her bloody head upon the robber's breast, there is not one word exaggerated or overwrought. It is emphatically God's truth, for it is the truth ... It involves the best and worst shades of our common nature; much of its ugliest hues, and something of its most beautiful; it is a contradiction, an anomaly, an apparent impossibility, but it is a truth. I am glad to have had it doubted, for in that circumstance I find a sufficient assurance that it needed to be told.[32]

Thus, Dickens concluded, the Newgate Controversy offered no reason for a literary novelist to abandon the subject of crime and social deprivation. Ultimately, the moral panic that he once feared could wreck his career had actually confirmed it. Serious social investigation could now commence.

And as for the literary application of the Flash tongue, Thackeray finally put it out of its misery in a false start to the sixth chapter of *Vanity Fair* called 'The Night Attack', written in the manner of *Jack Sheppard*:

One, two, three! It is the signal that Black Vizard had agreed on.

'Mofy! is that your snum?' said a voice from the area. 'I'll gully the dag and bimbole the clicky in a snuffkin.'

'Nuffle your clod, and beladle your glumbanions,' said Vizard, with a dreadful oath. 'This way, men; if they screak, out with your snickers and slick! Look to the pewter room, Blowser. You, Mark, to the old gaff's mobus box! and I,' added he, in a lower but more horrible voice, 'I will look to Amelia!'[33]

When Thackeray revised the novel in 1853, this passage was omitted, the author considering it no longer relevant as a contemporary satire. In 1849, a year after the publication of *Vanity Fair*, Henry Mayhew began his epic social investigation *London Labour and the London Poor* in the *Morning Chronicle*, while Pierce Egan, the man who may well have started it all, died peacefully at his home in Pentonville, aged seventy-seven or thereabouts.

Egan unwittingly created a scandal in the name of realism and authenticity, Ainsworth resurrected it by falling foul of emergent Victorian values, and as the debate expanded, it enabled Dickens to pursue a much more serious project of social investigation, with no more Flash dialogue, but equally in the name of realism and authenticity. One might well have seen George IV at a bare-knuckle bout, but it would be inconceivable to bump into Victoria and Albert ringside.

Chapter 4

Invasion of the Bodysnatchers

If the history of the anatomists teaches us anything, it is how far an unregulated free market can actually go. It is also a lesson in how much politicians are willing to deny or ignore rather than deal with a serious social problem, as we have already seen in the resistance to the establishment of an organised police force. This is a trend from which we are not immune today; but for all the horrors of the modern world, bodysnatching, at least, is the stuff of gothic fiction. This was not the case when, in 1828, a Parliamentary Select Committee was appointed 'to inquire into the manner of obtaining Subjects for Dissection in the Schools of Anatomy'. Back then, especially for the poor, it was a lot harder to rest easy in your grave, particularly between October and May (the anatomy school year), when a reasonably fresh corpse was worth at least eight guineas if you had the right connections and the stomach to dig it up.

This wasn't a new trade, but by the nineteenth century it was epidemic. Medical science was rapidly evolving. Surgeons had only split from the Worshipful Company of Barbers as a professional guild in 1745, forming the Company of Surgeons, the forerunner of the Royal College of Surgeons in London, which was created by Royal Charter in 1800. (This is why we don't call a member or fellow of the Royal College of Surgeons 'Dr'. Only physicians held medical degrees, not barber-surgeons.) As the profession established itself as an Enlightenment science based upon empirical research and experiment, two figures came to dominate its development, the Scottish anatomist and physician William Hunter, and his younger brother John, the 'Father of Modern Surgery'. Both men were innovative researchers and teachers. They stressed the importance of hands-on physiological knowledge, which could only be gained through the regular dissection of animals and human beings, enhancing diagnostic accuracy and the refinement of surgical technique. Books and lectures, they believed, were not enough.

Despite its advances, surgery was not pretty. There was no real understanding of infection, and no anaesthetic. Operating tables were made of wood, an ideal surface for bacteria to flourish, with a channel cut into it so that blood would run off into buckets filled with sawdust. Overly complicated surgical instruments were difficult to clean and again a breeding ground for all manner of nasty microorganisms. John Hunter called his patients 'victims', and they were tied down and held as necessary, conscious and screaming throughout the procedure, which was often conducted in front of a large class of medical students. The mortality rate was high, with many of the patients who were strong enough to survive the operation subsequently dying from infection. The young Charles Darwin originally intended to train as a surgeon, enrolling at the University of Edinburgh Medical School in 1825. After attempting – and failing – to view two operations to their completion he never went back. 'Hardly any inducement would have been strong enough to make me do so; this being long before the blessed days of chloroform,' he later said, admitting that 'the two cases fairly haunted me for many a long year.'[1] If you were on the operating table, and therefore denied the option of flight, your chances of survival were greatly enhanced if your surgeon was knowledgeable, precise, and above all, *fast*. This was the level of skill the Hunters and their graduates offered.

And practice made perfect. Corpses for dissection were supplied under the provision of the 1752 Murder Act, section V of which stated that 'in no case whatsoever the body of any murderer shall be suffered to be buried.' They were to be either anatomised or hung in chains so 'some further terror and peculiar mark of infamy be added to the punishment of death.'[2] But even the Bloody Code could not meet the ever-growing demand for the 'silent teachers', leaving dozens of medical students often forced to work on a single corpse, if one was available at all, or to practise on the 'clastic anatomie' papier mâché models developed by Dr Louis Auzoux of Paris. In a grotesque parody of the old adage that good business is where you find it, the black economy was therefore quick to rise to the challenge.

The Sack-'em-Up Men

Disgusting though the practice of disinterring a body undoubtedly was, it wasn't actually illegal. Grave robbery – that is, stealing the corpse's personal effects – was a criminal offence, as was disturbing a grave; the body itself, however, was not deemed to have an owner. Leaving aside the moral and religious questions, no law was broken as long as the grave was returned to its original state after it was violated. Taking the body was a misdemeanour, not an indictable offence. When the notorious resurrection man Thomas Vaughan and his wife were transported, it was not the two corpses found in their kitchen that did for them, but the fact that they had stolen their clothes. As a rule, the bodysnatcher's biggest problem was vigilante justice or running into a rival gang. To ordinary men and women, however, the thought was appalling. They feared they would not rise for the Last Judgement, while dissection and, worse, display was the fate of the common criminal. To medical men, this was a necessary evil in which the good done by the knowledge gained from anatomical study and surgical practice far outweighed the hurt caused to grieving families or the affront to the immortal soul of the deceased. Surgeons viewed themselves as scientists; corpses were merely specimens to study and, indeed, collect.

To those not of the medical profession, however, the practice of acquiring bodies for dissection without permission was a continuing obscenity, as can be seen in *The Surgeon's Warning*, an early poem by the future Poet Laureate, Robert Southey, published in 1799. This is a narrative poem in which a surgeon on his deathbed calls for a parson and an undertaker, beseeching them to save his remains from the resurrection men he has employed in the past:

> Bury me in lead when I am dead,
>   My brethren I intreat,
> And see the coffin weigh'd I beg
>   Lest the Plumber should be a cheat.
>
> And let it be solder'd closely down
>   Strong as strong can be I implore,
> And put it in a patent coffin,
>   That I may rise no more.[3]

He further begs that three armed men guard his coffin in a locked church for three weeks, until he is so decomposed as to not be worth having. They are to be kept happy with beer and gin, with a bounty of five guineas paid for ever bodysnatcher they shoot. All his instructions are duly carried out, but every night the sexton visits, offering the guards more gold on behalf of

'Mister Joseph', a satanic resurrection man, to abandon their posts. On the third night they surrender, for a guinea apiece, and leave the door unlocked. The sack-'em-up men come and cart him off:

> The watchmen as they past along
>   Full four yards off could smell,
> And a curse bestowed upon the load
>   So disagreeable.

> So they carried the sack a-pick-a-back
>   And they carv'd him bone from bone,
> But what became of the Surgeon's soul
>   Was never to mortal known.[4]

The implication of the final line is quite clear. The surgeon went to hell.

One of John Hunter's most talented students was Astley Paston Cooper, the son of a Norfolk clergyman and the novelist Maria Susanna Cooper. Like the Hunters, Cooper represents the combination of ambition, nepotism and entrepreneurship that characterised the medical profession at the turn of the nineteenth century. He had succeeded his uncle, William Cooper, as surgeon to Guy's Hospital, and he ensured in turn that prime appointments went to his nephews, one of whom, Bransby Blake Cooper, later wrote his biography, painting a vivid portrait of a big, ebullient man who never shed his thick regional accent. He also lectured anatomy at St Thomas' and, as was common, retained a lucrative list of private patients including Robert Peel and the Duke of Wellington. This was a good time to be a surgeon. The seemingly endless war with France, and the constant stream of military casualties, meant that practical surgical knowledge was in high demand, guaranteeing both students and status, and, for Astley Cooper, £21,000 a year. After Waterloo, he sent several of his assistants to Brussels to attend to the wounded, and in 1821 he was made a baronet after successfully removing an infected cyst from the King's head, subsequently serving as sergeant surgeon to George IV, William IV and the young Queen Victoria. He is remembered today as a pioneer of vascular surgery, his name eponymous with several previously undescribed diseases and anatomical structures, such as Cooper's testis (neuralgia of the testicles) and Cooper's pubic ligament.

Also like the Hunters, Cooper's surgical prowess was founded on a wealth of practical experience. He was a compulsive pathologist, dissecting animals and human beings on a daily basis. His biographer describes him pursuing stray dogs down the street for 'the prosecution of his investigations', and having struck up a relationship with the keepers at the Royal Menagerie he obtained the bodies of any animals that died at the Tower, including an elephant, which he dissected in the garden of his house in St Mary Axe, the carcass being too big to get inside. Cooper had other contacts as well, such as Tom Butler, a porter at St Thomas', and William Millard, the dissecting room superintendent, both of whom acted as agents between the eminent surgeon and the London bodysnatching community – 'a set of persons,' wrote his nephew, 'who were at that time essential to him, as to all other teachers of Anatomy and Surgery, to enable them to perform the duties which they had undertaken.'[5] Bransby Cooper's biography of Sir Astley walks a delicate line between his desire to honestly portray a man he greatly admired, which meant accepting and defending the position that bodysnatching was necessary and justified, while portraying his uncle as largely innocent of the law:

> Mr. Cooper was altogether unconscious that, as the enactments relating to dissection at that time stood, he was not only benefitting by an infringement of the laws on the part of the body-snatcher, but was himself, as the receiver after the disinterment, actually liable to be tried for misdemeanour, with a risk of incurring severe penalties. He therefore, ignorant of the hazard to which he was thus exposing himself, made no secret of the nature of his occupations in this apartment; contenting himself merely by painting the windows so that persons outside might not observe him while engaged in his investigations.[6]

The apartment with the painted windows was on the ground floor of Cooper's house, where he would often work on a cadaver before breakfast.

Bransby goes on to relate the first time his uncle fell foul of the watch, when a coachman unwittingly transporting three bodies hidden in hampers from his house to the hospital became suspicious. (Coachmen were a canny lot. One once took an unsuspecting medical student conveying a cadaver between schools straight to Bow Street.) Cooper managed to blind the watchman with science, but the latter left vowing to give the Lord Mayor a full account in the morning. Cooper beat him to it, and His Lordship assured him the matter would go no further. Bransby explains that this was the norm because magistrates were 'fearful of obstructing the progress of medical education', an attitude that led to 'the prevailing opinion among the members of the profession, that they were legally justified in such proceedings'.[7] This is a subject to which he returns several times, making the point that the Government had to look the other way in the interests of the country, 'for, without their passive permission of these transgressions, England in a short time would have stood lowest among European nations as to the condition of her Medical science.'[8] Cooper's biography therefore offers an unflinching wealth of detail on the trade, from the point of view of not only the resurrection men but their distinguished customers.

Under the patronage of Astley Cooper, the 'Borough Gang', originally led by the leering Cockney Ben Crouch (and later the Irishman Patrick Murphy), held the monopoly in supplying bodies to Guy's and St Thomas'. These were men, wrote Bransby, 'of the lowest, and most degraded character', but rough and unpredictable though they were, students and surgeons had to deal with them. Bransby describes the commencement of a typical school year in October (the 'dissecting season', when the weather cooled enough that 'subjects' would not go off so quickly), in which the resurrection men would mill about the dissection room with the new students, bargaining with the porters, promising exclusivity and haggling over the price. And if the price be not satisfactorily agreed, 'Then you may go and tell Sir— that he may raise his own Subjects; for not one will he get from us.'[9] Going elsewhere was not an option; any outside crew brought in willing to trade at a lower rate would be mysteriously informed against, bribed, beaten or otherwise driven off by the 'Borough Boys'. Crouch or Murphy would then return, settling on fifty quid down and an equitable rate for the subjects, less than the original asking price but more than the school had wanted to pay, usually nine or so guineas for an adult corpse, with children priced by the inch. Murphy would often obtain four or five down payments from as many schools, each of which he promised to supply exclusively. It wasn't unusual for a gang to make upwards of £1,000 during the school year.

One of the Borough Boys, Joseph Naples, kept a work diary or 'log book', a fragment of which survives, running from 28 November 1811 to 5 December 1812. Bransby Cooper had access to it, and it ended up in the Library of the Royal College of Surgeons. It was published with a commentary by the college librarian James Blake Bailey in 1896, and it offers a fascinating insight into the life of a resurrection man. The literary historian Donald Low called this 'surely the most hair-raising of all nineteenth-century diaries' and likens Naples's voice to that of Bill Sikes in

Oliver Twist.[10] This is a good comparison. As we have seen, it was Dickens's intention to portray the criminal underworld realistically, without glamour or sensation, and that's equally true of the tone of Naples's diary. What's most striking about it, and, indeed, most horrific, is how ordinary it is, how matter of fact, an early example of what Hannah Arendt would later characterise as the 'banality of evil'.

The first few entries are essentially representative of the whole, and are reproduced here with abbreviations and irregular spelling retained:

1811 NOVEMBER.

Thursday 28th. At night went Out and got 3, Jack & me Hospital Crib,[11] Benj[n], Danl & Bill to Harpers,[12] Jack & me 1 big Gates,[13] sold 1 Taunton D[o] S[t]. Thomas's.

Friday 29th. At night went out and got 3, Jack, Ben & me got 2, Bethnall Green, Bill & Danl. 1 Bartholo[w]. Crib opened;[14] whole at Bart[w].

Saturday 30th. At night went and got 3 Bunhill Row, sold to Mr. Cline,[15] S[t]. Thomas's Hospital.

Sunday 1st. We all look[d] out,[16] at Home all night.

Monday 2nd. Met at S[t]. Thomas's, Got paid for the 3 adults & settled; met and settled with Mordecei,[17] made Him up £2 5s. 6d. and Receipt of all demands. At Home all night.

Tuesday 3rd. Went to look out and brought the Shovils from Barthol[w]., Met early in the evening at Mr. Vickers, did not go out that night, Butler and me came home intoxsicated.

Wednesday 4th. At night went out and got 10, whole[18] went to Green[19] and got 4, Black Crib 1, Bunner| fields 5.

Thursday 5th. The whole at home all night.

Friday 6th. Removed 1 from Barthol. to Carpue.[20] At night went out and got 8, Danl, at home all night. 6 Back S[t] Lukes & 2 Big Gates: went 5 Barthol. 1 Frampton[21] 3 S[t]. Thomas's, 3 Wilson.[22]

Saturday 7th. At night went out & got 3 at Bunhill Row. 1 S[t]. Thomas's, 2 Brookes.[23]

Sunday 8th. At home all night.

Monday 9th. At night went out and got 4 at Bethnall Green.

Tuesday 10th. Intoxsicated all day: at night went out & got 5 Bunhill Row. Jack all most buried.[24]

There's a pattern of frantic activity punctuated by indolent drinking bouts; 'got drunk' appears numerous times in the log. There are also references to transactions with some of the most prominent surgeons of the day, including Astley Cooper, as well as run-ins with rival gangs – Israel Chapman, a minor player, gives them a run for their money – cemetery watchers, guard dogs, and internal disputes. Phases of the moon are noted, because it was not safe to go out on bright moonlit nights. The diary ends much as it begins, only with the gang packing bodies to send to Edinburgh.

The methods of the professional bodysnatchers were many and various. Gravediggers and sextons were bought off or recruited into the gang, and watchmen who could not be bribed were lured away under a variety of pretences or plied with drink. Watchers were watched, and if they ever fell asleep or slipped away to relieve themselves, their friends and loved ones were literally exhumed under their noses. On any night when the moon was not full, and depending on the depth of the grave, it was the business of no more than half an hour.

The technique was a closely guarded secret. All a seasoned resurrection man might disclose, were he a reader, would be that gothic writers like Samuel Warren, who imagined the laborious process of exhumation in the *Blackwood's* tale of terror 'Grave Doings' was way off the mark. In his serial *Passages from the Diary of a Late Physician*, Warren had assumed the necessity of opening up the entire grave, but this wasn't how they did it. Instead, members of the gang would take turns to furiously dig a narrow hole down to the head of the coffin, after which a long iron jemmy was inserted, the weight of the earth providing the force at the fulcrum to snap the top of the lid clean off. As the graves of poor and low-income people were preferred, the coffin usually broke quite easily. A rope was then used to draw out the corpse, which would be bent double and tied in a sack. The grave would then be restored to its proper order, with any hidden markers carefully replaced. It was a matter of professional pride to leave no sign of desecration. Only when dealing with multiply stacked coffins, which happened during periods of epidemic or other local disasters, would the entire grave need to be dug up. If a grave was especially deep, carefully returfed or covered with a heavy stone, the resurrectionists would tunnel in diagonally until the head of the coffin was exposed. This was easily removed, being less solid than the lid, after which the corpse could be turned on its side and extracted through the narrow gap. Bodies were then taken to a safe house, usually on a cart owned by one of the gang, and then generally delivered to the home of the surgeon, who would smuggle them into the hospital by Hackney carriage. So audacious were these men that it was not unknown for a resurrectionist to dress as a porter and carry the body in a sack on his back through town in broad daylight.

Pit burial of paupers was also still common practice in many British cities, cremation not becoming socially acceptable until the 1870s. Mass graves were kept open for weeks until filled almost to the brim with bodies. With only a few inches of dirt scattered over them, they were easy pickings for the resurrectionists. One of the most notorious burial grounds was Russell Court in Drury Lane, which was reached by a foul tunnel behind the theatre and overlooked on all sides by towering tenements. In *Bleak House*, Dickens recreated it as 'Tom all alone's', where Jo, the doomed crossing sweeper, brings the disguised Lady Dedlock to show her the resting place of her long-dead lover, Captain Hawdon:

> By many devious ways, reeking with offence of many kinds, they come to the little tunnel of a court, and to the gas-lamp (lighted now), and to the iron gate.
>
> 'He was put there,' says Jo, holding to the bars and looking in.
>
> 'Where? Oh, what a scene of horror!'
>
> 'There!' says Jo, pointing. 'Over yinder. Among them piles of bones, and close to that there kitchin winder! They put him wery nigh the top. They was obliged to stamp upon it to git it in. I could unkiver it for you with my broom if the gate was open. That's why they locks it, I s'pose,' giving it a shake. 'It's always locked. Look at the rat!' cries Jo, excited. 'Hi! Look! There he goes! Ho! Into the ground!'
>
> The servant shrinks into a corner – into a corner of that hideous archway, with its deadly stains contaminating her dress; and putting out her two hands and passionately telling him to keep away from her, for he is loathsome to her, so remains for some moments. Jo stands staring and is still staring when she recovers herself.
>
> 'Is this place of abomination consecrated ground?'
>
> 'I don't know nothink of consequential ground,' says Jo, still staring.
>
> 'Is it blessed?'

'WHICH?' says Jo, in the last degree amazed.

'Is it blessed?'

'I'm blest if I know,' says Jo, staring more than ever; 'but I shouldn't think it warn't. Blest?' repeats Jo, something troubled in his mind. 'It an't done it much good if it is. Blest? I should think it was t'othered myself. But *I* don't know nothink!'[25]

Desperate to avoid such a fate, poor families would often pay for loved ones to be buried in vaults that were little more than charnel houses, like the infamous Enon Chapel on Clement's Lane, where an interment cost fifteen shillings and denomination was of no account. Only a stone's throw from the Strand, Enon sat in a dark court flanked by rundown and overcrowded houses like some huge, bloated spider. Rats and weird-looking insects infested the buildings, and in the summer the stench was intolerable, regularly causing members of the congregation to pass out. When the Commissioners of Sewers investigated, it was discovered that the minister had managed to cram about 12,000 bodies into the tiny vault, which was separated from the chapel above by nothing more than thin wooden floorboards.[26] Not that these vaults were inviolate. Patrick Murphy once raided one by posing as a bereaved relative and then slipping the bolts of the trapdoor for later while the minister was showing him the space.

Then there were the simple dodges. Deals would be struck with the low-end undertakers, the 'death hunters' who served the workhouses and the poor communities. With the right intelligence, it was an easy matter for the wife of a resurrection man to present herself tearfully at the gates of St Giles' workhouse to claim the body of a recently deceased 'relative', while many a cheap funeral saw the clergyman read the service over a casket full of bricks. Even bodies stored in outhouses awaiting coroners' inquests were snatched. Not that the well-to-do were always spared, despite their deeper graves. Once a servant whose master had just passed away approached one of Mr Murphy's men and arrangements were made to the mutual satisfaction of all parties, the coffin being filled with sand the night before the funeral. Bransby Cooper even recounts a case when an off-duty resurrection man walking near St Thomas' saw a pedestrian stagger and fall, clearly having a heart attack. He rushed to the man's aid, and having discretely established that the stranger had dropped dead, called for passers-by to help him get his 'sick cousin' to the hospital.

Sometimes, the resurrection men would visit surgeons' homes in the dead of night, asking for money up front to bribe a watchman because of a particularly rich seam of death somewhere or other. Sometimes there would be a return on this investment, but often not. The surgeons, of course, had no recourse to the law if they were cheated, while the resurrection men could simply threaten to stop supplying the school if their customers started complaining, which could affect student recruitment and retention. Similarly, they might raise a price unexpectedly at the last minute, leaving teachers with no choice but to pay out of their own pockets. Sources, like prices, constantly shifted, with the schools of Edinburgh often supplied with bodies from the overnight mail from London and the Dublin packet, while when the citizens of London became more vigilant Liverpool gave up its dead for the capital. The provinces, meanwhile, were routinely raided, with bodies hidden in commercial packaging and delivered in barrels or crates supposedly full of salted fish or haberdashery. When subjects were scarce, prices could go as high as twenty pounds a corpse.

There were also, of course, countermeasures, and the job certainly became more arduous as the century progressed. Mortsafes were heavy iron cages, padlocked together and buried around the coffin. These were originally developed in Scotland, and the remains of many can still be found in churchyards near the old medical schools of Edinburgh. Variations on the concept included stone sarcophagi, heavy slabs covering fresh graves, and Edward Bridgman's patent iron coffin (retailing at £31 10s) because, declared the advertisements, 'Many hundred dead bodies will be dragged from their wooden coffins this winter.'[27] Branches and brambles were mixed into the soil to make it harder to dig out, loose stones and broken glass were scattered on walls, spring-guns were set, like the ones used against poachers, and armed guards were hired to watch graves until the sun rose. Pitched battles were not unusual, especially in Ireland, where feelings ran particularly high, there being (probably unfounded) rumours of street children in Dublin being abducted and murdered for dissection. James Blake Bailey quotes the following report from an unidentified Irish newspaper in 1830, under the headline 'Desperate Engagement with Body-snatchers':

> The remains of the late Edward Barrett, Esq, having been interred in Glasnevin churchyard on the 27th of last month (January), persons were appointed to remain in the churchyard all night, to protect the corpse from 'the sack 'em-up gentlemen', and it seems the precaution was not unnecessary,

for, on Saturday night last, some of the gentry made their appearance, but soon decamped on finding they were likely to be opposed. Nothing daunted, however, they returned on Tuesday morning with augmented force, and well-armed. About ten minutes after two o'clock three or four of them were observed standing on the wall of the churchyard, while several others were endeavouring to get on it also. The party in the churchyard warned them off, and were replied to by a discharge from fire-arms. This brought on a general engagement; the sack 'em-up gentlemen fired from behind the churchyard wall, by which they were defended, while their opponents on the watch fired from behind the tomb-stones. Upwards of 58 to 60 shots were fired. One of the assailants was shot he was seen to fall; his body was carried off by his companions.[28]

Generally speaking, though, resurrectionists avoided defended graveyards if they could, unless they were confident that the guards were either bribable, gullible enough to be lured away, or just plain useless and unreliable. Instead, they sought out more and more obscure burial grounds. The most likely cause of violence was therefore an encounter between rival gangs. The victors would often vandalise the cemetery and then inform on their competitors. Thomas Vaughan, it was said, could leave a churchyard looking like a ploughed field.

On one occasion, in the winter of 1823, Tom Vaughan was particularly irked by the repeatedly impressive hauls of Patrick Murphy and his right-hand man, Patrick Connolly, during a period of otherwise increased watchfulness on the part of the general public. Murphy and Connolly jealously guarded their secret source of supply, the private burial ground attached to the independent chapel at Holywell Mount in Shoreditch. The place was managed by a single superintendent, one Mr Whackett, who also acted as gravedigger. When Whackett locked up at dusk, he always left the recent graves marked and the bolts of the gate undrawn, having given Murphy a key in return for a piece of the action. Several London crews were keen to either join the harvest or queer the pitch, but it was Vaughan, with his mate Bill Hollis, a cabby who had worked with the Borough Gang, who got wind of Whackett. They duly paid him a visit at his place of employment, initially claiming that they were Murphy's accomplices, and when that didn't work demanding he share the job with them anyway, or be exposed. Whackett denied all knowledge of Murphy and refused to cooperate. Vaughan kept at him until Whackett lost his temper and stormed over the road to the nearest pub, pointing at Vaughan and Hollis through the window and announcing that they were bodysnatchers attempting to bribe him to let them raise from his ground. The bar emptied out and it was only the resurrection men's fleetness of foot that saved them from a brutal beating.

Furious, Vaughan ran to the local magistrate, bursting into a crowded court, and telling him to send officers to Holywell Mount, where they would find every grave empty. A large crowd descended on the ground, breaking the gates and surging in. Whackett was detained, and when the despoiled graves were exposed the mob threw him into the deepest hole and started shovelling earth in. It was only the intervention of a peeler that saved him from being buried alive.

Murphy neither forgave nor forgot, and his revenge can be found in the court report of the *North Wales Gazette*, dated 18 March 1824:

> At the last Maidstone Assizes, Vaughan, a notorious resurrection man, was convicted of stealing five dead bodies, and sentenced to two years' imprisonment, but contrived to escape, and a reward of £10 was offered for his apprehension. A week since, Kinsey, the vigilant officer of the Town Hall, Southwark, received private information that this marauder was practising at Manchester, and lost not a moment in going in quest of him … Yesterday morning at one o'clock, he passed through the Borough on his way to Maidstone with his prisoner.[29]

Vaughan did two years at Maidstone Gaol. The 'private information' that gave him up came from Patrick Murphy.

Under Proper Regulations

It was clear that something had to give, allowing medical science to progress while challenging the ghoulish trade in dead bodies that everyone knew was happening but which no government had hitherto acknowledged or addressed. Finally, in 1828, a House of Commons Select Committee was appointed 'to inquire into the manner of obtaining Subjects for Dissection in the Schools of Anatomy, and into the State of the Law affecting the Persons employed in obtaining or dissecting Bodies'.[30] In her seminal study

Death, Dissection and the Destitute, the historian Ruth Richardson has described this as 'a means to an end', pointing out the clear influence of the father of Utilitarianism, Jeremy Bentham, whose 'fundamental axiom' was the principle that 'it is the greatest happiness of the greatest number that is the measure of right and wrong.'[31] The author of the subsequent report, for example, was 'avowed Benthamite' Henry Warburton, the MP for Bridport, while correspondence on the subject between Bentham and Sir Robert Peel, then the Home Secretary, predate the Select Committee by nearly two years.[32] In 1826, Bentham was already suggesting that charity hospital patients, in return for free medical care, should consent to giving up their bodies for dissection against a £100 forfeit payable by next of kin, while repealing the judicial dissection of murderers, thereby removing the stigma that the anatomy table was a criminal punishment in the minds of the public, particularly those that were so poor they had to use charity hospitals. Richardson therefore argues persuasively that the committee was something of a PR exercise on an effectively done deal.

Of the fifty-odd witnesses called, twenty-five were medical men, most notable Astley Cooper, another friend of Peel's and then President of the Royal College of Surgeons, and, sensationally, three were resurrection men. Their identities were disguised, and they are designated in the report 'A.B.' (almost certainly Ben Crouch), 'C.D.' (who Bailey suggests was the diarist Joseph Naples), and 'F.G.' (an unidentified accomplice of Naples and Crouch, possibly Connolly, who came out of the trade quite well off and may thus have been rewarded for appearing). The Select Committee gathered a quantity of evidence on the progress of medical science and the necessity of anatomical knowledge, and the processes and problems attendant in obtaining specimens. Comparisons with continental practices were considered, and opinions sought as to potentially alternative sources of supply.

The report opens with the examination of Sir Astley Cooper, which sets the substance and tone of the Committee's line of enquiry throughout. Cooper comes across as remarkably frank; and although an argument can undoubtedly be made that he represented an elite group of professionals and aristocratic politicians asking and answering loaded questions designed to impose another terrible and self-interested burden on the poor, the pragmatic voice of the scientist can equally be heard. It is a fascinating performance. 'Without dissection,' he begins, answering the opening question as to its necessity, 'there can be no anatomy, and that anatomy is our polar star, for, without anatomy a surgeon can do nothing, certainly nothing well.'[33] Clinical competence and its value to society is a theme he returns to many times, and when asked 'Can Anatomy be sufficiently learnt in any way but by dissection of the actual body?' his reply is refreshingly direct and assured: 'Certainly not!'[34]

Cooper's revelations on bodysnatching were also remarkably candid, as well as canny, suggesting that anyone (by implication, anyone in the committee chamber) could be a subject. 'The law does not prevent our obtaining the body of an individual if we think proper,' he said, continuing, 'for there is no person, let his situation in life be what it may, whom, if I were disposed to dissect, I could not obtain … The law only enhances the price, and does not prevent the exhumation.' In discussing the resurrection men, a group he describes as 'the lowest dregs of degradation', he also suggests that his mortal remains are no more inviolate than the rest: 'There is no crime they would not commit, and as to myself, if they would imagine that I should make a good subject, they really would not have the smallest scruple, if they could do the thing undiscovered, to make a subject of me.'[35] There seems to be a genuine anxiety here, but Cooper was also working the room, deflecting the complicit and symbiotic criminal behavior of his profession back towards the resurrection men. 'The great difficulty teachers have to contend with,' he explained, 'is the management of those persons, and it is distressing to our feelings that we are obliged to employ very faulty agents to obtain a desirable end.'[36]

The resurrection men examined also drew attention to their many trials, most notably the increased number of armed guards watching the burial grounds. 'Every ground in London is watched by men put into them at dark, who stop till daylight with fire arms … The risk is almost beyond describing,' complains 'A.B.', concluding that, 'it is very dangerous, because they have constables; either a man risks his life or his liberty. They would not mind shooting a man as dead as a robber, if they caught him in a church-yard.'[37] 'C.D.' similarly testified that 'we had our men shot away from us, and it was very dangerous.'[38]

Cooper's solution to all this distress was a change to the law, which was really the point of this entire exercise, as can be seen by the directive questioning. When asked, 'Have you been at all led to consider whether it would be expedient to obtain a supply from the bodies of those persons who die in workhouses, that are unclaimed by relatives or friends?' he had prepared a very detailed reply:

> Upon this point I am extremely anxious to read to the Committee
> the information I have taken some pains to obtain respecting
> the Mary-le-bone infirmary and workhouse, and which I think

may be here useful ... The claimants in the parish are 6,383; of the out-poor there are four sources of burials. In the first place, they bury those dying in the infirmary; in the second, they bury those dying in the workhouse, who are attended by its apothecary; in the third, they bury those who die in the parish, attended by general practitioners; and in the fourth, they bury insane persons from a house which they have at Hoxton. The deaths in the workhouse are 110 annually; the deaths in the infirmary are 238; the still-born are 64; the parish poor not in the house, 161; and lunatics, 12; making a total of 585 persons buried in that workhouse in the year: one-fifth of those buried are unclaimed, 84 only are buried by their friends; of those who claim and attend the funerals, very few would claim if they were to be at the expense of the funeral.[39]

Cooper was followed by Benjamin Collins Brodie, the surgeon at St George's, who was asked: 'You heard that part of the evidence of Sir Astley Cooper, which related to the giving up the bodies of those who die in workhouses, and are unclaimed; do you concur with him in opinion?' Brodie concurred.[40]

But logical though this stance might be to the utilitarian philosopher and the gentleman surgeon, this was going to be a hard sell when it came to the general population, and much of the report appears written to lay the foundations of what amounts to a rebranding of dissection. The resurrection men established that their victims were invariably from the poorer classes as, said 'F.G', 'we could not obtain the rich so easily; because they were buried so deep,'[41] while the medical men were unanimous in their call to repeal the Murder Act because, as Cooper explained, 'The law enforcing the dissection of murderers, is the greatest stigma on Anatomy which it receives, and is extremely injurious to science.'[42] Cooper was also not alone in advocating that all subjects obtained as proposed should and would receive a 'decent burial' at the school's expense, and that the use of the unclaimed dead meant that 'the fittest persons in society for dissection, are those who have no friends to care about them; the dead body of course does not feel either injury or disgrace, and where there are no friends to feel it, the mischief to society can be none at all.'[43] The report's key recommendation was thus that, 'the bodies of those who during life have been maintained at the public charge, and who die in workhouses, hospitals and other charitable institutions, should, if not claimed by next of kin within a certain time after death, be given up, under proper regulations, to the Anatomist.'[44] The writing was on the wall. But while the Select Committee was still sitting, a terrible series of crimes that would change public opinion were already happening in Edinburgh.

The Doctor and the Devils

William Burke and William Hare were not bodysnatchers; nonetheless, it was the trade that led to their notorious killing spree. Both were Irish immigrants in their mid-thirties. Burke was a cobbler and Hare and his wife, Margaret, kept a two-room lodging house in Tanner's Close in Edinburgh, the only building in a dark and narrow court in the roughest part of the Old Town, where a third share in a bed could be had for 3d a night. Burke and his woman, Helen 'Nelly' McDougal, took up permanent residence there in the autumn of 1827 after their lodgings burnt down, and the couples quickly gained a reputation locally for their love of strong drink and wild behavior.

Burke was educated but feckless. He had a military background and came from a respectable family, although he had deserted his first wife and children some years before and ended up as a navvy on the Union Canal. He was quite a charmer and well liked in the neighbourhood. Hare, by comparison, was volatile, illiterate and uncouth, and had come into his modest business only by marrying his landlord's widow. On Halloween night 1828, Burke, now living with his cousin, John Broggan, bribed two fellow lodgers, James Gray, an old soldier, and his wife Ann, to stay in the Hare's house for the night, so he and Nelly could entertain a relative from the old country with their friends. Returning briefly to collect some warmer clothing for their kids sometime around nine, they found Burke and Hare and their wives carousing with a middle-aged Irish woman called Margaret Docherty, whom Burke had lured back earlier that evening claiming his mother was a distant relative. The next morning, she was gone, Burke explaining that Docherty had become belligerent, so he had sent her on her way. 'She's quiet enough now,' he added cryptically. Mrs Gray became suspicious when Burke wouldn't let her near a pile of straw at the foot of her bed. She took a look when the Burkes went out and found the body of Margaret Docherty concealed in the straw, her mouth caked with blood and saliva. Horrified, she told Mrs Hare, who offered the couple a tenner to keep their opinions to themselves. Instead, Mr and Mrs Gray went straight to the police.

When the police arrived at the bleak lodgings, the body was long gone, but the bloodstained straw and the murdered woman's clothes stuffed under the miserable bed told the tale. Burke, Hare, their wives and Broggan were all taken in for questioning, and the next morning the police raided the famous anatomy school of Dr Robert Knox in Surgeon's Square. They found Docherty's corpse in the dissecting room, which James Gray positively identified as the woman he'd seen drinking with Burke and Hare. Broggan was deemed not to be involved and released; the others were arrested.

The trial that followed on Christmas Eve and Christmas Day appalled and captivated the public, stoked by the kind of hysterical media response that had similarly characterised the Ratcliffe Highway Murders. Burke and Hare had been busy over the last year. As we've seen, the resurrection trade was tightly controlled by the criminal gangs, and this useless pair of drunken psychopaths could not have possibly broken into it. Instead, they took bodysnatching to its logical conclusion in a grotesque parody of manufacture and capital: they produced the bodies themselves, bypassing the grave completely. Their grim project began in November 1827, not long after Burke and Nelly had moved in to Tanner's Close, when an elderly lodger died owing Hare rent. The friends decided that it was reasonable to recoup this loss by selling the body. Not really knowing what to do, they went to Surgeon's Square and approached a group of young men they rightly presumed to be students, Jones, Miller, and Fergusson (later Sir William Fergusson, Serjeant Surgeon to Queen Victoria and President of the Royal College of Surgeons). The students referred them to Dr Knox's school. Returning with the body in a sack, they were amazed to receive £7 10s from Jones after the doctor himself had checked the corpse, the assistant telling them that he 'would be glad to see them again when they had another to dispose of'.

The money got the couples through the winter, after which they figured out that the best way to repeat their previous success was to give nature a helping hand. This is chillingly described in Burke's first confession:

> Early last spring, 1828, a woman from Gilmerton came to Hare's house as a nightly lodger, Hare keeping seven beds for lodgers: That she was a stranger, and she and Hare became merry, and drank together; and next morning she was very ill in consequence of what she had got, and she sent for more drink, and she and Hare drank together, and she became very sick and vomited, and at that time she had not risen from bed,

and Hare then said that they would try to smother her in order to dispose of her body to the Doctors: That she was lying on her back in the bed, and quite insensible from drink, and Hare clapped his hand on her mouth and nose, and the declarant laid himself across her body in order to prevent her making any disturbance, and she never stirred, and they took her out of bed and undressed her, and put her into a chest, and they mentioned to Dr. Knox's young men that they had another subject, and Mr. Miller sent a porter to meet them in the evening at the back of the Castle; and declarant and Hare carried the chest till they met the porter, and they accompanied the porter with the chest to Dr Knox's classroom, and Dr. Knox came in when they were there; the body was cold and stiff. Dr. Knox approved of it being so fresh, but did not ask any questions.[45]

This was Abigail Simpson, a salt seller, although several of their victims died without a name.

The sequence of murders that followed is difficult to precisely determine. Burke made two confessions, one to the procurator fiscal, the other in the form of an interview for the *Edinburgh Courant*, and although the victims tally, the order changes. Hare's statement offers yet another sequence, although the details of the actual murders largely coincide. According to Burke's original confession, Miss Simpson was succeeded by a miller called Joseph, who was suffocated with a pillow while he was in bed with a fever; an unnamed Englishman, again ill in bed; an unidentified elderly lady enticed to Tanner's Close for a drink by Margaret Hare and killed by her husband; Mrs Haldane, another old woman; a cinder woman known to Burke called Effy; an unnamed woman with her young grandson (a murder Burke claimed haunted him); and, chillingly, the daughter of Mrs Haldane, Peggy. They also killed a young prostitute called Mary Paterson at Burke's brother's house in Canongate; their washerwoman, Mrs Hostler; a relative of Helen's first husband called Ann McDougal; and a well-known disabled street person, James Wilson, known locally as 'Daft Jamie'. At some point, Hare killed a woman by himself and tried to conceal the sale from Burke, leading to a quarrel and Burke moving to the house of his cousin two streets away, where Margaret Docherty was murdered. They also did for an unidentified drunk woman that a policeman was helping home when Burke intervened, claiming that he knew her. They killed sixteen men, women and children in all, all at the bottom of society and rarely, if ever, missed, all sold to Knox for between £8 and £10. Nine were killed in Hare's house, two in his stables, four at John Broggan's house, and one at Burke's brother's house in Canongate, although neither of the latter men were implicated in the murders. In Burke's first confession, he also says he 'thinks' he killed an old female lodger when Hare was not around in May 1828, between Joseph the Miller and the English victim.

Aside from the little boy and 'Daft Jamie' (who didn't drink), their ruthless *modus operandi* did not change. They would lure someone back to one of the murder houses or focus on a vulnerable lodger or acquaintance, getting them compliantly drunk on whisky before suffocating them, a method of execution that was essentially undetectable before the coming of modern forensics and which came to be known as 'Burking'. As Burke himself admitted, 'Neither Hare nor myself ever got a body from a church-yard'.[46] They always dealt with Knox, who never questioned the fact that the bodies showed no signs of being buried, although William Fergusson did, apparently, recognise Mary Paterson. It is likely they recognised 'Daft Jamie' as well, because his head and club feet were removed before he was given to the students.[47]

Although police suspected Docherty and several others had been murdered, it was difficult to prove beyond circumstantial evidence, such as the friends of victims identifying personal effects kept by the killers. Docherty's remains were examined by the toxicologist Robert Christison and the forensic expert William Newbigging, and although they thought deliberate asphyxiation highly likely, they had to concede that this could not be medically proven. Apart from Docherty, there were no bodies either. As part of his investigation Christison also interviewed Knox, who believed, he said, that Burke and Hare obtained such fresh corpses by purchasing them from low lodging houses immediately after death. Knox was deemed innocent, though Christison described him as 'deficient in principle and heart'.[48] The deadlock was broken by Hare, who agreed to turn King's Evidence against Burke in return for immunity from prosecution. Because a spouse could not be forced to testify against their partner, his wife Margaret was also off the hook, leaving Burke and McDougal charged with the murders of Mary Paterson, 'Daft Jamie' and Mrs Docherty, the evidence being strongest in these cases. Mary Paterson was not alone when she was enticed to visit Tanner's Close. Her friend Janet Brown was with her; she survived by leaving early, and was subsequently told that Mary had eloped to Glasgow with a travelling salesman. She was thus a witness to Mary's last movements before vanishing off the face of the earth, and she recognised

Mary's skirt and petticoats among Helen McDougal's belongings. Similarly, a local tradesman told police that he'd seen Burke's nephew wearing 'Daft Jamie's' breeches.

An angry mob thronged the court, and 300 special constables were drafted in to contain the crowd while the army was put on standby. Knox and his assistants were named as witnesses but only David Paterson was called to briefly confirm Knox had received bodies from Burke and Hare. Burke was convicted – the jury taking less than an hour to deliberate – but the case against Helen was 'not proven', a verdict in Scottish law meaning that the prosecution case had failed to secure a conviction but that the jury was not persuaded of the accused's innocence. She had to be kept in protective custody to save her from the crowd, while the Hares remained locked up during an unsuccessful private prosecution brought by James Wilson's mother. All left Edinburgh quietly, the Hares going their separate ways. Travelling to Dumfries, Hare was recognised by one of Mrs Wilson's lawyers and had to spend a night in the cells to save him from being lynched by another mob before fleeing for the English border. His wife was similarly recognised trying to get passage to Ireland, narrowly escaping with her life to Belfast. Despite various rumours and urban legends, they then drop out of history, although folklore has it that Hare was thrown into a lime pit and blinded, ending his days as a beggar on Oxford Street, with alternative stories placing him in both Ireland and America.

Robert Knox, once the most popular lecturer on anatomy in Britain, was not prosecuted; in fact Burke's statements went to great lengths to declare his innocence. He was however tried and convicted in the court of public opinion, and his house was attacked by a large crowd who burned him in effigy. He was subsequently exonerated by a Committee of the Royal Society of Edinburgh, but his reputation never fully recovered and by 1831 he had been forced to resign from the Royal College of Surgeons of Edinburgh. After fairing no better teaching in Glasgow, eleven professors blocked his application for the chair in pathology at Edinburgh University, and in 1847 he was expelled from the Royal Society. He ended his days as pathological anatomist at the Free Cancer Hospital (The Royal Marsden), dying in relative obscurity.

Leaving the world no poorer, the apparently contrite Burke was hanged in Edinburgh on 28 January 1829. A crowd estimated at the time to be in excess of 20,000 people turned out to watch him dance, their hatred rising to a roar with every paroxysm as he slowly strangled under his own body weight. His corpse was publicly dissected in the anatomy theatre of the university's Old College by Professor Alexander Monro, and his skeleton donated to the Anatomical Museum of the Edinburgh Medical School, where it remains on display to this day. As with Thurtell and the 'Gill's Hill Tragedy', the so-called 'West Port Atrocities' became the subject of a ghoulish nursery rhyme:

> Up the close and doun the stair,
> But and ben[49] wi' Burke and Hare.
> Burke's the butcher, Hare's the thief,
> Knox the boy that buys the beef.

And that should have been enough to stop it. In March the same year, Henry Warburton submitted his *Bill for preventing the Unlawful Disinterment of Human Bodies, and for Regulating Schools of Anatomy*, based on the recommendations of the Select Committee on Anatomy but neglecting to repeal the old Murder Act. Although public revulsion at the recent West Port murders was still running high, there remained significant opposition. The Radical MP and pamphleteer William Cobbett, for example, quoted Lord Harewood in the House – 'If we can sell the dead bodies of the people, what is it to prevent us selling their living bodies?' – and argued, 'But they tell us it was necessary for the purposes of science. Science? Why, who is science for? Not for poor people. Then if it be necessary for the purposes of science, let them have the bodies of the rich, for whose benefit science is cultivated.'[50] The College of Surgeons petitioned against the bill, and although it passed the House of Commons it was withdrawn in the Lords after the opposition of the 'old-High Churchman' William Howley, then the Archbishop of Canterbury.

It took the murder of another child to finally change public opinion. Carlo Ferrari, an Italian boy from Bethnal Green, who made his living showing white mice on the street, was only fourteen years old when he was killed by the 'London Burkers' John Bishop, Thomas Williams and James May on 5 November 1831. The men were members of a notorious gang of resurrectionists who graduated to offering street urchins cheap lodgings and then drugging them with rum and laudanum and drowning them head-first in a well. (G.W.M. Reynolds would later base his folk devil villain 'The Resurrection Man' in *The Mysteries of London* on this crew.) There was immense public sympathy for Ferrari, though he was not the only victim, much as the untimely demise of 'Daft Jamie' had provoked in Edinburgh. May was transported, and Bishop and Williams went to the gallows. In December, Warburton introduced a revised Bill in the Commons, which passed in both Houses, becoming law on 1 August 1832. The Anatomy Act created licensed teachers of anatomy overseen by four inspectors who reported to the Home Secretary and tracked every subject donated for dissection. Surgeons and their students were granted legal access to unclaimed corpses from prison and the workhouse, while the bodies of executed murderers were now to be hung in chains or buried in the last prison in which they had been confined, ending the association between punishment and surgical dissection.

The surgeons had gotten away with it, while the poorest members of society had been exploited first by the resurrection men, then opportunistic serial killers and, finally, the Government, all in the interests of medical science, of course. But while many now felt an additional horror in dying in the workhouse that the utilitarians would never understand, the era of the sack-'em-up men was finally at an end.

Chapter 5

The Real Oliver Twist

Tragic though the murders of the poor street children were, it is unlikely that they'd have fared much better had they never come into contact with the London Burkers, a situation explored in probably the best-known novel on the subject to come out of the nineteenth century.

Compared to the criminal romances of the 1830s, which celebrated the outlaws of the previous century like Dick Turpin and Jack Sheppard as heroes, Dickens's novel *Oliver Twist, or The Parish Boy's Progress* (1839) represented a new style of hardcore social realism, at least as far as the author was concerned. In this iconic English novel, a young orphan is drawn into a den of thieves in the notorious London rookery of Saffron Hill. Here he joins a group of street urchins schooled in crime by the avaricious fence Fagin, while the survivors of his previous generation of pupils, the drunken and codependant Bill and Nancy, have grown into the roles of housebreaker and prostitute. The workhouse-born Oliver is seduced by the apparent freedom of Jack Dawkins, the 'Artful Dodger', a miniature version of Bill Sikes and the leader of a gang of pickpockets mentored by Fagin that offers the orphan his first experience of family. Dickens's device is to contrast this fallen group with the more wholesome, Christian and middle-class households of the philanthropic Mr Brownlow and the innocent Rose Maylie, the dramatic doubles of Fagin and Nancy. Oliver is saved by birth and Christian charity – he turns out to be Rose's nephew – while Bill beats Nancy to death, wrongly believing she's informed against him; he is accidently hanged trying to escape across the rooftops of the slum. The Artful Dodger is transported and Fagin goes to the gallows.

Oliver Twist is a hero's journey and a 'coming of age' story, it's subtitle referencing the Christian allegory *The Pilgrim's Progress* by John Bunyan (1678). It's never been out of print and it was a bestseller in its own day, subject to numerous unlicensed theatrical adaptations. It's been multiply adapted for film and television, although what Dickens would have made of the musical is anyone's guess. He loathed the plays in the main, and was apt to declare that he was being robbed. John Forster later described an attempt to watch one of the first in December 1838: 'I was with him at a representation of his *Oliver Twist* the following month at the Surrey Theatre, when in the middle of the first scene he laid himself down upon the floor in a corner of the box and never rose from it until the drop-scene fell.'[1]

But the original was also very political, anticipating the 'Condition of England' novels of the 1840s. It wasn't a historical novel or a costume drama, it was a cultural response. Dickens's prominent narrative voice was savagely critical of the authors and provisions of the 1834 Poor Law Amendment Act. Like the Anatomy Act, this was another piece of utilitarian legislation. It was based upon the doctrine of 'less eligibility', meaning that workhouses should serve as a last resort and deterrent, the *Poor Law Report* of 1834 stating that: 'The first and most essential of all conditions, a principle of which we find universally admitted, even by those whose practice is at variance with it, is that his [the pauper's] situation on the whole shall not be made really or apparently so eligible as the situation of the independent labourer of the lowest class.'[2] The alternative was survival of the fittest on the streets: you worked, if you could find it, you begged, you sold your body, you stole, or you starved.

Baby Farming in Brixton

This was a world that Dickens knew well. He had reported on it at length as a young journalist, but he also knew it from personal experience. Although few close to him knew the truth, Dickens's father, John, had gone to the Marshalsea debtors' prison in February 1824, owing £40 10s, his mother and younger siblings following in April. When he was just twelve years old, Dickens was taken out of school and sent to work at Warren's Blacking Warehouse, a waterfront factory on the Hungerford Stairs, in a dank and filthy rookery hidden behind the Strand. John Dickens was released after three months, but the family remained poor and Charles was forced to continue working at the factory. Despite concealing his origins, they constantly surfaced in Dickens's fiction. He sent Mr Pickwick to the Fleet debtors' prison (in an uncharacteristically bleak section of the otherwise comic *Pickwick Papers*), Mr Micawber to the Marshalsea, and his alter ego, David Copperfield, to 'Murdstone and Grinby's Wine Warehouse'. In *Little Dorrit* (1857), the protagonist of the title, Amy Dorritt, is born in the Marshalsea. And however successful he became, Dickens constantly worried about money. He had seen how easy it was to fall from one class to another.

As Dickens knew from bitter experience, it was hard work being a kid in the nineteenth century, especially if you were born into a pauper family. In his epic *Inquiry into the sanitary condition of the labouring population of Great Britain*, published in 1842, the architect of the new Poor Law, Edwin Chadwick, showed that half the children born in the United Kingdom died before their fifth birthday. Adults didn't fare much better. The life expectancy of a professional man was thirty, while for labourers it was just seventeen, dropping to thirteen in the undrained slums of the industrial north. That put the death rate at twenty-three per 1,000. You could be seen off by any number of virulent and epidemic diseases; influenza, pneumonia, tuberculosis, cholera, typhoid, measles and smallpox were rife, while many children were listed as dying of 'atrophy', a euphemism for starving to death. Accidents were common, usually as the result of drunkenness, ignorance and neglect, with mothers often forced to leave very young children unattended to go to work. Open fires were a menace; clothing made from natural fibres was highly flammable, and coroners' reports throughout the century routinely list infant deaths from burning and scalding. Their parents unable to afford doctors, sick children were often unintentionally poisoned by patent medicines, or chemicals intended for surface cleaning or pest control picked up in error by candlelight. (The distinct cobalt-blue poison bottle with a ridged pattern didn't appear until the early 1870s.) In 1871, for example, three girls with colds were fatally poisoned at the Crumpsall Workhouse in Manchester when a teaching assistant picked up a bottle of carbolic acid by mistake in the dark. The cough medicine was next to it on the shelf. Because cots and even the most primitive cribs were beyond the means of many parents, it was common for large families to sleep in the same bed, leading to numerous accidental suffocations, babies often smothered by their drunken fathers. 'Found dead in bed' is another cause of death frequently listed by coroners.

Then there were the deaths that were not so accidental. Sometimes another mouth to feed was simply too much, and the death rate of children born out of wedlock was consistently over twice that of those with married parents. With such a high infant mortality rate, doctors were often indifferent as to whether a sleeping child had been accidently or intentionally asphyxiated. Hundreds of tiny corpses were tossed into parks and gardens every year, or left on doorsteps and in churches, or dumped in dustholes, canals or under railway arches; and for each body found, it was likely another went undiscovered. More were hidden in attics and cellars, while the Thames held as many bodies as the Ganges; the *Marylebone Mercury* routinely reporting on 3 August 1859, for example, that 'The body of a baby boy was found floating in a water-butt of a house in Upper Boston Street. Attention had been alerted when the wife of a tenant noticed a peculiar taste in the water.'[3]

Or you might find yourself entrusted to a 'baby farmer', usually a woman, who took on the unwanted children of the poor for a fee. For a one-off payment of between five and twenty pounds, a baby farmer would adopt a child permanently, freeing the parent or parents of the burden. Children were kept in appalling and frequently lethal conditions to maximise profits. It wasn't possible to raise a child to adulthood on a few pounds, and a brisk turnover was most desirable, meaning that these kids were quite literally worth more dead than alive.

Margaret Waters was a baby farmer in Brixton. She drugged and starved the children in her care, and was believed to have murdered at least nineteen of them. She was convicted of murder in 1870 and hanged at Horsemonger Lane Gaol. Amelia Elizabeth Dyer, the 'Ogress of Reading', was a trained nurse with mental health problems who operated as a baby farmer under a variety of aliases. Like Waters, at some point she moved from fatally neglecting her charges to killing them herself. Her preferred method was strangulation. Dyer was active for twenty years, and is suspected of killing as many as 400 children. She was finally exposed after a bargeman pulled a package out of the Thames containing a baby girl (later identified as Helena Fry). The bundle had been inadequately weighted, and the wrapping paper still had legible traces of a name and address. Dyer was located (operating as 'Mrs Thomas'), and put under police surveillance. The river was dredged near the spot where Helena was found, and six more infant bodies were discovered. She was arrested and convicted of murder in the spring of 1896, and hanged at Newgate on 10 June. In 1939, the writer William Stewart made a case for Dyer being Jack the Ripper, mutilating women to cover up botched abortions she'd performed, elaborating on Sir Arthur Conan Doyle's 'Jill the Ripper' theory that the killer could have been a midwife or cross-dressed man disguised as one to get closer to his victims without causing alarm, as well as to evade capture. Stewart ultimately concluded that the double-murderer Mary Pearcey was the strongest candidate, but while he makes an interesting case for both women, the evidence is circumstantial at best.[4]

Dyer's case, in particular, led Parliament to pass the Infant Life Protection Act of 1897, which empowered local authorities to control the registration of 'nurses' responsible for more than one infant under the age of five for a period longer than forty-eight hours, marking the beginning of proper regulations for adoption and fostering. But not all baby farmers were serial killers. Some would just put the children on a train, or take them to an unfamiliar part of town and abandon them.

Some parents, meanwhile, were just sick of poverty, hopelessness and failure, and saw death as the only way out. Such was the case of the bankrupt druggist and father of six, Samuel Hill Derby of Salford, who in 1888, apparently with the consent of his wife, poisoned himself and his entire family with prussic acid mixed with treacle. In his suicide note, he poignantly wrote that his children were 'better off now than millionaires'.[5]

And if you could survive that lot, your options as a poor child were still pretty uninviting. If, like Oliver Twist, you were a workhouse boy, you might well find yourself an indentured parish apprentice, a practice that continued for several years after the Poor Law Amendment Act. In Dickens's novel, Oliver is offered to the undertaker, Mr Sowerberry, as a 'parochial 'prentice' along with the sum of five pounds 'upon liking', a phrase, explains the author, 'which means, in the case of a parish apprentice, that if the master find, upon a short trial, that he can get enough work out of a boy without putting too much food into him, he shall have him for a term of years, to do what he likes with.'[6] Children could be apprenticed at seven, for a minimum of seven years, and until the Parish Apprentice Act of 1844, the practice was largely unregulated and not far off slavery. Girls, on the other hand, would most likely go into service at sixteen, with an average working day from 6.00 am to 10.00 pm, and the possibility of being routinely raped by the master of the house and dismissed without reference if they fell pregnant. There was also honest work to be found in factories and mines, of course, and after Althorpe's Factory Act became law in 1833, children aged nine to thirteen only had to work nine-hour shifts, although the 1842 Report of the Children's Commission on Mines found that young workhouse apprentices were still working underground up to sixteen hours a day.

Schools of Crime

For many kids, the independence of surviving on the streets may well have seemed preferable to working. Begging was always an option; you could sweep chimneys, there was also bone grubbing and rag gathering, you could be a crossing sweeper, brushing horse shit out of the way of middle-class pedestrians in the hope of a tip, or become a 'mudlark', wading in the filthy water of the Thames searching for anything you could use or sell: old nails, a lump of coal, scrap iron, rope or bones… You could also scavenge for easier pickings, such as cigar ends, which could be shredded into tobacco, or become a 'pure-finder', as described by Henry Mayhew in his epic study of London street folk, *London Labour and the London Poor*:

> Dogs' dung is called 'Pure', from its cleansing and purifying properties … The pure-finders meet with a ready market for all the dogs' dung they are able to collect, at the numerous tan yards in Bermondsey, where they sell it by the stable-bucket full, and get from 8d to 10d per bucket, and sometimes 1s and 1s 2d for it, according to its quality. The 'dry limy-looking sort' fetches the highest price at some yards, as it is found to possess more of the alkaline, or purifying properties; but others are found to prefer the dark moist quality.[7]

You slept rough, or in unsanitary and overcrowded lodgings if you were lucky – pure-finders kept their buckets with them. Life was likely to be short, and there were no benevolent Mr Brownlows reaching down, like God, to save you. Even as late as 1876, Dr Barnado estimated that there were around 30,000 neglected children under the age of sixteen sleeping on the streets of London. When one reads the first-hand accounts of the lives of the 'street-children' in Mayhew, kids aged way beyond their years by endless toil that made barely enough money for basic survival, the life of the 'boys on the cross' – youthful criminals like Dickens's Artful Dodger – looks increasingly inviting. Overall, was the risk of punishment much worse, or even much more fatal, than a life sentence of poverty and labour? Was starving slowly to death any better than thirty seconds of agony at the end of a rope, or the life of a convict labourer in Van Diemen's Land? And at least in prison you had food and shelter.

It was not unusual in the rookeries for children under ten to be accomplished thieves and Newgate alumni, a situation compounded for the post-Waterloo generation by the rise in unemployment caused by the return of soldiers from Europe. The term 'juvenile delinquency' dates from this period. And, like those similarly labelled nowadays, nineteenth-century juvenile delinquents were natural rebels. They shared a disdain for authority, a desire to impress their peers, and an edgy sense of bravado. Prison was 'boarding school', where one might learn from the older convicts, transportation was 'going to sea' and seen as a great adventure, and if they went to the gallows it was important to 'die game', dressing well and going out defiantly. In *Oliver Twist*, for example, the gang sees the Artful Dodger's transportation so young in life as something worthy of respect:

> 'Never mind, Charley,' said Fagin soothingly; 'it'll come out, it'll be sure to come out. They'll all know what a clever fellow he was; he'll show it himself, and not disgrace his old pals and teachers. Think how young he is too! What a distinction, Charley, to be lagged at his time of life!'
> 'Well, it is a honour that is!' said Charley, a little consoled.[8]

Given the hopeless circumstances under which many of the urban poor existed, with little or no possibility of earning an honest living wage, many kids had little choice but to stare down the shadow of the Tyburn Tree and carry on thieving. 'The children of idle, drunken, and dishonest parents, are suffered to infest the streets in a state of destitution,' the magistrate John Thomas Barber Beaumont told the Committee on the State of the Police of the Metropolis in 1816, continuing that:

> the first instructions and ideas these little creatures receive are to procure the means of life by begging and thieving. I have seen children not more than seven or eight years of age initiated into the trade of picking of pockets, under the eye of adults, seemingly their mothers. In Covent-garden Market, and other places affording partial shelter, and in private houses in Saint Giles's, and in public-houses in Whitechapel, boys and girls take up their nightly abode in a state of promiscuous depravity.

Beaumont believed that the best course of action was to remove the children from the environment. 'By separating them from their parents and other bad connexions,' he said, 'and giving them some education, they might soon be made useful members of society, instead of their continuing for life a burthen and a terror to it.'[9]

But there was not even provision in the prisons and the infamous convict hulks moored in the Thames to separate very young children from hardened criminals, let alone remove them from the influence of immoral relatives and the flash houses to which Beaumont alluded. Education there was, but of entirely the wrong sort. Beaumont was right in his assertion that the young thieves were being trained by their elders, who called them 'Tyburn Blossom', who 'in time will ripen into fruit borne by the deadly never-green.'[10] Thomas Evance, a magistrate at the Union Hall police office, described a familiar pattern by which children were either orphaned or deserted by parents that couldn't afford to keep them, but were considered old enough by the parish (six) to earn their own keep, after which:

> there are a number of designing thieves constantly on the lookout for children, who are naturally more inclined to be idle than to work, and who commence with petty thefts at the wharfs, and other places where property is exposed; these the confirmed thieves seize hold of and make them the catspaw in doing those things which they otherwise would themselves, and for which they would probably suffer detection and punishment, hoping that, in consideration of their youth, commiseration may be excited in the breasts of the Magistrates, and that they may be dismissed.[11]

It was widely agreed by reformers and law enforcement officials that London's numerous 'flash houses' were schools of crime where very young street children were seduced into profligacy and vice and recruited by older criminals. Flash houses were a combination of low lodging house, unlicensed public house, and brothel, frequented by all classes of the 'flash crowd', the criminal fraternity. They were therefore hubs of underworld intelligence, where robberies were planned, and stolen goods fenced. The police knew them, and often turned a blind eye for a suitable remuneration. Strangers were not welcome.

John Nelson Lavender, a Bow Street Runner based at the Queen Square office, was asked by the Chair of the Committee, Henry Grey Bennet, 'Do you not think that in houses of that description the boys and girls are trained up in such a system of vice as to lead afterwards to the perpetration of greater crimes?' The policeman agreed, elaborating on a wider network of recruitment. 'There is no doubt at all about that,' he said, 'but the way in which girls are brought into this sort of mischief is by old bawds[12] going about the town, and laying their hands on every girl who has a pretty face; and they actually seduce the boys before they think of such things.'[13] Decades later, the Russian novelist Fyodor Dostoyevsky was appalled at the age of the prostitutes on the Haymarket, writing in the magazine Время in 1863 that 'Little girls of about twelve seize you by the hand and ask you to go with them.'[14] The Reverend

Joshua King, a clergyman from Bethnal Green (Bill and Nancy's manor), singled out the worst of the local 'disorderly houses' that he knew of:

> The Seven Stars and Three Sugar Loaves are a receptacle for suspicious characters, at hours when all other public-houses are closed; and at The Sun, a club significantly termed a cock and hen club, has been, and I believe still is held.
>   In which boys and girls meet? [Asked Bennet.]
>   Yes, and get drunk and debauch one another.[15]

There was also The Black Horse in Tottenham Court Road and The Rose in Long Acre, the landlords of both being well-known thieves, and The Bear, a notorious establishment that was directly over the road from the famous Bow Street police office. In *Oliver Twist*, the flash house favoured by Fagin, Sikes and Nancy was The Three Cripples (based on The One Tun on Saffron Hill):

> Cunning, ferocity, and drunkenness in all its stages, were there, in their strongest aspects; and women: some with the last lingering tinge of their early freshness, almost fading as you looked: others with every mark and stamp of their sex utterly beaten out, and presenting but one loathsome blank of profligacy and crime; some mere girls, others but young women, and none past the prime of life; formed the darkest and saddest portion of this dreary picture.[16]

As the Dickens scholar Humphry House argued – noting that Dickens ceased to be a journalist as much as a novelist only in 'his reticence about what he thought might be offensive' – in the real world of *Oliver Twist*, 'Nancy's job would certainly have been to use her sex as much as possible with boys like Charley Bates and the Dodger.' Oliver's life in London, he concludes, 'would have been drenched in sex'.[17]

The Reverend Horace Salisbury Cotton, Ordinary of Newgate, even confirmed that 'persons have presented themselves at Newgate, calling themselves sisters and relations of the boys, who had been prevented afterwards from coming, from its being found out that they were common prostitutes, and kept by the boys.'[18]

The Quakers William Crawford and Peter Bedford, who were also witnesses, had already established a private committee and co-authored a report on the 'Causes of the Alarming Increase of Juvenile Delinquency in the Metropolis'. They described the flash houses as 'pestiferous haunts' and 'nurseries of crime' in which 'are to be found the most experienced and notorious thieves; boys and girls, from nine years of age' and 'women of the most profligate description; associating indiscriminately'.[19] Juvenile promiscuity is a recurring theme, and one that Henry Mayhew picks up in *London Labour and the London Poor* over a generation later, writing that 'Perhaps the most remarkable characteristic of these wretched children is their extraordinary licentiousness.'[20] Bedford and Crawford's report was, however, groundbreaking in its attempt to understand young offenders, rather than simply condemning them. Their committee would often intercede on a child's behalf to have a death sentence commuted or to place them in school or work, and they saw the good in the kids, or the potential for good, their report frequently noting the intelligence of the children. In *Oliver Twist*, Bill Sikes laments the intervention of the committee after a child he'd been grooming is rescued:

> 'I want a boy; and he mustn't be a big un. Lord!' said Mr. Sikes, reflectively, 'if I'd only got that young boy of Ned, the chimbley-sweeper's! He kept him small on purpose, and let him out by the job. But the father gets lagged; and then the Juvenile Delinquent Society comes, and takes the boy away from a trade where he was arning money: teaches him to read and write, and in time makes a 'prentice of him. And so they go on,' said Mr. Sikes, his wrath rising with the recollection of his wrongs, 'so they go on; and, if they'd got money enough (which it's a Providence they haven't) we shouldn't have half a dozen boys left in the whole trade, in a year or two.'[21]

It is for this reason Oliver is forced into housebreaking.

Although death sentences were passed on children, executions were relatively rare, and usually for serious offences. Until the 1823 Judgement of Death Act gave judges the discretion to pass lesser sentences for any crime other than treason or murder, there were over 200 capital crimes on the statute books, the Bloody Code, many of them trivial by today's standards, for example blasphemy, shoplifting, stealing a letter, picking a pocket, coining, and the theft of any private or commercial property to the collective value of five shillings or more. By the turn of the century, over a thousand men, women and teenagers a year were being sentenced to death, although the majority of these cases, about 95 per cent, were commuted to transportation. The youngest person to be executed in Britain in the nineteenth century was the 14-year-old John Amy Bird Bell, who was hanged outside Maidstone Prison on 1 August 1831, for the murder of 13-year-old Richard Taylor. Along with his younger brother, James, who was eleven, Bell had killed Taylor for the nine shillings he had collected from the parish for his crippled father. Nearly 5,000 people turned out to watch. Two years later, a 9-year-old boy was convicted of housebreaking at Maidstone Assizes and condemned to death, but he was reprieved after a public outcry. Before the death of Bell, an illiterate country pauper, the youngest victims of Jack Ketch were both hanged at Newgate; Henry Lovell in 1819 for highway robbery, and John Smith for burglary in 1825. They were both fifteen.

Bedford and Crawford saw the severity of the English Penal Code as an issue that needed to be addressed. Their report also highlighted the contributory factors of poverty and neglect, lack of schools and jobs, the lure of street gambling as a gateway to crime and vice, and problems with policing (there weren't enough, and many officers were easily bribed). The report concludes with an appendix containing several anonymous case studies, which offer an insight into the ordinary lives of the street children. They are all quite Dickensian, for example:

> A.B. aged 13 years. His parents are living. He was but for a short time at school. His father was frequently intoxicated; and, on these occasions, the son generally left home, and associated with bad characters, who introduced him to houses of ill fame, where they gambled till they had lost or spent all their money. This boy has been five years in the commission of crime, and been imprisoned for three separate offences. Sentence of death has been twice passed on him.

> E.F. aged 8 years. His mother only is living, and she is a very immoral character. This boy has been in the habit of stealing for upwards of two years. In Covent Garden Market there is a party of between thirty and forty boys, who sleep every night under the sheds and baskets. These pitiable objects, when they arise in the morning, have no other means of procuring subsistence, but by the commission of crime. This child was one of the number; and it appears that he has been brought up

to the several police offices upon eighteen separate charges. He has been twice confined in the House of Correction, and three times in Bridewell. He is very ignorant, but of a good capacity.

G.H. aged 15 years. During the time that he should have been in school, his parents suffered him to range the public streets. He there mixed promiscuously with boys of bad character. He entered into their schemes, and continued in connexion with them, until he had committed a capital offence, for which he was tried, and received the sentence of death. Thus situated, he attracted the attention of the Committee. Intercession was made for him. His life was spared, and he is now in a situation where he is receiving the benefit of instruction, whilst he is training up in habits of industry.[22]

The inversion of the healthy family unit is a bleak and common denominator in these stories. Children are either directed to steal by their parents, or neglected, orphaned or abandoned, in which case they must fend for themselves. In either situation, however pernicious the gangs or profligate the children, it was clear that they were being enabled and exploited by adults, much, it has to be noted, as they would have been had they found more conventional employment.

Real versions of Dickens's Fagin therefore abounded, both male and female. It is often asserted by literary historians that the character was based on the notorious London fence Isaac 'Ikey' Solomon, largely because of their shared faith. In his seminal study, *Dickens and Crime*, for example, Philip Collins takes the matter for granted. 'Fagin was, as everyone saw,' he wrote, 'based on the famous Jewish fence, Ikey Solomon, and his methods of employing and training boy pick-pockets were the standard practice, and remained so for several decades.'[23] But the similarities are tenuous at best, and there's a kind of scholarly anti-Semitism at work in the assumption that the 'very old shrivelled Jew, whose villainous-looking and repulsive face was obscured by a quantity of matted red hair' and 'dressed in a greasy flannel gown' described by Dickens had to be inspired by the rather urbane Solomon simply because both were London Jews.[24] Fagin is just as likely to be a fictional hybrid of several enterprising criminals known to the police in the early part of the century who corrupted children.

There was, for example, Lippy Allen of Bell Lane, Spitalfields, who raised his son to steal while he disposed of the loot. The boy's mates were similarly employed, but although Lippy was well in with local law enforcement, he would only put his hand in his pocket to save his son. Mrs Jennings of Whitecross Street, St Luke's, also brought her son up a thief. Like Bill Sikes, he was an expert housebreaker or 'cracksman' and his mother was a sophisticated fence, running an ever-changing crew of boys and girls out of a flash house in Red Lion Market, over whom she appeared to have absolute and malevolent control. She even had a secret room in her house for the temporary storage of stolen goods, accessed through the doors of a large cupboard. Another source of income were the men her girls lured back to the house, got very drunk and then robbed with their young boyfriends, often turning them back out into the street insensible and in a state of undress. 'Mother' Cummings of St Giles, another fence, criminal mentor, and madam, kept a flash house in George Street where beds could be rented either all night or by the hour. She ran a gang of very young thieves and whores, her favourite a workhouse boy called Billy, and was known for her violent and jealous temper. Like Mrs Jennings, her girls were trained to rob their clients blind.

Other operators worked out of small shops, like Mrs White of Wigmore Street, who kept a shoe shop in Barret's Court where she also sold domestic items like brushes, pails and coal scuttles, things that could be pinched from just inside the door of a middle-class house by one of her boys; or Mrs Diner of Holborn, whose shop in Field Lane sold only silk handkerchiefs, the owner's initials carefully picked out with a needle, a trick Fagin teaches Oliver. Then there was Mr Brand of Tottenham Court Road, who had a rag shop that was largely a front for fencing lead, and Mr Reed of Fitzroy Place, whose rag and glass shop was, in realty, a school for young apprentice cracksmen. Also of Fitzroy Place was one Mr Lawrence, who notionally sold Banbury Cakes out of a basket at fairs and fights, as well as a crafty glass of gin, while children in his employ picked his customers' pockets.[25]

Ikey Solomon, however, was in a class of his own. And although there's no proof that he ever trained child criminals, rightly or wrongly his name is now forever linked with Dickens's Fagin. The reality is just as colourful, and Solomon, a sophisticated and successful criminal who escaped from Newgate but then gave up his freedom for the woman he loved, could have easily sprung from the pages of one of the criminal romances of the day that Dickens so opposed. His name, in the press and in folklore at the height of his fame, when he stood in the dock at the Old Bailey in the summer of 1830, was as familiar as that of the underworld icons of the previous century, like Dick Turpin, Jack Sheppard and Jonathan Wild. He was, in many ways, the nineteenth century's first gangland celebrity.

The Prince of Fences

As a young man, the so-called 'Prince of Fences' had been one of the 'swell mob', described by Mayhew as 'the elegantly dressed and expert pickpocket promenading in the West-end and attending fashionable assemblies', though he would have cut his teeth as a 'natty lad', lifting handkerchiefs from tailcoats as a child.[26] Like many Eastenders, he was the child of Jewish immigrants (one of nine). His father came from northern Bavaria, and he was born and raised in Houndsditch, close to the heart of the London Jewish community in Whitechapel, where his future wife, Hannah 'Ann' Julian, was born a couple of years after him, sometime in the mid-1780s.[27]

Solomon's career as a pickpocket came to an abrupt end for the same reason we know so much about the likes of Mrs Jennings and 'Mother' Cummings – these were all characters well known to the police, whether or not anything could be proven against them. In 1810, Solomon and an accomplice called Joel Joseph were working the crowd at a speech by the radical politician Sir Francis Burdett in New Palace Yard. They'd had a good day and were attempting to leave quietly through Westminster Hall when they were recognised by John Vickery, a policeman attached to the Worship Street office. The pair made a run for it, but were trapped because the doors at the upper end of the hall were locked. Solomon dropped a pocketbook and when Joseph was collared he was stuffing bank notes into his mouth. The owner of the wallet was traced and the prisoners' defence that they had found the wallet and intended to return it to the owner was subsequently rejected by a jury. Both men were sentenced to be transported for life. Joseph was sent to Australia, but Solomon, as was not uncommon, served his time on the prison hulk *Retribution*. He was released in error in 1816, when he was confused with another prisoner with a similar name, after which he surrendered himself on the advice of his father and received a pardon, partly as a reward and partly to cover up the mistake that had set him free in the first place.

From this point on, the legend takes over. There is no record of Solomon's activities over the next decade, but when he attained celebrity status, several broadsheet mongers attempted to fill this void. *The Life and Exploits of Ikey Solomons, Swindler, forger, fencer, and brothel-keeper* by 'Moses Hebron' (c. 1830)[28] does exactly what it says on the tin, and presents Solomon as the master of a 'nugging house' in Angel Court, a base from which he also operated as a receiver of stolen goods and a moneylender, with half the Bow Street magistrates and officers in his pay, also running a sideline in counterfeit jewellery and pornographic literature, which he supposedly disseminated through London synagogues. The anonymous author of *Adventures, Memoirs, Former Trial, Transportation, and Escapes, of that Notorious Fence, and Receiver of Stolen Goods, Isaac Solomons*, meanwhile, had Ikey down as a card sharp, a confidence trickster and a smuggler, while *The Life and Adventures of Isaac Solomons, The Notorious Receiver of Stolen Goods* essentially knocked off 'Moses Hebron', adding only a new account of his trial.[29] There isn't a shred of documented evidence for any of this, but when Solomon's head once more appears above the parapet, he is one of the most affluent and successful fences in London. He had spent the last decade building an empire. By now a father of six children, operating out of the family home in Bell Lane, Spitalfields, with assets valued at between £18,000 and £20,000 (that's between 1.7 and 1.8 million GBP today), his business network comprised a small army of thieves, from pickpockets to bank robbers, with continental contacts for laundering stolen bank notes.

Solomon had come to the attention of the wider public in May 1826, when he escaped capture after his home was searched by warrant and £200 worth of watch movements recently stolen from the McCabe and Strachan warehouse in Lombard Street was discovered by police in a locked room at the top of the house. Although now in hiding, Solomon continued his trade unabated for another year, with the clandestine support of his family, until he was recognised on the street by a policeman from the Lambeth Street office and arrested near the lodgings he rented under an assumed name in Islington. He was found to have a number of watches on him and a large quantity of cash – over £200 in notes and gold – and his rooms were packed with stolen loot, from numerous silk handkerchiefs and suits of clothes to bolts of Irish linen. Although legend has it that Solomon offered McCabe and Strachan £200 to drop the original charges and a grand to another Lambeth Street police officer to let him escape, he was committed to stand trial at the Old Bailey on six counts of theft and receiving stolen goods and transferred to Newgate on 15 May 1827.

Newgate Prison in Solomon's day was no longer quite the 'bottomless pit of violence' memorably described by Alexander Smith in 1714 as the 'Tower of Babel where all are speakers and no hearers', having been rebuilt after it was destroyed by fire during the Gordon Riots of 1780.[30] Sanitation and ventilation was much improved, and the virulent form of typhus, known as 'gaol fever', that had plagued the prison in the last century was a thing of the past. The prison was now regularly visited by a doctor who reported back to the sheriffs and aldermen of the City.

There were still a variety of fees expected to be paid to the keeper and his warders by the prisoners, though, for everything from coal, candles and bedding to admission to the Press Yard, the most desirable part of the prison, a 'garnish' whereby new arrivals had to buy cellmates drinks, and a charge for being released upon receiving a pardon. Criminals of all ages and experience were also still held together, from young, petty thieves to old lags and condemned murderers, and these mixed with debtors and political prisoners. 'The days were passed in idleness, debauchery, riotous quarrelling, immoral conversation, gambling, instruction in all nefarious processes, lively discourse on past criminal exploits, elaborate discussion of others to be perpetrated after release,' reported the newly appointed Inspectors of Prisons in 1835, continuing, 'No provision whatever was made for the employment of prisoners ... Drink, in more or less unlimited quantities, was still to be had ... Women saw men if they merely pretended to be wives; even boys were visited by their sweethearts.'[31] From 1783, a platform erected outside, the 'New drop', had replaced the public gallows at Tyburn, and the prison was largely a remand centre, holding prisoners awaiting trial, transportation or execution.

Ikey Solomon, however, had a plan. He instructed his 'agent', James Isaacs of Bury Street, to apply for bail. This meant he had to appear in person before a judge at Westminster Hall. Prisoners were conveyed by Hackney carriage, accompanied by two guards. Of course, he had no chance of being granted bail, but on the return journey he managed to escape from the carriage and disappear into the tangle of streets and alleys around Petticoat Lane. Details of the escape are obscure, with the Keeper of Newgate later claiming that the coachman had been discovered to have been Solomon's father-in-law, who had taken an irregular route to meet accomplices waiting in Whitechapel. Some newspaper reports suggested that the party had actually stopped for a drink at Solomon's suggestion, after which his guards were drugged. Others said his wife was travelling in the coach, and the turnkeys diverted in order to drop her off. Or perhaps someone finally accepted a bribe. Again, there are various versions, but the escape itself was very real, and embarrassing for new Prime Minister George Canning's coalition government, not to mention James Isaacs, who was effectively acting as his solicitor, and the two men who were supposed to be guarding him. He'd only spent ten days in Newgate.

After Solomon's escape, which was worthy of the eighteenth-century rogue Jack Sheppard, the police turned their baleful eye on the rest of his family, arresting his wife, Ann, a month later on suspicion of receiving stolen goods. Identification of the items proved difficult, however, as all personal and maker's marks had been removed. Only some textiles were traced to an old robbery, but as this had occurred prior to her husband's arrest Ann was not deemed responsible under law and the charges were dropped. Next, the Solomon's eldest son, John, was also arrested on suspicion of holding stolen goods at a second family house on Henry Street, but was released due to insufficient evidence. Barely a week later, Solomon's father, Henry, was arrested after his house at Gravel Lane was searched and stolen watches and jewellery were discovered. Henry denied everything but this time the charges stuck, although his sentence was respited until the next sessions owing to his health. Ann unwisely continued to run the family business from home, and the house was raided again by police at the end of August, with a warrant issued by the Royal Mint to search for counterfeit money. This time, the police took the house apart, digging up the yard and lifting floorboards, unearthing a large storage space under a concealed trapdoor. They found over 500 base sovereigns, used for coining, and a vast number of watches, ornaments and items of jewellery, as well as piles of clothes and bolts of cloth. Four coach-loads of stolen goods were taken to Hatton Garden police office, where dozens of local tradespeople turned up to identify their property. Ann protested that as the majority of this loot was hidden, she knew nothing about it, but she was arrested along with her son, Moses, and her servant. The latter were both released without charge, but Ann was committed to stand trial on three counts of receiving stolen goods and one charge of possessing 540 counterfeit sovereigns with intent to circulate. The coining charge was not proceeded with, despite being the subject of the original warrant, and Ann was acquitted of two of the three receiving charges on the same grounds that had seen her go free in June. She could not, however, account for a watch that had only been reported stolen a week and a half prior to the search, and was found guilty. Ann was sentenced alongside her father-in-law in September. Henry received six months in prison, a lenient sentence because of his age (he was then at least seventy); Ann was sentenced to transportation for fourteen years.

Ann petitioned the King, as did one of her prosecutors, Joseph Ridley, the owner of the fatal watch, being so taken with the 'elegant' and 'unfortunate woman'. But it was to no avail. She remained in Newgate until 24 February 1828, when she was placed aboard the convict ship *Mermaid* with her four youngest children, arriving at Hobart in Van Diemen's Land at the end of June. Her two oldest boys, John and Moses, arrived of their own volition soon afterwards, closely followed by their father.

Ikey's previous whereabouts remain largely a mystery, although he himself subsequently wrote that he'd 'sailed to America' in a petition to the Home Secretary written in 1830. Legend has it that he lived in Manhattan and made his living forging bank notes, although the only record of him in this period is on the ship *Coronet*, which he boarded for Van Diemen's Land at Rio de Janeiro.[32] But wherever he had been, as soon as news reached him of his wife's predicament he immediately travelled to join her. This was a huge risk. Ann had been assigned to the house of Richard Newman as a convict servant. Newman was on the staff of Josiah Spode, the Chief Police Magistrate, but out of sympathy for Ann and her children he didn't immediately report Ikey. Unfortunately, the two families soon quarrelled for reasons that are now unclear. In Solomon's letter to the Home Secretary he blamed Newman. This was an (unsuccessful) petition to reclaim property seized by the police in 1827. The tone throughout is that of the victim, with the author's life on the run described in terms of 'the extreme hardship which I have suffered'. His claim that Newman tried to swindle him should therefore probably be taken with a pinch of salt, as should his assertion that his wife was 'an innocent woman' who had been maliciously and falsely accused by others, her virtue sullied by association.[33] Only his oft-stated love for Ann feels sincere, and his rush to join her is difficult to explain in any other terms. In Hobart, however, it would appear that in reality his wife was comfortable with Newman and his wife until her husband and sons arrived, after which relations quickly degenerated. Ann was sensible enough to play the vulnerable housewife on her own, but together the criminal clan must have been a handful for a middle-class bureaucrat like Newman.

Transported convicts were mostly given 'public works' duties (government jobs ranging from general maintenance to office work and even security), or, like Ann, they were assigned to settlers, merchants or government employees as servants. A third category, 'hard labour', was reserved for the most violent and hardened criminals, who had continued to offend on the colony. This group worked in irons and were kept physically separate from the main community of prisoners on a camp at Port Arthur, guarded by soldiers with dogs. As in ordinary life, the lot of the servant depended on the disposition of the master, and Ann had been lucky with the Newmans until her mask slipped. Because of the breakdown in relations – it was reported by several parties that Ann and Mrs Newman fought like cat and dog – Ikey was exposed, Newman was reprimanded by Spode for sheltering him, and Ann was sent to the 'Female Factory', a depot for unassigned women prisoners, with her children going to an orphan school.

Having broken no laws in Van Diemen's Land, Solomon remained at large with his sons. He was reasonably well heeled, and able to buy a house in Hobart, from which he lobbied the Lieutenant Governor, Colonel George Arthur, for the release of his wife and reassignment to the new family home. He offered several concessions, including a commitment to remain in Hobart Town, essentially as a convict, for the duration of Ann's sentence. The local press took up his cause, creating a narrative of redemption through love. Several respected Hobart businessmen supported Ikey's efforts, and in March 1829, Ann was assigned to her husband as his servant, under a bond of £2,700 put up by her sponsors to be forfeited should she make any attempt to leave the island.

Solomon, however, remained a wanted man in England, and as soon as his identity was verified (three convicts knew him personally from Newgate), Arthur reported this to the Home Office, which promptly issued six warrants for his arrest and extradition. Ikey was detained, but he immediately applied for a writ of *habeas corpus* on what amounted to a legal technicality involving jurisdiction and the right of the Home Office to direct the Australian Colonial Office. He also questioned the evidence of the original charges. He was aided in this by the council of Joseph Tice Gellibrand, who had an axe to grind against Arthur having been previously dismissed from his post of Attorney General to the island in favour of the Lieutenant Governor's nephew, and who also edited the opposition newspaper, the *Tasmanian and Australasian Review.* The writ was granted by the Supreme Court in January 1830, but as Solomon was undeniably an escaped convict, bail was set at £2,000 with four additional bonds of £500 required from men willing to stand surety against him failing to return to England at the first opportunity to stand trial. This was an impossible undertaking, and Solomon thus remained in prison, despite the legal ruling dismissing the warrant on which he'd been arrested. This was an embarrassment for the colonial government, and despite public opinion and continued opposition from Gellibrand's paper, the Lieutenant Governor issued his own warrant with the support of the colony's Executive Council, and Ikey was quietly put on His Majesty's Ship the *Prince Regent* on 25 January, arriving once more at Newgate on 27 June.

Ikey was tried with positively indecent haste. The first indictments were read at the Old Bailey on 8 July. East End Jews packed the public galleries in support and the broadsheet writers went into overdrive. There were eight counts of theft and receiving stolen goods, five in the City of London and three in Middlesex, including the case of the McCabe and Strachan watch parts. He was acquitted of the five London indictments, which included three charges of burglary (carrying a potential life sentence), but McCabe and Strachan did for him. The stolen goods had been found on his property, and instead of offering any explanation he had bolted and gone into hiding. He was also convicted of stealing twelve pieces of Valencia cloth, found at his Islington lodgings, and on 12 May he was sentenced to be transported for fourteen years, although he claimed that the jury was prejudiced and objected strongly to the press describing him as 'notorious'. He arrived back at Hobart Town on the first day of November.

During his voyage on the *William Glen Anderson*, Solomon had gotten wind of a plan by some of the other convicts to seize the ship. Seeing no profit in this for himself, in fact quite the reverse, the gentleman thief alerted the commander of the guard, Lieutenant Colonel H. Breton, who later gave an account of the foiled mutiny to a parliamentary select committee in which Solomon is named and praised as the informer. He was rewarded with the relatively cushy colony job of 'javelin man', an administrative assistant at Richmond Gaol, a few miles outside Hobart, and allowed to live with his wife at their sons' house in town.

All seemed well that ended well. Both Ann and Ikey's prison records are unremarkable in the first half of the 1830s, aside from a minor breach of discipline that saw the latter imprisoned for a month in Richmond in the winter of 1832 for 'abusive language' and 'turbulent and disorderly conduct', compounded by a supposedly false accusation made against a gaoler called McNeilly. In 1834, Ikey was transferred to a clerical position at Port Arthur, just under 40 miles from Hobart. A year later, he was granted a ticket of leave and paroled, two years earlier than his sentence conventionally required, on the condition that he lived outside the state capital. He chose to settle in New Norfolk, a small town about 20 miles north-west of Hobart, where he owned property. But there was trouble in Paradise. During her husband's absence (40 miles was a long way in that part of the world in those days, as Joseph Gellibrand learned to his cost in 1837, disappearing without a trace between Geelong and Melbourne), Ann had fallen in with a wealthy settler and ex-convict called George Madden and become his lover. Although also married, Madden doted on her and she had no intention of giving up the material benefits of their relationship and moving to the sticks with her husband. Instead, she proposed Ikey maintain two family houses, one for her in Hobart and another for himself in New Norfolk. She would continue to see Madden.

This did not go down well, and Ann's convict record notes that she was sent back to the Factory on 20 July 1835, for 'disorderly conduct in using opprobrious epithets to her Husband and otherwise ill-treating him, Disturbances having continued in the Family ever since the Warning given them on the 3rd July and appearing to arise from a combination between Mother and the Children against the Father'.[34] John G. Wilson, a young lodger at the Solomon house, wrote an earnest letter to the Police Magistrate at New Norfolk laying the blame at Ikey's door, recalling the unlikely support of Joseph Ridley in London, and one is left with the sense that Ann must have been a very charismatic, sexually magnetic woman, able to command considerable devotion from any man under her spell. Her husband, for example, had abandoned the life of the free and wealthy gentleman in South America to go to her in Van Diemen's Land. His life and his surviving letters demonstrate a keen intelligence; he must have known that he would ultimately join her as a convict. Wilson eventually married the Solomon's daughter, Nancy (known as 'Anne'), so he may have been trying to curry favour with her by defending the mother, though it is notable that Anne was the only one of the Solomon children that remained loyal to their father.

Nonetheless, Anne petitioned for her mother's release from the 'Factory', and on 5 November she was paroled. Ikey was allowed to return to Hobart in 1838, where he opened a tobacconist's shop. Although estranged, the couple were both conditionally pardoned on 27 May 1840, meaning they were free but unable to leave the colony. Ann's sentence was served in full in 1841, Ikey's three years later. He died in September 1850, at the age of sixty-five or thereabouts. Despite contemporary rumours in London that he had made another fortune in the colony, and legends that persist to this day in Australia and Tasmania that he continued to run a criminal empire from the front of his shop in Hobart, he died a poor man, leaving an estate to his wife valued at £70.

Looking at the life of Ikey Solomon, it is difficult to detect much of Dickens's Fagin in him besides his race, a casually anti-Semitic move that was not unusual for the time. In Ainsworth's *Jack Sheppard*, for example, Jonathan Wild has a grotesque Jewish henchman called Abraham. Dickens attempted to moderate this in revisions to later editions of *Oliver Twist* after criticism from the *Jewish Chronicle* and a family acquaintance, Eliza Davis, who became a regular correspondent, although he could not resist explaining that Fagin was the way he was 'because it unfortunately was true of the time to which that story refers, that that class of criminal almost invariably was a Jew'.[35] If you read Dickens's public and private correspondence, it's clear he could never be wrong. As Peter Ackroyd wrote of the great man's attitude to slaves during the American Civil War, 'In modern terms, Dickens was a "racist" of the most egregious kind, a fact that ought to give pause to those who persist in believing that he was necessarily the epitome of all that was decent and benevolent in the previous century.'[36] And while the popular and academic Dickens establishment will invariably cite Ikey Solomon as the model for Fagin, there is no mention of the original prince of fences in either Dickens's correspondence or the first biography by John Forster, his closest and oldest friend. Fagin rather belongs to a long tradition of stereotypical Jewish villains in English literature, from the child murderers of Chaucer's *The Prioress's Tale* to Christopher Marlowe's psychopathic Barabas in *The Jew of Malta* and Shakespeare's Shylock. And after Fagin there was Svengali.

Fagin is condemned at the end of the novel, a sentence that was dramatically appropriate though not factually accurate – for his crimes, he would almost certainly have been transported. Oliver visits him in prison, and, as with the Magdalene-like Nancy, there is a moment of redemption when he whispers the location of the papers that prove Oliver's birthright. After this, he reverts to a pathetic figure scheming for his life, whom Oliver prays for as he goes to the gallows. For the fallen in Dickens, redemption, if it comes at all, comes only in the afterlife.

Ikey Solomon was a much more complex and enigmatic figure than the literary counterpart that has been forced upon him. He was a dapper, resourceful and literate man who fought his way up from the rookeries of London, becoming one of the richest and most successful criminal masterminds of his age, long before the Jews Relief Act and Lionel de Rothschild entering Parliament effectively heralded Jewish emancipation in England. He considered himself a businessman, and as far as anyone knows he never killed, or caused to be killed, anyone. And when the game was finally up, he got away clean, voluntarily choosing to relinquish his freedom to be with his wife. The fact that there was no happy ending should not detract from the nobility of that act, even if it was the only honest thing Ikey Solomon ever did. The only argument that could relate him to the uncouth and pitiable Fagin would be that Dickens was continuing his stated project to negate the fashionable anti-heroes of Newgate novels, and had decided when faced with one in reality to remake him a ragged and duplicitous grotesque. Otherwise, Fagin is nothing more than a convenient racist stereotype, and any similarity with Ikey Solomon is purely coincidental.

This is not to say that there were not many men, and women, like Fagin. In the underworld, children were simply another resource to be exploited and, if necessary, discarded, by unscrupulous adults, until social reformers like Thomas Barnado, Charles Booth and Joseph Rowntree began to make a difference towards the end of the century. And if these lost boys and girls survived to adulthood, they would most likely lead the lives, and the deaths, of men and women like Bill and Nancy. In this sense, Dickens's *Oliver Twist* was brutally accurate, and his portrayal of poverty and crime in London in many ways defines the image our own culture has of his period. As he said himself in his preface to the novel, 'It is true.' In fact, propriety stopped him from going any further, as did his rival G.W.M. Reynolds, who in *The Mysteries of London* piled horror upon horror in his sensational depiction of Saffron Hill in the time of Oliver Twist. What Dickens called the 'miserable reality' was always worse, but in *Oliver Twist*, as in his later, more mature novels, the journalist in him got as close to the truth as his publishers and audience would allow. It is only the novel's resolution that is unrealistic. In the real world of the street children of London, Oliver would not have been saved.

Chapter 6

Fallen Women

Like the old adage that in the city you are never more than 6 feet away from a rat, as London and the great industrial centres of the north grew, their bourgeois inhabitants were never too far from the poverty and crime of the underworld. But although they might encounter thieves from time to time, whether through a pocket picked or in the pages of a popular novel like *Oliver Twist*, nowhere did these worlds collide more fully than in the burgeoning Victorian sex industry.

Although estimates of the number of prostitutes active at any given time in London and across the country varied wildly, the trade was unashamedly obvious. They were active in Liverpool, Manchester, Edinburgh and Glasgow, and in the fleshpots of Ipswich and Diss. As afternoon became evening, parks, pubs and urban sub-centres across the land were occupied by an army of painted ladies and the darting child prostitutes that had so appalled Dostoyevsky, from the itinerant 'hedge whores', wraithlike dockyard bunters, and slightly shabby provincial ladybirds, to the Drury Lane Vestals and the glamorous courtesans of London's West End, collectively owning the streets and the alley corners. When the crusading journalist W.T. Stead first encountered what he called these 'wretched ruins of humanity' and 'women trampled and crushed into devils by society', for example, he wasn't describing the rouge-caked girls of London's Haymarket and wicked Windmill Street, but women walking the smoky streets of Darlington.[1] 'Women of the town' were, it was said, 'as common as a barber's chair in which a whole parish sit to be trimmed', and this was a situation that persisted, largely unchanged by legislation, throughout the century.[2]

The Great Social Evil

If there was an epicentre, it was the warren of streets and alleys at the upper end of the Haymarket, London's theatre district and the broad street connecting Pall Mall with Piccadilly, Tom and Jerry's old stamping ground. As one 'shrewd and clever' girl told Mayhew's man, Bracebridge Hemyng, explaining a typical day:

> What are my habits? Why, if I have no letters or visits from any of my friends, I get up about four o'clock, dress ('en déshabillé')[3] and dine; after that I may walk about the streets for an hour or two, and pick up any one I am fortunate enough to meet with, that is if I want money; afterwards I go to the Holborn, dance a little, and if any one likes me I take him home with me, if not I go to the Haymarket, and wander from one café to another, from Sally's to the Carlton, from Barn's to Sam's, and if I find no one there I go, if I feel inclined, to the divans.[4] I like the Grand Turkish best, but you don't as a rule find good men in any of the divans.[5]

The haunts this woman mentions puts her somewhere in the middle rank of her profession, neither high nor low. These were ordinary 'night houses', known to the police – who maintained a strong but distant presence – as a bit bawdy but not particularly dangerous. Were she one of the more elegant class of consort, she would have cited places like the Café Royal[6] in Princes Street, run by the formidable old tart Kate Hamilton, the Argyll Rooms in Great Windmill Street (supposedly a dancing academy), the Alhambra in Leicester Square, or the Cremorne Gardens in Chelsea, the last of the great London pleasure gardens, famous for ballet, bowling, exotic animals and ornamental gaslights; a popular place for fashionable picnicking by day and amorous transactions by night.

In the 'Modern Babylon' – a popular term for London first used by Benjamin Disraeli in his novel *Tancred* (1847) – the 'Great Social Evil' of prostitution was perceived in such monstrously pervasive terms that F.W. Newman, the younger brother of the Cardinal, saw charitable attempts at prevention as 'comparable to mopping out the ocean'.[7] There was a general and growing hysteria around the subject, fuelled by the evangelism of the age, which was both epic and reductive. In reality, prostitution in Victorian England was a much more complicated business, which, as ever, the social investigators attempted to categorise and contain, as did the popular novelists. Obvious examples include Dickens's Nancy and the ruined and equally doomed Esther in Mrs Gaskell's *Mary Barton* (1848), with some more transgressive portrayals in pornography and the penny dreadfuls. The character of Ellen Monroe, for example, in *The Mysteries of London*, progresses from mesmerist's assistant, artist's model, dancer, and actress (all Victorian codes for prostitution) to, finally, the lover of a corrupt politician. A bold and resourceful woman, she blackmails the MP into marriage after having his illegitimate child, surviving the story (unlike her husband, Nancy and Esther), and ultimately inheriting his estate. But Reynolds's unorthodox treatment of the subject was far from the norm. Fine art, similarly, provided gentile models of the 'fallen woman', most notably in William Holman Hunt's artfully symbolic *The Awakened Conscience* (1853) and Dante Gabriel Rossetti's unfinished but nonetheless influential painting *Found* (c. 1855). Such portrayals did much to create a powerful image of the prostitute as either the Magdalene redeemed (Dickens, Hunt) or the soiled dove (Gaskell, Rossetti), images that coexisted uneasily with the prevailing cultural narrative of physical and moral contagion. As ever, middle-class commentators looked down upon the working and underclasses with whom they increasingly shared their cities, fascinated and repelled by what many saw as an urban environment rife with depravity, vice and sexual danger.

The daughters of the underworld were thus perceived in stark and threatening contrast to the bourgeois concept of feminine domesticity celebrated, for example, in Coventry Patmore's leaden sequence of narrative poems collectively entitled *The Angel of the House* (1854–62), which idealised women as dedicated wives and mothers, and paragons of modesty and virtue. But in 1840, the year after Dickens finished *Oliver Twist* – long before Bracebridge Hemyng was conducting interviews and Dr William Acton set out to 'heal the sick prostitute and to cleanse her moral nature' – the French writer and activist Flora Tristan was already talking to the working girls of London.[8]

Flore-Celestine-Therèse-Henriette Tristan-Moscoso was a fascinating woman. Like Mary Wollstonecraft before her, she was a pioneer of feminist theory, who is mostly remembered nowadays, if she's remembered at all, as the grandmother of the artist Paul Gauguin. As a social explorer, she represents the ideological opposite of late Georgian commentators like Hazlitt and Egan, who were essentially on safari, as well as Dickens's belief in Christian charity and Henry Mayhew's Victorian blue book analytics. She is closest, politically, to Utopian Socialists like Charles Fourier (whom she knew personally), and the early work of Marx and Engels. Her *Promenades dans Londres* (or 'London Journal') pre-dated Engels's study *The Condition of the Working Class in England* by four years and *The Communist Manifesto* by eight, and her polemical style is also echoed in the sensational serials of the Chartist Reynolds, who had learned his trade in Paris. Gauguin later described her as a 'blue stocking socialist and anarchist', and the sign of the *Place Flora Tristan* in Paris describes her as a 'Militante Féministe'.[9]

Fiercely independent, Tristan was motivated to write by a deep resistance to patriarchal authority and a lifelong struggle with poverty. She was born in Paris in 1803, the illegitimate child of a Peruvian aristocrat who died intestate, leaving his young mistress and children destitute. Flora supported her mother and, unable to marry the man she loved because of the social stigma of her birth, made a match at seventeen with an apprentice lithographer named André Chazal. After bearing Chazal two sons, Flora felt increasingly trapped, leaving her husband when she was pregnant with her third child (Gauguin's future mother, Aline). Posing as single and childless, she travelled to Peru, presenting herself to her uncle, General Juan Pío de Tristán y Moscoso, and claiming her paternal inheritance as the oldest child of the oldest son. Her claim was rejected, though Don Pio granted her a small allowance. She remained in Peru in the aftermath of the recent war of independence, and like Che Guevara a little over a century later, she became increasingly radicalised after witnessing first-hand the appalling living conditions of South American peasants, a process she described in an autobiography written in Paris in 1838 entitled *Peregrinations of a Pariah*. This was a colourful and melodramatic book, in which Tristan presented herself as a romantic revolutionary descended from an Inca princess, while her uncle, the last Spanish Viceroy of Peru, was depicted as an avaricious idiot reliant on his niece's wise political counsel, and her husband was dismissed as a drunk and a gambler. Understandably miffed, Don Pio stopped Flora's allowance and had her books burned in the street and her effigy shot in the public square at Arequipa. Her husband, meanwhile, tracked her down in Paris and shot her outside her apartment. The attempted murder sent Chazal to prison for twenty years and turned Flora into a literary celebrity. She followed her memoir by rushing the novel *Méphis* into print the same year, in which she explored the male exploitation of women through the story of a wife forced to sleep with a wealthy nobleman by her husband, implicitly linking marriage to prostitution. She then promptly abandoned the path of easy fame to concentrate on the class struggle, particularly the plight of working-class women, travelling to England, then the heart of the Industrial Revolution.

Despite her dislike of the English climate, about which she complained constantly, Flora explored what she called 'The Monster City' extensively, visiting factories, schools, prisons, and asylums. 'In London one draws gloom with every breath,' she wrote, continuing:

it is in the air; it enters at every pore. Ah, there is nothing so lugubrious, so spasmodic as the look of the city on a day of fog, rain or bleak cold! When one is in the grip of such influences, one's head is heavy and aching, one's stomach has trouble functioning, breathing becomes difficult for lack of pure air, one feels an overwhelming lassitude; then one is seized by what the English call 'spleen'! One feels deep despair! immense grief! without knowing why; bitter hatred for those one was accustomed to love the most, finally a loathing for everything and an irresistible desire for suicide.[10]

She went to Parliament, and also met with Chartists, the working-class activists calling for electoral reform; she even attended the races at Ascot Heath. She talked to the Irish in the rookeries of St Giles, and Jews in and around Whitechapel, Ikey Solomon's old manor, feeling enormous empathy for those she saw as the outcasts of capitalist society. She was especially drawn to the girls of the street, writing that, 'Never have I been able to see a prostitute without being moved by a feeling of compassion for our societies, without experiencing contempt for their organisation and hatred for rulers who, strangers to decency, to any respect for humanity, to all love of their fellow creatures, reduce her whom God created to the lowest degree of abasement!'[11]

What made Tristan's view of prostitution so unique was that she saw the women as the victims of patriarchy, whereas the common view at the time was that the women themselves were the threat. 'It is almost impossible that a young man can escape without having his morals contaminated,' Dr William Tait had written, for example, of the dark streets of Edinburgh in 1842. 'His path is beset on the right hand and on the left, so that he is at every step exposed to temptation. From boyhood to mature age, his life is one continued struggle against it ... He cannot pass along the street in the evening without meeting with, and being accosted by women of the town at almost every step.'[12] As Peter Stallybrass and Allon White have argued, 'It was above all around the figure of the prostitute that the gaze and touch, the desires and contaminations, of the bourgeois male writer were articulated.'[13] The Old Testament fear of temptation and fall thus remained the dominate narrative throughout the century. In 1881, forty years after Dr Tait explored the path of temptation, the future Conservative MP, C.E. Howard Vincent (then the director of the newly created CID at Scotland Yard), told a House of Lords Select Committee that 'a boy must be a paragon of virtue, who, at 16 or 17, can walk from 11 o'clock at night till half-past 12 in the morning, from the top of the Haymarket to the top of Grosvenor-place, without being solicited to such an enormous extent, that he is almost certain to fall.' And masculine authority, even military prowess, was no defense: 'there is scarcely a senior boy at Eton,' Vincent had continued, 'a cadet at Sandhurst, or a subaltern in the army, who will not agree with me as to the enormous danger there is.'[14] Tristan argued, however, that as long as the genders were not equal, with women denied the same rights to education, trades and, after marriage, property as men, the likes of Tait and Vincent must 'Put the blame therefore on the social order and let women be exonerated,' while rather than trying to legislate against prostitution, 'Governments must strive instead to eradicate its causes and to regulate its practice.'[15]

Tristan devoted an entire chapter of her *London Journal* to prostitution. The theoretical sections lean heavily on Dr Michael Ryan's contentious book *Prostitution in London* (1838), which shared a similar opinion to her own, the author having prefaced the work:

> According to our contradictory, anomalous, and absurd laws, statute, common, ecclesiastical and civil — women are most shamefully and inhumanly exposed to seduction, prostitution, adultery and ruin; they seem to be considered the lawful prey to the lust, treachery, cruelty, and artifices of licentious and profligate men, who may seduce and then abandon them at will, as is evinced by that infamous charter of libertinism, the Poor Law Bill; by the irrational and unchristian Marriage Laws, which encourage adulterers, fornicators and seducers, while they severally punish helpless and degraded women.[16]

Nonetheless, it is Tristan's personal observations of her 'sisters' on the street and in the flash houses that carry the most emotional power, culminating in a politically charged and infernal description of an orgy at a 'finish', one of the higher-class half-taverns/half-brothels off the Haymarket where a gentleman might finish off the night after dinner and a show:

> The finishes are temples raised by English materialism to their gods! The servants who minister unto them are richly dressed; the owners of the finishes respectfully greet the *male* guests who come to exchange their gold for debauchery.

Around midnight, the habitués begin to arrive. Several of these taverns are meeting places for society; it is where the elite of the aristocracy gather. At first the young lords lie on the sofa-like benches, and they smoke and jest with the women. Then after several libations, the alcoholic vapours of champagne and madeira go to their heads. The illustrious scions of English nobility, the honourable Members of Parliament take off their coats, waistcoats and braces. They make themselves at home in a public tavern as if they were in a private boudoir. There is no reason for them not to feel quite at home; after all they pay a high price for the right to show their contempt. As for the contempt they inspire, they could not care less. The pace of the orgy increases; it reaches its peak between four and five in the morning.

It takes a good deal of courage to sit through it all, a silent spectator of what goes on!

What a noble use these noble English lords make of their immense wealth! How handsome they are, how generous, when they have lost their senses and offer fifty or a hundred guineas to a prostitute if she will lend herself to all the obscenities conceived by intoxication.

There are all sorts of entertainments in the finishes. One of the most appreciated is to ply a woman with drink until she falls reeling on the floor and then to make her swallow vinegar mixed with mustard and pepper. The mixture almost invariably produces horrible convulsions. The unfortunate creature's gasps and contortions provoke laughter, and the honourable society is enormously amused. Another much appreciated entertainment in these fashionable gatherings is to throw a glass of anything at all on the drunken woman lying senseless on the floor. I have seen satin dresses whose colour could no longer be ascertained; they were merely a confusion of filth. Countless fantastic shapes were traced in wine, brandy, beer, tea, coffee, cream and so forth – debauchery's mottled record. The human creature can sink no lower!

The sight of such satanic depravity is revolting and alarming. The atmosphere is nauseating. The air is heavy with foul vapours: the smells of meat, drink, tobacco smoke and others even more fetid. They catch in your throat; your temples throb; you are seized with dizziness. It is horrible! However, the prostitute's only hope of success is to go through this experience *every night*, because she has no hold whatsoever on the sober Englishman. The sober Englishman is chaste to the point of prudishness.[17]

The women being so ill-used in these places tended to be veterans, 'blowens' in the vulgar tongue, and well past their prime. Pretty young things did not as a rule work the finishes, which were waiting for them in their middle years, if they survived on the street that long. In the finishes, a woman had to be prepared to do anything.

And if the gentleman about town didn't find his way to such places on the grapevine, there were written guides describing pubs, clubs, gambling houses, theatres and disguised 'introducing houses' where prostitutes could be met, often including listings for individual women. The Eganesque *New Swell's Night Guide to the Bowers of Venus* (c. 1847) was an indication that the Corinthians were not yet all washed and sanctified. This detailed handbook for dandies in the underworld was subtitled 'A Curious Account of the Cyprian Beauties and Their Little Love Affairs; The Principle Introducing Houses, West-End "Walks", Chanting Slums, Flash Cribs, and Dossing Kens, with all the Rowdy-Dowdy and Flash Patter of Billingsgate and St Giles'. Being a Complete Stranger's Guide to Life in London!' To find a clandestine introducing house, the guide advised that, 'Enumerating the localities of several French Houses situate in the West End the man of town must be on the *qui vive* to observe, thus:– a brass or zincographic plate may denote corset making, millinery, &c., when in fact these ingenuities merely conceal the temple of Venus and Voluptuarians.'[18]

With her biblical rhetoric and left-wing disdain for the aristocracy, it's notable how different Tristan's scene is in tone to Pierce Egan's light-hearted description of the gentlemen out on a bit of a spree in the 'All-Max' in Smithfield, a well-known Regency 'finish'. Tristan wrote with a fervour that would have given any Chartist orator or Radical MP a run for his money, although while they were calling for reform what she wanted was revolution. 'Prostitution is the ugliest of all the sores produced by the unequal distribution of wealth,' she wrote, 'which, much more damningly than crime, bears witness against the organisation of society. Prejudice, poverty, and serfdom all combine their pernicious effects to produce this revolting degradation.' Her solution was true gender equality: 'We can say that until woman is emancipated, prostitution will grow ever greater.'[19]

After her study of London, Tristan's ideas on the relationship between the subordination of women and the capitalist exploitation of the workers coalesced into a utopian, proto-communist call for internationally organised labour, which she outlined in her book *L'Union Ouvrière* (*The Workers' Union*) in 1843. Social progress, she believed, could be measured by the status of women in society; the emancipation of the workers was therefore indivisible from the emancipation of women, an issue taken up much later by Engels in *The Origin of the Family, Private Property, and the State* (1884). She considered this to be a necessary continuation of the process of liberation initiated by the French Revolution, essentially laying the foundations of modern feminism. This could not have been further from the mainstream English bourgeois position, Bracebridge Hemyng writing that 'immorality had spread more or less all over Europe, owing to the demoralizing effects of the French Revolution.'[20] Undertaking a *Tour de France* through the major industrial cities to promote this idea was productive but exhausting. Flora had never fully recovered from the wounds inflicted by her husband, and she died of a stroke in Bordeaux in November 1844, at the age of forty-one. Four years later in 1848, the year of European Revolution, 8,000 French labourers marched to her grave to place a monument there, singing songs from *The Workers' Union.* When *The Communist Manifesto* concluded with 'Workers of the world, unite!' it was quoting Flora Tristan.

Notionally less radical, but nonetheless both contentious and influential, was Dr William Acton's book *Prostitution, Considered in Its Moral, Social, and Sanitary Aspects in London and Other Large Cities and Garrison Towns with Proposals for the Control and Prevention of its Attendant Evils* (1857). This was a landmark study that sought to define the prostitute and her trade, its title indicating the interlinking themes of morality, class and public health that characterised the anxieties of the Victorian elite and middle classes. Acton was a gynaecologist, and his book on prostitution followed immediately on from *The Functions and Disorders of the Reproductive Organs, in Childhood, Youth, Adult Age, and Advanced Life, Considered in the Physiological, Social, and Moral Relations*, written the same year, in which he had argued that 'The majority of women (happily for them) are not very much troubled with sexual feeling of any kind,' and 'As a general rule, a modest woman seldom desires any sexual gratification for herself. She submits to her husband's embraces, but principally to gratify him; and, were it not for the desire of maternity, would far rather be relieved from his attentions.'[21] To Acton, sexual desire in the female indicated nymphomania.

He also held a common belief at the time that human bodies were a closed system, possessing a finite amount of energy. Physical overexertion, especially sexual, was therefore considered dangerous because it wasted energy and, in men, precious bodily fluids, one ounce of semen supposedly containing the 'life-power' of forty ounces of blood.[22] Intercourse was therefore strictly for procreation, and Acton devoted much of his later career to warning against the horrors of masturbation. We have him to thank for the myth about going blind. This was allied with the other principal concern in sexual health, venereal disease. Acton regarded prostitution as 'an inevitable attendant upon civilized, and especially closely-packed, population', which he deemed to be 'ineradicable'. His purpose, then, was not to stop it, but to make an argument for government intervention, 'to treat it as they do such ordinary nuisances as drains, sewers, and so forth, by diminishing its inconvenience to the senses, and, in fact, rendering, its presence as little noticeable as possible.'[23]

Acton begins by enumerating three types of prostitute:

> The 'well-dressed, living in lodgings' prostitute ... eschews absolute 'street-walking'. The 'well-dressed, walking the streets' is the prostitute errant, or absolute street-walker, who plies in the open thoroughfare and there only, restricting herself generally to a definite parade, whereon she may always be found by her friends, and hence becomes, of course, 'perfectly well known to the police'.
> The 'low prostitute, infesting low neighbourhoods', is a phrase which speaks for itself.[24]

He then sub-divides again, this time into three distinct 'classes': 'the "kept woman" ... who has in truth, or pretends to have, but one paramour, with whom she, in some cases, resides; the common prostitute, who is at the service, with slight reservation, of the first comer, and attempts no other means of life; and the woman whose prostitution is a subsidiary calling'.[25] He analysed several estimates of the number of prostitutes in London, ranging from Colquhoun's 50,000 at the turn of the century and a police report to Parliament in 1839 citing 6,371, to the Bishop of Exeter's claim of 80,000, which was endorsed by one Mr Talbot, 'secretary of a society for the protection of young females'.[26] Through a series of his own calculations, based on birth and marriage statistics, Acton proposed that 'we shall find that 210,000, or one in twelve, of the unmarried females in the country above the age of puberty have strayed from the path of virtue.'[27] Working on these numbers – which, like most such statistics, should be taken as a matter of speculation over calculation – the spread of venereal disease was seen as shockingly exponential. Quoting two other doctors, Duchâtelet and Barr, who claimed that prostitutes could have over twenty clients a day, Acton darkly hinted that all could be infected; and if the woman was healthy, all it would take was one client who was not, which probability rendered all but certain. On these figures, millions could potentially be infected by a small group of prostitutes, as if bitten by vampires. The health of the male population, and therefore the country, morally and physically, was clearly under threat, and many read Acton's earnest and reasonably measured report as a sign of the moral decay of a nation whose major cities were infested with disease-ridden women. What was, then, essentially a medical treatise became a bestseller, read fearfully by a culture that often likened itself to the Roman Empire, and thus feared a collapse into decadence.

Whatever his views about closed systems and the evils of masturbation, Acton's work was pragmatic rather than sensational, seeking to explore the medical and social issues surrounding prostitution for both sexes, and making recommendations for regulation, such as, 'putting an end so far as possible to the overcrowding of families, and making better provision for the relief and suitable employment of women'. He also proposed 'to remodel the laws relating to seduction, making the seducer substantially responsible for the support of his bastard offspring, — providing facilities for procuring affiliation orders — and assisting the pregnant woman during her confinement'.[28] As a doctor, he knew the miseries of venereal disease and was appalled both by popular ignorance and government indifference. As much as anything, his book was an attempt to initiate rational public debate. Because of his beliefs about female sexuality, he also challenged the popularly held opinion that women chose prostitution because they were somehow naturally lustful and wicked, highlighting instead a range of social conditions, many of them connected to poverty and lack of decent options for employment (although he later supported the Contagious Diseases Acts, which effectively criminalised all women suspected of being prostitutes). 'If in this wide world, teeming with abundant supplies for human want,' he concluded, 'to thousands of wretched creatures no choice is open save between starvation and sin, may we not justly say that there is something utterly wrong in the system that permits such things to be.'[29]

Acton greatly admired the work of the journalist Henry Mayhew, the 'traveller in the undiscovered country of the poor', who, aided by Henry

Wood and Richard Knight, had meticulously documented London street life in a series of articles for the *Morning Chronicle* published in three volumes in 1851.[30] A fourth 'extra volume', co-written with Bracebridge Hemyng, John Binny and Andrew Halliday, was published in 1861, four years after Acton's study, covering the lives of swindlers, beggars, thieves and prostitutes. The young barrister, Samuel Bracebridge Hemyng, was the future creator of the quintessentially British schoolboy hero Jack Harkaway; his section, entitled 'Prostitution in London', occupies a large part of the work. Using Mayhew's tried and tested formula of statistics, novelistic description and first-hand interviews, Hemyng surveyed the complex trade from the kept mistresses and 'prima donnas' of the Haymarket set who scandalised the London season to the wretched creatures at the end of the line, like the burnt-out ex-whore he found sleeping on the floor of an empty 'hole' in a low lodging house and opium den in Bluegate Fields:

> Her face was shrivelled and famine-stricken, her eyes bloodshot and glaring, her features disfigured slightly with disease, and her hair dishevelled, tangled, and matted. More like a beast in his lair than a human being in her home was this woman. We spoke to her, and from her replies concluded she was an Irishwoman. She said she was charged nothing for the place she slept in. She cleaned out the water-closets in the daytime, and for these services she was given a lodging gratis.[31]

Like Acton, Hemyng's work exposed the moralising myth of the doomed harlot in favour of a much more dynamic group. Similarly, Tristan's hellish vision had only told half the story. As the 'shrewd and clever' girl from the Haymarket had gone on to say:

> Strange things happen to us sometimes: we may now and then die of consumption; but the other day a lady friend of mine met a gentleman at Sam's, and yesterday morning they were married at St. George's, Hanover Square. The gentleman has lots of money, I believe, and he started off with her at once for the Continent. It is very true this is an unusual case; but we often do marry, and well too; why shouldn't we, we are pretty, we dress well, we can talk and insinuate ourselves into the hearts of men by appealing to their passions and their senses.

'Her testimony,' concluded Hemyng, 'is sufficient at once to dissipate the foolish idea that ought to have been exploded long ago, but which still lingers in the minds of both men and women, that the harlot's progress is short and rapid, and that there is no possible advance, moral or physical; and that once abandoned she must always be profligate.'[32]

It is also notable, as both Acton and Hemyng confirmed from their own investigations, that prostitution at almost all levels was controlled by women. Brothels, lodging houses and 'accommodation houses' (where rooms could be rented by the hour) were invariably run by women, generally former prostitutes, and the majority of full- and part-time 'ladies of the town' worked for themselves. There were no 'pimps', as we understand the term today, merely procurers – again, women – who might bring clients and new girls together (especially ones who could pass for virgins) for a commission. It was also obvious that, like the choice of the child criminals, an honest living was likely to be so poorly paid, arduous, uncertain and unhealthy, if not downright dangerous, that it was no choice at all. Despite the risk of disease, a violent punter, or arrest (the 1824 Vagrancy Act had criminalised prostitution and 'living off immoral earnings'), prostitution was the only option – other than the stage – whereby a woman with no assets could earn a good living for herself. Acton said as much in his study, admitting that the prostitute's life was likely to be no harder than that of a 'virtuous' working-class woman with children and/or a piecework job in a rag trade sweatshop:

> If we compare the prostitute at thirty-five with her sister, who perhaps is the married mother of a family, or has been a toiling slave for years in the over-heated laboratories of fashion, we shall seldom find that the constitutional ravages often thought to be necessary consequences of prostitution exceed those attributable to the cares of a family and the heart-wearing struggles of virtuous labour.[33]

Occupying the space between the two worlds were the 'dollymops', usually young women with non-residential jobs and therefore not under constant supervision who supplemented their income as casual and part-time prostitutes, sometimes out of financial necessity – when Mayhew interviewed seamstresses in the late 1840s, he concluded that at least a quarter of them were also prostitutes – and sometimes for fun.

Professionals often objected to the amateur dollymops – there was enough competition as there was – while procurers loved them for their newness and freshness, and by that route several slid full-time into the trade. One such girl was 'Yellow-haired Kitty', whose cheery voice can be heard in the notorious pornographic memoir *My Secret Life* by 'Walter', an anonymous confessional epic published privately in eleven volumes in 1888. Kitty was blond, plump and fifteen, and 'Walter' picked her up in the Strand when he was about twenty-five. He wrote that 'There was a frankness, openness, and freshness about this girl which delighted me,' and, being inexperienced, she was happy to talk to him in a very unguarded way, rather like one of Hemyng's subjects, only over sex rather than a glass of gin:

> 'I ain't gay,' said she astonished. 'Yes you are.' 'No I ain't.' 'You let men fuck you, don't you?' 'Yes, but I ain't gay.' 'What do you call gay?' 'Why the gals who come out regular of a night dressed up, and gets their living by it.' I was amused.[34]
>
> 'Don't you?' 'No, Mother keeps me.' 'What is your father?' 'Got none, he's dead three months back. Mother works and keeps us. — She is a charwoman and goes out on odd jobs.' 'Don't you work?' 'Not now,' said she in a confused way. 'Mother does not want me to, I take care of the others.' 'What others?' 'The young ones.' 'How many?' 'Two — one's a boy, and one's a gal.' 'How old?' 'Sister's about six, and brother's nearly eight, — but what do you ask me all this for?' 'Only for amusement. — Then you are in mourning for your father?' 'Yes, it's shabby, ain't it? — I wish I could have nice clothes, I've got nice boots — ain't they?' cocking up one leg — 'a lady gived 'em me when father died, — they are my best.'[35]

Kitty sews and watches her younger siblings, sneaking out when she can. She mostly solicits for the excitement and for treats, poignantly admitting that she's often hungry and likes to spend her money on pastry, pies and sausage rolls. Ignorant of the value of innocence, she lets slip she was deflowered for five shillings. 'Walter' privately reflects that he'd recently paid £200 to do the same to a girl called Louise.

The Maiden Tribute

Although shockingly young, Kitty was well over the age of consent when she met 'Walter' in the mid-1840s, which had been twelve since the

Offences Against the Person Act of 1828, rising to thirteen in 1875. She had entered a market so overcrowded that stories of young girls kidnapped and forced into prostitution that tended to circulate in moralising tracts which formed the evangelical mythology of prostitution were, as Acton noted, almost entirely without foundation. The simple truth was that there was no point or profit in kidnapping and grooming someone – although a sceptical Hemyng met a woman in a brothel at Portland Place who claimed this had happened to her – because the supply of willing girls was so great. 'Walter' knew Kitty for several years, and she comes across in his bizarre diaries as resourceful and relentlessly positive, a survivor at the lower end of a harsh and unforgiving economy. She eventually met a good man, to whom she promised to be faithful, telling 'Walter' this the last time they had sex without any sense of irony.

If anyone was grooming children to be criminals, it was most likely to be parents or guardians, the kids already hardened by poverty and vice and perfectly complicit. They were, as Kellow Chesney put it, 'conditioned to depravity'.[36] The Offences Against the Person Act of 1861 had created the offence of 'child-stealing', making it illegal to 'lead or take away, or decoy or entice away or detain' an unmarried girl under the age of sixteen. (Boys could legally marry at fourteen, girls twelve.) Any sort of removal required the father's consent, and therein lay the problem when it came to legally protecting young girls. As Howard Vincent told the Lords' Select Committee in 1881:

> I believe in the generality of cases ... that these children live at home; this prostitution actually takes place with the knowledge and connivance of the mother and to the profit of the household ... These procuresses, or whatever you may call them, have an understanding with the mother of the girl that she shall come to that house at a certain hour, and the mother perfectly well knows for what purpose she goes there, and it is with her knowledge and connivance, and with her consent that the girl goes.[37]

As Acton had argued in the fifties and Tristan in the forties, this was in fact merely a symptom of a much wider social problem, but it largely suited successive governments to follow the established narrative of iniquity and promiscuity among the underclasses rather than addressing the very real problems of slum housing and an unequal, uncertain and still largely unregulated labour market. In the end, the politicians were coerced into action by a masterly managed campaign of public moral outrage.

William Thomas Stead – known to his colleagues and supporters as 'The Chief' – was a crusading journalist in the most literal sense. The son of a Methodist minister, he was possessed of the absolute certainty of his cause that characterised the righteousness of the imperial Victorian frame of mind. As the new editor of the Conservative *Pall Mall Gazette* (a forerunner of the *London Evening Standard*), which he had joined as assistant editor in 1880, Stead set about pretty much single-handedly inventing the modern tabloid newspaper, developing what Matthew Arnold described as the 'new journalism', adding opinion pieces, maps and diagrams, breaking up long articles with eye-catching subheadings, and interviewing significant public figures (including dead ones; as an ardent Spiritualist he once 'interviewed' the ghost of Catherine the Great on the Russia Question).

His approach was not universally popular among gentlemen of letters. Until Stead's stewardship, Arnold had enjoyed a long association with the *Gazette*. 'We have had opportunities of observing a new journalism which a clever and energetic man has lately invented,' he wrote of the new management. 'It has much to commend it; it is full of ability, novelty, variety, sensation, sympathy, generous instincts; its one great fault is that it is feather-brained. It throws out assertions at a venture because it wishes them true; does not correct either them or itself, if they are false; and to get at the state of things as they truly are seems to feel no concern whatever.'[38] Similarly, the Prime Minister, William Gladstone, said that Stead had 'done more harm to Journalism than any other individual ever known'.[39] George Bernard Shaw, meanwhile, described him as 'stupendously ignorant' and 'extraordinarily incapable of learning anything',[40] and the poet Algernon Swinburne always referred to the *Pall Mall Gazette* as the 'Dunghill Gazette'.[41]

Stead had run a sensational campaign calling for slum clearance based around the nonconformist pamphlet *The Bitter Cry of Outcast London* by the Reverend Andrew Mearns (1883), which had led to a Royal Commission, and he successfully lobbied the Government to send General Gordon to Khartoum and to refit the Royal Navy. As the young editor of the *Northern Echo* he had campaigned with the feminist and social reformer Josephine Butler against the Contagious Diseases Acts of 1864, 1866, and 1869, which subjected women suspected of being prostitutes in port and garrison towns to compulsory examinations for venereal disease and confinement in 'lock hospitals'. (Male clients, however, went unmolested.) In this period, he described his rise in editorial journalism to a friend as a 'glorious opportunity of attacking the devil'.[42] Stead's limitless ego and his sense of personal mission, combined with his ruthless professional ambition, led to what was without doubt his most famous moral and political crusade, fought against child prostitution and the so-called 'white slave trade', whether it was real or not.

'The Maiden Tribute of Modern Babylon' was a series of four articles written by Stead that appeared in the *Pall Mall Gazette* between 4 July and 13 July 1885. These were a *tour de force* of tabloid journalism and showmanship, heralded by a 'Frank Warning' to readers:

> Therefore we say quite frankly to-day that all those who are squeamish, and all those who are prudish, and all those who prefer to live in a fool's paradise of imaginary innocence and purity, selfishly oblivious to the horrible realities which torment those whose lives are passed in the London Inferno, will do well not to read the *Pall Mall Gazette* of Monday and the three following days.

Having guaranteed that his already extensive readership would rather die than miss the next issue, Stead did not disappoint. He used the Greek myth of Aegeus' tribute to King Minos as a controlling metaphor for the sacrifice of innocents: 'This very night in London, and every night, year in and year out, not seven maidens only, but many times seven, selected almost as much by chance as those who in the Athenian market-place drew lots as to which should be flung into the Cretan labyrinth, will be offered up as the Maiden Tribute of Modern Babylon.'[43] The original piece was divided into short, punchy sections, with titles like 'The Violation of Virgins', 'The Confessions of a Brothel Keeper', 'The London Slave Market', 'Strapping Girls Down', and, most sensationally of all, 'A Child of Thirteen Bought for £5'. The article concluded with a masterful piece of gothic prose, setting the scene on a narrative cliff edge and then leaving the rest to the readers' imaginations:

> All was quiet and still. A few moments later the door opened, and the purchaser entered the bedroom. He closed and locked the door. There was a brief silence. And then there rose a wild and piteous cry – not a loud shriek, but a helpless, startled scream like the bleat of a frightened lamb. And the child's

voice was heard crying, in accents of terror, 'There's a man in the room! Take me home; oh, take me home!'[44]

The graphic revelations of an apparent trade in young girls run out of sinister brothels, with padded rooms, drugs, and evil procuresses, was straight out of the popular sensation fiction of writers like Charles Reade, J.S. Le Fanu, and Wilkie Collins. As each new instalment went to print, London was thrown into a state of moral panic not seen since the Newgate Controversy. Extra editions had to be printed to meet demand.

The point of all this was the failure of Parliament to pass into law the Criminal Amendment Bill 'to make further provision for the Protection of Women and Girls' and to raise the age of consent to sixteen. This had been a long time coming. The original bill had been initiated by Benjamin Scott, the Chamberlain of the City of London and a founder member, with Alfred Dyer, of the London Committee for Suppressing the Traffic in British Girls for Purposes of Continental Prostitution. An ally of Stead and Josephine Butler, Scott had long campaigned to raise the age of consent. He had approached Lord Granville, Gladstone's Secretary of State for Foreign Affairs, to appeal for legislation to protect young girls from being taken abroad for 'immoral purposes', although investigations thus far had demonstrated that although English girls did travel abroad to work in European brothels, it was entirely of their own volition. The result was the Lords' Select Committee of 1881, the report of which made a series of recommendations, including raising the age of consent, which became the basis for the bill. In 1883, it sailed through the House of Lords, but was dropped in the House of Commons. It was reintroduced the following year but sacrificed by the Government to get the Third Reform Bill through. It was reintroduced again in 1885, again getting through the Lords, only with the proposed age of consent lowered to fifteen. It was debated in the Commons on the eve of the Whitsun recess, where it was once more killed by a combination of indifference and spirited rebuttal by the Tory MP George Cavendish-Bentinck concerning the curtailment of civil liberties.

The anti-vice activists were particularly outraged by this intervention, as Cavendish-Bentinck's friendship with Mary Jeffries, the owner of eight brothels in the city and a house of whipcord in Hampstead, was one of the worst kept secrets in London. Mrs Jeffries – a Victorian Cynthia Payne with numerous shadowy links to members of the Government and the aristocracy – had recently been the subject of a private prosecution brought by the London Committee for 'keeping a disorderly house' (a high-class brothel in Chelsea).

Scott and Dyer suspected her of white slavery and child prostitution and had hoped the case would generate publicity, but Mrs Jeffries pleaded guilty after a preliminary consultation with the judge on the understanding that the evidence would not be made public. She was fined £200, which she paid immediately and in cash, before going back to work.

Supported by Scott and Dyer, Josephine Butler, the Archbishops of Canterbury and Westminster, the Bishop of London, the Congregational Union and the Salvation Army, Stead formed a 'Secret Committee' and went to war. With the help of Bramwell Booth, son of William and the first Salvation Army Chief of Staff, and a born-again prostitute called Rebecca Jarrett whom he had met through Butler, Stead had set out to prove the white slave trade existed. Using a procuress, Nancy Broughton, he bought a 13-year-old girl called Eliza Armstrong ('Lily' in the text) from her drunken mother in Marylebone. The child was chloroformed and taken to a brothel off Regent Street by Stead and Jarrett, where Louise Mourez, a midwife and abortionist, confirmed she was a virgin. Stead played the part of a drunken libertine. The child was not harmed, and after Stead enacted his pantomime in the brothel, Eliza was passed on to Booth. Another one of the 'Committee', the Swiss Salvationist Madame Combe, then took Eliza to Paris and Stead wrote up his lurid account for the *Gazette*, as far as he was concerned, his point proven.

The public outcry was loud and swift, although Cavendish-Bentinck attacked Stead in the House and W.H. Smith refused to stock the *Gazette*. Thousands rallied in Hyde Park calling on the Government to address the scandal, despite the rather obvious fact, as Chesney has argued, that Stead had not proved his claim that such transactions were a regular part of the trade, simply that there were people out there who could be persuaded to sell their children. As Mary Ann Irwin has noted, Stead was using 'white slavery' as a powerful metaphor, oversimplifying the problem of prostitution and offering a simple solution.[45] Seeing the way the wind was blowing, Parliament hastily resumed the debate on the Criminal Law Amendment Bill, although its progress was hampered by the intervention of the recently formed Society for the Prevention of Cruelty to Children, freshly emboldened by Stead's efforts. MPs resisted; Stead named each of them in the *Gazette*. Soon, any opposition to the bill was publicly deemed to be tantamount to child abuse, and 'Stead's Act' was passed into law on 14 August. The last hurdle had been an amendment clause added by the Liberal MP Henry Labouchère that 'Any male person who, in public or private, commits, or is a party to the commission of, or procures, or attempts to procure the commission by any male person of, any act of gross indecency with another male person, shall be guilty of a misdemeanour, and being convicted thereof, shall be liable at the discretion of the Court to be imprisoned for any term not exceeding two years, with or without hard labour.[46] This was the so-called 'blackmailer's charter' that made homosexuality illegal, the law that convicted Oscar Wilde in 1895. The age of consent was finally raised to sixteen, with children's evidence admissible in court without an oath; heavier penalties for rape, procurement and brothel-keeping were introduced, and the old legal ambiguities that had allowed bawdy lodging houses to function largely unimpeded were swept away. Prostitution at all levels became a clearly delineated criminal offence, ending the era of the old school Covent Garden Nuns.

Mary Jeffries, meanwhile, was mentioned by name in the second instalment of 'The Maiden Tribute', 'recruiting for the house of evil fame', but it was not her that was prosecuted this time but Stead. Rival newspapers, most notably *The Times*, had begun to dig and it soon came out that the man in the room had been Stead. As the journalists closed in, Mrs Armstrong suddenly recognised 'Lily' as her daughter and went to the police, claiming she'd been duped and that she thought Eliza was going into domestic service. Also, the father's consent had not been given. Stead, Jarrett, Booth, Mourez, Combe and another 'Secret Committee' member, Sampson Jacques, were all charged under the Offences Against the Person Act, for abduction and indecent assault (the midwife's examination). Stead defended himself, and the Archbishop of Canterbury, Edward Benson, and Frederick Temple, the Bishop of London, spoke in his defence, arguing that his motives were pure. Combe and Booth were acquitted, the rest convicted, with sentences ranging from one to six months' hard labour. Stead got three months. In summing up, Mr Justice Henry Charles Lopes appeared to speak for the many politicians who remained furious with 'government by journalism' by criticising the original articles, for which Stead was not on trial:

> I regret to say that you thought fit to publish in the *Pall Mall Gazette* a distorted account of the case of Eliza Armstrong, and that you deluged, some months ago, our streets and the whole country with an amount of filth which has, as I fear, tainted the minds of the children that you were so anxious to protect, and which has been—and I don't hesitate to say, ever will be—a disgrace to journalism.[47]

Mourez did not survive her sentence (like Jarrett, she received six months), but Stead flourished, continuing to edit the *Gazette* from prison. On his release, he published a pamphlet entitled *My First Imprisonment*, and every year thereafter, on 10 November, the anniversary of his conviction, he would proudly wear his prison uniform, which had been presented to him as a gift by the governor of Holloway Prison.

As the age of the Victorian streetwalker came to an end, the modern media event was born. Larger than life to the end, Stead died at the start of another, going down with the *Titanic* while travelling to a peace congress in New York at the personal invitation of US President William Howard Taft. The rival journalist Frank Harris later wrote of Stead's dramatic demise that he was 'rather relieved when he went down in some shipwreck and we were rid of him'.[48]

Chapter 7

The Greeks Had a Word for It

When Mr Justice Henry Charles Lopes castigated W.T. Stead for deluging the country with 'filth', he was, of course, explicitly linking 'The Maiden Tribute' to pornographic literature, a trade that continued despite the mid-century passage of the first Obscene Publications Act and the famous prudishness of late Victorian culture. To a man of Stead's religious convictions, this must have stung, even though, as Donald Thomas has noted, the style was reminiscent of the '*fin-de-siècle* sado-erotic fantasy', a form that reached its zenith somewhere between the mysterious underground novel *Teleny* in 1893 and the chastisements of the magnificent Mrs Harcourt in the anonymous *Sadopaideia* (1907).[1] Despite their ongoing struggle with the Society for the Suppression of Vice – and its successor, the National Vigilance Association, of which Stead was a council member – the publishers and booksellers of Holywell and Wych Streets continued to sell *académies* ('art photographs') and 'literature of an incandescent kind' from the backs of their shops that went far beyond the calculating coyness of 'The Maiden Tribute'.[2] As with the oldest profession, times were admittedly changing, and many of London's most notorious pornographers were on their way to decamping to Paris in light of Section Four of the Post Office Protection Act of 1884, which made it an offence to send 'indecent, obscene, libellous, or grossly offensive' material through the post. Not that Stead and the judge would know this, but the first volume of 'Walter's' explicit memoir was also only three years away from discreet and private publication in Amsterdam.

Literature of an Incandescent Kind

Pornography has been around much longer than the word to describe it, as antiquarians had discovered to their horror during the excavations of Pompeii and Herculaneum. Alongside the elegant marble statues traditionally associated with Ancient Rome, diggers had unearthed frescoes depicting couples making love not just in brothels but in the homes of artisans, merchants and politicians, in the quarters of their servants and their slaves, as well as the public baths. Erect phalluses were carved into paving stones and doorways as symbols of protection, and beautifully rendered statues of deities cavorting with both animals and human beings were proud centrepieces of any fashionable home. Erotic art had clearly been an everyday part of Roman life.

A particularly impressive and representative example was unearthed at the Villa dei Papiri, named for its charred but intact library, a country house about halfway up the slope of Mount Vesuvius, believed to have been built by Lucius Calpurnius Piso Caesoninus, the father-in-law of Julius Caesar. In addition to being the most complete classical library ever discovered, the villa was also notable for its owner's large collection of statuary, which included an intact and intricately carved marble, about 6 inches tall, of the god Pan on his knees penetrating a she-goat. 'It is impossible not to admire the expression of sensuous passion and intense enjoyment depicted on the Satyr's features,' wrote the French antiquarian Cesar Famin, adding, 'and even on the countenance of the strange object of his passion.'[3] King Charles of the Two Sicilies himself placed the statue of Pan and the goat under the supervision of the royal sculptor, Joseph Canart, with strict injunction that no one should be allowed to see it.

Academics and politicians knew that these artefacts were of priceless archaeological and cultural value. They could not be destroyed, but neither could they be publicly exhibited. The solution was concealment. Like Pan and the goat, the erotic artefacts of Pompeii and Herculaneum were hidden. At the suggestion of Francesco Gennaro Giuseppe, Duke of Calabria and later Francis I, over a hundred pieces were locked away in a special room in the Museo Borbonico known as the 'Gabinetto degli Oggetti Osceni' or 'Cabinet of Obscene Objects'. Access to these objects was limited to 'persons of mature age and of proven morality', which basically meant male scholars of notable social rank, who were deemed to be capable of rising above the baser instincts that exposure to these artefacts might provoke.[4] A royal permit was required, and obviously women, children and members of the lower orders need not apply. What had begun as an Enlightenment project – the excavation of the ruins – had now become, in effect, proto-Victorian, and other 'secret museums' were established in Florence, Dresden and Madrid housing 'obscene relics' from not only Rome but also Egypt and Greece. In 1865, the British Museum established its own *Museum Secretum* to house the erotic components of the private art collection of the antiquarian George Witt, whose bequest contained what amounted to an 'all or nothing' clause. Much of this material has now found its way into the main collections, but some of it is still under lock and key, including a terracotta replica of the statue of Pan and the goat.

Europe had fashioned itself in the Greco-Roman image – a model for 'Civilisation', with obvious parallels in particular drawn between the might of the Roman Empire in the past and the British in the present. That this image was now demonstrably tarnished was potentially catastrophic to the collective sense of cultural identity. Following the work of the French philosopher Michel Foucault, historians such as Lynda Nead and Walter Kendrick have argued that classicists overcame their dilemma by creating a new physical and cultural space, where both knowledge and morality were preserved, inventing the category of the 'obscene object' and then segregating it, with access both restricted and carefully monitored. This was a political act; the contents of the secret museums were part of classical culture, but not, officially, the part that Europe had inherited. Instead, they represented the dark decadence that had destroyed Rome and which the modern world had to resist. Art, therefore, should only stimulate aesthetically and intellectually, never physically. Nead, in fact, has made a strong case for the origin of the word 'obscene' as we understand it in the Latin term *ob scena*, which refers to the space off to the side of a stage.[5]

While the presence of the material was not denied, museum authorities behaved as if it did not exist, in exactly the same way that sex was central to the human condition yet never acknowledged in polite society. From about 1800, a new word was found to describe this material: *pornography*, from the Ancient Greek πορνογράφος (*pornográphos*), which in turn was derived from πορνεία (*porneía*, 'fornication, prostitution') and γράφω (*gráphō*, 'I depict'), a classical term originally applied to writings and illustrations about or by prostitutes. As Foucault wrote:

> Sexuality was carefully confined; it moved into the home. The conjugal family took custody of it and absorbed it into the serious function of reproduction. On the subject of sex, silence became the rule. The legitimate and procreative couple laid down the law. The couple imposed itself as model, enforced the norm, safeguarded the truth, and reserved the right to speak while retaining the principle of secrecy. A single locus of sexuality was acknowledged in social space as well as at the heart of every household, but it was a utilitarian and fertile

one: the parents' bedroom. The rest had only to remain vague; proper demeanour avoided contact with other bodies, and verbal decency sanitized one's speech. And sterile behaviour carried the taint of abnormality; if it insisted on making itself too visible, it would be designated accordingly and would have to pay the penalty.

He called this the 'monotonous nights of the Victorian bourgeoisie'.[6]

In the eighteenth century, recognisably modern literary pornography had evolved alongside the English novel as developed by writers like Daniel Defoe and Samuel Richardson. The best-known and most groundbreaking example is *Memoirs of a Woman of Pleasure*, popularly known as 'Fanny Hill', written in the Fleet Debtor's Prison by the former soldier John Cleland and published in 1748. *Fanny Hill* – the name a slang English translation of *mons veneris* – belongs in the Enlightenment tradition of pornography as revolutionary satire, most notably in the work of the Marquis de Sade. It both leans on and subverts Hogarth's series of moralising illustrations *A Harlot's Progress* (1732) by giving its heroine a happy and prosperous end, combining the whore's dialogue of the *pornográphos* with a parody of Christian confession. It is also filthy and often extremely funny; never resorting to obscenity, Fanny narrates using elaborate euphemisms, for example: 'Her sturdy stallion had now unbuttoned, and produced naked, stiff, and erect, that wonderful machine, which I had never seen before, and which, for the interest my own seat of pleasure began to take furiously in it, I stared at with all the eyes I had.'[7] The first instalment got Cleland and his publisher, Ralph Griffiths, arrested and charged with 'corrupting the King's subjects', but despite popular legends of Cleland renouncing the book and Griffiths going to the stocks, both were actually released on recognizance with Cleland preparing an abridged and self-censored version of the novel in 1750.[8] Thomas Sherlock, the Bishop of London, protested to the Secretary of State, the Duke of Newcastle, regarding this new edition, urging him to 'give proper orders, to stop the progress of this vile book, which is an open insult upon Religion and good manners, and a reproach to the Honour of the Government, and the Law of the Country'.[9] But nothing much came of this, and the novel continued to sell steadily alongside several pirated editions with the Government paying little or no attention until the Victorians banned it a century later.

In Cleland's day, there was no English law relating to obscenity, only a judicial ruling from 1727 when the notorious hack publisher and bookseller

Edmund Curll had to be prosecuted for 'obscene libel' over his translation of the seventeenth-century French 'whore dialogue' *Vénus dans le cloître*. As Bishop Sherlock's failed intervention indicates, the regulation of supposedly obscene material and the protection of public morals traditionally fell to the Church and other independent watchdogs, until the State took on an increasing role in the second half of the nineteenth century.

Leading the charge in the new century was the Society for the Suppression of Vice, founded by the anti-slavery campaigner and independent MP William Wilberforce in 1802, largely to the indifference of the general public. Numerous private prosecutions were brought by the Society, including repeated indictments against publishers of *Fanny Hill*. Working closely with the police and customs officials, the preferred method of their agents was entrapment. For example, the Proceedings of the Central Criminal Court for 16 August 1847 show Thomas Dugdale (brother of the notorious publisher William Dugdale) indicted for unlawfully selling and publishing obscene prints after a SSV sting:

> GEORGE WILLIAM SHARP. I am clerk to Messrs. Pritchard and Collett, solicitors to the Society for the Suppression of Vice, No. 57, Lincoln's Inn Fields. On the 27th of July last, about half-past nine o'clock in the evening, in consequence of instruction I received, I went to the station-house at Bow-street, and after being there searched by a policeman, I went to No. 51, Holywell-street, Strand, followed by the policeman—I went into the shop and asked for a book, which the prisoner showed me, and which I produce—I paid a guinea for it—I then left the shop, and went, closely followed by the policeman who had searched me, to the Society's chambers, where he took from my pocket the book I had bought off the defendant.

The prisoner pleaded guilty and threw himself on the mercy of the court, adding that 'I have no desire to demoralize society.' He was found guilty and sent to prison for a year.[10] The Dugdale brothers were giants in the industry, and all did serious time as a result, William dying in Clerkenwell Prison aged sixty-eight.

William Dugdale was the eldest son of a Quaker tailor from Stockport. Aged eighteen, he had moved to London and gone to work for William Benbow, the nonconformist preacher and radical publisher, who supported his political output by also publishing pirated pornography, mostly translations and material from the previous century. William went into business for himself as a publisher and bookseller in 1822, trading out of Seven Dials, one of the rookeries of St Giles and an area known for what Henry Mayhew called 'Street Literature' (chapbooks, Newgate calendars, ballads, literary counterfeits, penny magazines, political and religious tracts) where Pierce Egan had also cut his teeth. Implicated by rumour but never charged in the Cato Street Conspiracy – a plot to murder the British Cabinet and Prime Minister, Lord Liverpool, exposed in 1820 – William's first big score was a knock-off of Byron's *Don Juan*, followed by an English translation of *Memoirs of a Man of Pleasure, or The Adventures of Versorand* by Henri-François de La Solle (1761), and a pirated edition of *Fanny Hill*.

Like his mentor, Dugdale soon rose to dominate the trade in politically and sexually subversive material. He prudently moved his offices and published under a variety of aliases in an attempt to keep one step ahead of the SSV spies, finally settling down at number 37, Holywell Street in 1839, under the famous sign of the half moon, reputedly the oldest shop in London. His brothers ran shops at Numbers 50 (John) and 51 (Thomas), while his son, William John, was based at Number 35. The doors were solid and heavily fortified, allowing staff several minutes to burn stock before the police broke them down during a raid, a not uncommon occurrence.

Dugdale's name appears as publisher more than any other in Henry Spencer Ashbee's trilogy of pornographic bibliographies, a typical entry being:

> *Nunnery Tales; or Cruising under False Colours: A Tale of Love and Lust.* London: Printed for the Booksellers.
>
> 8vo.; size of letter-press 5 by 2⅝ inches; a line on the title-page of the first volume; 3 vols.; pp. 134, 128, 137; 24 coloured lithographs, obscene and badly done; original edition; published by W. Dugdale in the years 1866, 1867, 1868; vol. the third is dated, and bears moreover on its title-page, 'with appropriate engravings'; sold at 2 guineas per volume.
>
> Disguised in female attire, the young Augustus gains admission into a convent of which his aunt is the superior. He passes the first night in her bed. Aided afterwards by her, by the confessor of the house, father Eustace, who is in reality his own parent, and by the older nuns, he succeeds in enjoying every sister in the Convent. The abbess and the other nuns relate in turn their experiences and exploits, by which means the three

volumes are made up. The work is entirely deficient in tone and character. The orgies and amorous encounters, were they even possible, would be more in keeping in a low brothel, than in the most abandoned of nunneries, with the nature, rules, and habits of which the author displays utter ignorance. Add to this bad printing and numerous typo-graphical errors, and the reader may feel assured that the book is entirely beneath the notice of any literary man. One passage is sufficiently strange to be pointed out; it occurs at p. 70 of vol. I, and is a very circumstantial description of the manner in which green-sick sisters were relieved by the application of a turkey's neck when a man was not available. I cannot refrain from ending my notice with the highly spiced words in which Dugdale was wont to announce the book in his catalogue: 'every stretch of voluptuous imagination is here fully depicted, rogering, ravishing, ramming, one unbounded scene of lust, lechery and licentiousness.'[11]

Other titles from Dugdale speak for themselves; they include: *The Virgin's Oath, Intrigues in a Boarding School, Adventures of a Gentleman, The Authentic Memoirs of the Countess De Barre, Injured Innocence, The Birchen Bouquet, The Battles of Venus, How to Raise Love, The Confessions of a Lady's Maid, The Adventures of a Bedstead, The Mysteries of Whoredom, Love Letters of Arabella and Flora, The Wedding Night, Revelries and Devilries, The Bed-Fellows, The Confessions of a Young Lady, The Ladies' Tell-tale, The Lustful Turk, Scenes in the Seraglio, The Victim of Lust*, and *Lascivious Gems*, an anthology 'set to suit every fancy' including 'The Diary of a Nymphomaniac', 'Letter from a married man to a sensible wife' ('after a week's debauch with Nelly'), and 'A Night in St John's Wood', in which:

> Mr. F. Puttitinfar describes his meeting, at 'Mots', an old acquaintance, Kitty Graham, formerly a common prostitute, now a fast girl, living in style upon a legacy of £60,000 left her by a duke by whom she has been kept. Kitty invites Puttitinfar to accompany her home, where he finds to his surprise that Miss Graham keeps six other frail sisters to minister to her pleasures. The eight join in an orgie, into which flagellation and other irregular practices are introduced.[12]

Holywell Street, in the parish of St Clement's, was the heart of darkness, a positive cradle of filth hidden behind the Strand, its name, said the *Morning Post*, 'A bye-word and a proverb for obscene and blasphemous publications'.[13] 'J. Paul', the printer of *The New Swell's Night Guide*, had his premises at Number 2.

Wych Street, which ran parallel, where a century before Jack Sheppard had been apprenticed and Dugdale had also rented two shops, was worse, with brothels in among the bookshops. Lyon's Inn, the run-down and disreputable Inn of Chancery where William Weare had practised, was in the medieval backstreets between the two, until the area was cleared in 1901 as part of the Aldwych redevelopment. (The site where Holywell and Wych Streets converged to the west of St Clement Danes, and to which Gladstone's statue balefully glares, is now occupied by Australia House.) This was old London, known locally as 'The Backside of St Clements', with narrow alleys packed with dusty second-hand bookshops and dingy courts crammed between ancient, overhanging buildings, some of them dating back to the days of Elizabeth I. Way back before the Fire of London, the trade had been textiles, which, like nearby Fleet Street, had given way to book-selling and printing, initially supplying the nearby Inns of Court. By the end of the eighteenth century, as literacy increased among the working classes along with their political consciousness, the area became the home of the radical press, until the State came down hard in fear of an English revolution following the French, imposing evermore strict controls on print throughout the Napoleonic Wars. As sexual satire had always been part of subversive, political literature, many of the hacks of Holywell Street ditched the politics but kept the pornography, following the money and selling to upper-class pleasure seekers like the esoteric bibliographer Henry Spencer Ashbee, who could afford to pay two or even three guineas for a dirty book or five shillings for a series of highly artistic 'French' lithographs, the development of the daguerreotype having quickly led to erotic images. These became more cheaply available after the wet plate process made unlimited photographic prints an option, employing all the visual conventions (poses, acts and positions) associated with pornography today. 'The windows,' lamented one pedestrian who had blundered down the wrong passage off the Strand, 'display books and pictures of the most disgusting and obscene character, and which are alike loathsome to the eye and offensive to the morals of any person of well-regulated mind.' He wrote a strong letter to *The Times* on the matter, but preferred to remain anonymous.[14] In *The Mysteries of London*, G.W.M. Reynolds, on the other hand, called the area 'the home of the literature of radicalism and a type of bawdy publishing dedicated to exposing the hypocrisy and immorality of the ruling classes', but then, the Chartists had always hung out there.[15]

In addition to the bookshops and printers, there was also what Mayhew called a 'traffic in paper' going on outside, with both sides claiming the other was informing against them. 'Literary patterers' hawked their wares in the street; their business, said Mayhew, having 'almost as many divisions as literature' itself, including, of course, the 'Indecent Street-Trade'.[16] Then there was the 'Sham Indecent Street-Trade':

> The plan now adopted is to sell the sealed packet itself, which the 'patter' of the street-seller leads his auditors to believe to be some improper or scandalous publication. The packet is some coloured paper, in which is placed a portion of an old newspaper, a Christmas carol, a religious tract, or a slop-tailor's puff (given away in the streets for the behoof of another class of gulls). The enclosed paper is, however, never indecent.[17]

This was a classic gypsy switch, always conducted out of doors, where the purchaser would be wary of opening the packet.

Dugdale and his brothers were busted numerous times, but fines made little difference in such a lucrative trade, while if one was sent to prison the others kept the business running. As a publisher, he was a shameless hack, with a talent for reprinting and packaging material, anything to make money and give the impression of newness for his hungry clientele. His methods included reprinting old books with new titles and inexpertly revised text and passing them off as new works; dividing single books into two or three volumes – padding each segment as necessary – and selling each edition for a couple of guineas; and pirating books published by his rivals. He claimed many of his books were translations from the French, and repackaged so much that it is impossible to know in which language they originated. Ashbee described his editing, book-blocking and illustrations as 'of villainous execution'.[18]

More Deadly than Prussic Acid

Dugdale had been playing cat and mouse with the SSV for years, and on 9 May 1857, he appeared before Lord Chief Justice John Campbell on a charge of obscene libel following a complaint from the Society, at least his ninth prosecution. This was the first of two related obscenity cases presided over by Lord Campbell that day, the second involving William Strange, the Radical politician William Cobbett's former publisher, nicked for selling the saucy periodicals *Paul Pry* and *Women of London*. Dugdale was on trial for a variety of stock, including obscene prints and the anonymous epistolary novel *The Lustful Turk, or Lascivious Scenes from a Harem* originally published by John Benjamin Brookes in 1828, an erotic gothic with an oriental setting that Lord Campbell that day declared to be legally 'obscene'. The novel takes the form of a series of letters written by its heroine, Emily Barlow, who is kidnapped by Moorish pirates en route to India and presented as a gift to the Dey of Ottoman Algiers:

> For the first time in my life I caught a view of that terrible instrument, that fatal foe to virginity. With unutterable sensations I felt his naked glowing body join mine, again my lips were glued to his, softening me to ruin with his inflamed suctions. In a delirium little short of pleasure, panting with desire, I waited my coming fate...[19]

Like *Fanny Hill*, this was an influential and reasonably well-written book, with a Byronic flavour using the familiar erotic archetype of the virgin becoming insatiable once carnally initiated. *The Lustful Turk* was probably one of Dugdale's best products, but as a repeat offender this book and its companions cost him one year's hard labour; Strange got three months. This did not go down well, and Dugdale became increasingly excitable during the trial, first protesting the circumstances of his arrest and loudly proclaiming his innocence, then begging the court for mercy on account of his children, and finally producing a penknife and going for the witness for the SSV before being hastily restrained by the officers of the court.

Lord Campbell was horrified, particularly by the low prices of the periodicals, which were sold on the street for a penny. In his summing up, he argued that the traditionally high price of erotic literature had functioned as a kind of natural check on its influence, but that cheap and easily obtainable pornography would have a pernicious effect on society at all levels.[20] In common with the Newgate Controversy and the rationale of the secret museums, the concern was with the working classes gaining access to inflammatory material. The House of Lords was then debating a bill to restrict the sale of dangerous chemicals in light of the high-profile murder case of Dr William Palmer, the 'Rugely Poisoner', over whose trial Lord

Campbell had also presided. Palmer had been convicted of killing his old friend, John Parsons Cook, probably with strychnine, to collect on a series of lucrative bets that Cook had won while both were on a long run at the Shrewsbury races. He also tried to defraud Cook's family of £4,000, which he claimed to have been owed. Although it was his friend's murder that sent him to the gallows, Palmer was also suspected of killing his brother, his wife and his mother-in-law after taking out substantial life insurance policies in their names, and of murdering four of his own children to minimise household expenditure, the deaths (all by poison) officially attributed to a variety of natural causes by another local and very elderly doctor. Campbell saw parallels between the cases of Palmer, Dugdale and Strange, and therefore hijacked the debate on the sale of poisons with the startling announcement that, 'from a trial which took place before me on Saturday, I have learnt with horror and alarm that a sale of poison more deadly than prussic acid, strychnine or arsenic – the sale of obscene publications and indecent books – is openly going on.'[21]

Campbell introduced a bill to restrict the sale of pornography and to grant statutory powers to the police to seize and destroy obscene material. There had been some legal tweaks up to that point, largely due to the persistent lobbying of the SSV, for example the addition of 'wilfully exposing to view, in any Street, Road, Highway, or public Place, any obscene Print, Picture, or other indecent Exhibition' to the Vagrancy Act of 1824 (extended in 1838 to display inside a shop or house). The 1853 Customs Consolidation Act had also prohibited the importation of 'indecent or obscene' prints, but the publication of obscene material remained a common law misdemeanour with relatively minor penalties attached. Once again, the SSV had Holywell Street in its sights, and had worked hard during the trial of Dugdale and Strange to convince Campbell of the dangers of cheap, unregulated pornography. His proposed bill carried much stricter penalties, although it did not define what 'obscene' actually meant, a feature that became the focal point of much formal opposition, Lord Lyndhurst arguing that:

> My noble and learned Friend's aim is to put down the sale of obscene books and prints; but what is the interpretation which is to be put on the word 'obscene?' I can easily conceive that two men will come to entirely different conclusions as to its meaning.[22]

The Tory Lord Lyndhurst, supported by the Lord Chancellor, Robert Rolfe, 1st Baron Cranworth, and Lords Brougham and Wensleydale, feared that great works of art could fall within the scope of Campbell's Act, and that it would grant the police too much power to enter and search any building and then seize and destroy any material they thought might be deemed 'obscene'. Constables, the Lords noted, were hardly reliable arbiters of literary or artistic merit. Campbell responded that his bill was 'intended to apply exclusively to works written for the single purpose of corrupting the morals of youth, and of a nature calculated to shock the common feelings of decency in any well-regulated mind'.[23]

Although a legal definition was not set until Chief Justice Cockburn's ruling in Regina v. Hicklin (1868), a case involving an anti-Catholic tract, that an 'obscene' publication was any item that had a tendency 'to deprave and corrupt those whose minds are open to such immoral influences, and into whose hands a publication of this sort may fall', the concept of intentional corruption was already apparent in Campbell's language during the original debate. He dug in, and argued that pornography should be subject to the same regulation as other transgressive or contraband items, repeatedly invoking the spectre of Holywell Street by name:

> in Holywell-street the keepers of these abominable publications set decency and law at defiance. If there were the same powers of searching for these books as for 'uncustomed goods' or as in gambling houses for dice or cards, the public might have been relieved of these contaminations.[24]

With the laconic resistance of old Regency players like Brougham and Lyndhurst, who saw Dugdale's output as considerably less risqué than much of the art and literature of the Romantic period, the passage of the bill was by no means easy. It was further complicated by the Indian Mutiny, then at its height, which broke up Campbell's Commons readings with emergency debates on the siege of Delhi and the imperial crisis. Holywell Street and Delhi, the old capital of the Mughal Empire and the heart of the rebellion, thus became synonymous in the public consciousness as dangerous spaces that threatened the integrity of the Empire. With the support of *The Times*, the *Telegraph*, the *Illustrated London News* and an army of clergymen and concerned citizens mobilised by the SSV, the Obscene Publications Act passed into law in September 1857, sweeping opposition aside in one of England's periodic moral panics and knee-jerk reactions in which politicians attempt to legislate morality.

Above left: Bow Street Runners 'roast a dab'.

Above right: Patrick Colquhoun (1745–1820), the father of modern policing.

Below: The profane burial procession of John Williams, the presumed Ratcliffe Highway Murderer, 31 December 1811.

Above: The execution of John Thurtell outside Hertford Gaol on 9 January 1824.

Below: Tom and Jerry cavorting with high-class courtesans in *Life in London*.
'Bob Logic' (Pierce Egan) is tinkling the ivories.

Above: The return match between World Champion Tom Cribb and the former slave, Tom Molineaux, at Thistleton Gap in 1811. Molineaux was defeated in the eleventh round.

Right: Ainsworth's Jack Sheppard escapes from Newgate with the aid of his two prostitute lovers, Poll Maggott and Edgeworth Bess. Illustrated by George Cruikshank for *Bentley's Miscellany*.

Charlie Bates 'explains a professional technicality' to Oliver Twist. Also illustrated by George Cruikshank for *Bentley's Miscellany*.

Above left: W.H. Ainsworth by Frederick Waddy, *Once a Week*, 1873. Originally captioned 'The Biographer of Jack Sheppard', it is clear that even after thirty-four years, Ainsworth had not been forgiven for romanticising the Georgian criminal. (The Elizabethan dress is a reference to Ainsworth's historical novels.)

Above right: Based on the 'London Burkers', the penny dreadful villain the 'Resurrection Man' makes a 'stiff 'un' with his murderous family.

Below: 'Burke Murdering Margery Campbell' by Robert Seymour, the original illustrator of Dickens's *Pickwick Papers.*

'Resurrectionists' by 'Phiz' (Hablot Knight Browne – another Dickens illustrator), from the Newgate calendar *The Chronicles of Crime*.

Above left: Sir Astley Paston Cooper (1768–1841), English surgeon, anatomist and unapologetic user of bodysnatchers.

Above right: A late Georgian flash house.

Below left: Street kids selling matches not long after Waterloo.

Below right: The dapper Ikey Solomon – supposedly Dickens's model for Fagin – drawn during his sensational trial in June 1830.

Field Lane, off Saffron Hill in Holborn, where Fagin kept his crib. Note how the artist has attributed Dickensian names to local businesses.

Above left: Flora Tristan (1803–44), 'Militante Féministe', presented as a pin-up in *Les Belles Femmes de Paris*.

Above right: Crusading journalist William Thomas Stead (1849–1912), still attacking the devil in 1905.

Below: 'The Royal Saxe Coburg Saloon', a Haymarket 'Finish' named in mockery of Victoria and Albert, depicted in a fold-out illustration to *The New Swell's Night Guide*.

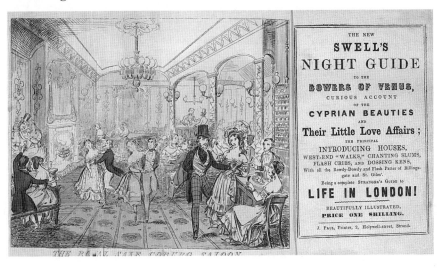

A NIGHT HOUSE—KATE HAMILTON'S.

Above left: The Café Royal in Princes Street, Leicester Square, the most famous of the mid-Victorian 'night houses', where fashionable men-about-town could meet high-class prostitutes.

Above right: The real Harry Flashman, Captain Edward Sellon, 'joins the ladies in the drawing room'. From his posthumously published autobiography, *The Ups and Downs of Life*.

Below left: Anon, daguerreotype, c. 1855.

Below right: Victorian businessman Henry Spencer Ashbee (1834–1900) as his decadent alter-ego, 'Pisamus Fraxi', erotic bibliophile.

He sits in a beautiful parlour
With hundreds of books
on the wall
He drinks a great deal of Marsala
But never gets tipsy at all

The *Illustrated London News*, reporting on the empire, politics, royalty, fashion, culture and technology…

POLICE THE ILLUSTRATED NEWS

LAW COURTS AND WEEKLY RECORD

No. 1,228.   SATURDAY, AUGUST 27, 1887.   Price One Penny.

THE END OF THE WHITE CHAPEL TRAGEDY

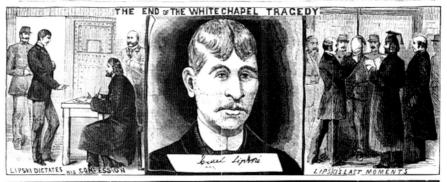

LIPSKI DICTATES HIS CONFESSION   LIPSKI'S LAST MOMENTS

SHIPWRECK—ELEVEN PERSONS DEVOURED BY SHARKS.

TERRIBLE TRAGEDY AT DERBY RESULT OF MIDLAND STRIKE!   ATTACKED BY BEES

…The *Illustrated Police News*, death porn. (This 1887 issue covers the execution of Israel Lipski, killer bees and shark attacks.)

Thomas De Quincey (1785–1859), English opium eater and the inventor of murder.

THE NEW

Newgate Calendar

CONTAINING THE

Remarkable Lives and Trials of Notorious Criminals, Past and Present.

No. 7,—Vol. 1.   Splendidly Illustrated.   Price One Penny.

THE EXTRAORDINARY DREAM OF MARIA MARTEN'S MOTHER.

THE MURDER OF MARIA MARTEN IN THE RED BARN AT POLSTEAD.

——o——

CHAPTER V.

It was a fine autumn morning that Walter Singleton sat sipping his chocolate in the handsome breakfast-parlour of a house in Red Lion Square. The apartment was most tastefully furnished, and everything in keeping, from the well-selected pictures decorating the walls to the smallest ornament on the mantel-shell. The breakfast equipage, which was exceedingly elegant, was laid for one person only.

The door of the room was noiselessly opened, and Jim Kenloy entered, bearing the newspaper and two or three notes in his hand.

'The Extraordinary Dream of Maria Marten's Mother', from *The New Newgate Calendar*.

Trial, Sentence & Execution of
KATE WEBSTER
For the Murder of Mrs. Thomas, at Richmond.

Behold a wretched woman dying,
  Condemned to death for murder, see,
Kate Webster now in anguish crying.
  'Twill end the famed Barnes mystery.
The Jury they have found her guilty,
  Mrs. Thomas, you from there on high,
Behold your murderess now lamenting,
  You'll be revenged—she's condemned
     to die.

'Tis done, and I my death am waiting,
  Kate Webster cries, why was I born,
To hear each witness against me stating,
  For me it fills each heart with scorn
As link by link they were unfolding.
  My fearful death I there could see,
The hangman I shall be beholding,
  And meet a doom of infamy.

Can ere a wretch ere hope for mercy,
  Was ever woman so vile as me,
I hope that God above will pardon,
  And forgive when I'm in eternity.
Take warning by a wretched creature,
  Who now in sorrow her death does wait,
While tears are streaming down every
     feature,
  No one will pity my awful fate.

I thought I ne'er should be discovered,
  That fearful crime I could conceal,
But when the box it was discovered,
  My mistresses murder it did reveal,
When captured my heart was sinking,
  That boy Porter the truth did say,
From guilt and death I now am shrinking,
  In a murderer's grave I must lay.

Farewell to all, my child, my father,
  For me the solemn bell will toll,
Oh, would a child I had died rather,
  May God have mercy on my soul.
Oh, mistress dear, while you in heaven,
  Your pity pray and pardon give,
And may I hope to be forgiven,
  When on earth I no longer live.

Wandsworth Gaol,
Tuesday, July 29th, 1879.

This morning as soon as daylight set in, a body of people assembled in the vicinity of the Gaol, under the impression that something might be seen of the prisoner but the execution was carried out within the prison walls. The gallows was erected in the large yard of the prison, a few feet from the ground. The only persons present were the Governor, Chaplain, the Sheriffs, Marwood the Executioner, the representatives of the press, and a few gentlemen who had been granted the privilege to be present. When the bell of the prison began to toll, the prisoner appeared to feel the awful position she was in. On arriving at the scaffold, she turned round and thanked the officials for their attention to her during her confinement. She was then placed in the necessary position. The executioner having drawn the cap over her face, retired from the scaffold, and the signal having been given, the bolt was withdrawn, and the unhappy criminal was launched into eternity. A black flag was hoisted outside the gaol to denote that the execution had taken place.

On Sunday, April 13th, a black bag, sunk with two bricks, was taken out of the Thames below London-bridge. It was conveyed to the police-station and examined as it was conjectured it might be the one which had contained the missing remains of the mutilated body, which through decomposition might have floated out.

On the boy however, being sent for to see if he could indentify it, he said it was not the same bag he carried. The bag is kept in the possession of the police, as it is considered possible that even perhaps a second bag might have been thrown in the water.

Old Bailey, 1879.

On Wednesday, July the 2nd, at the Central Criminal Court, before Justice Denman and a common jury, Kate Webster was placed in the dock on the charge of having on March 2nd, last, wilfully killed and murdered Julia Martha Thomas, at Richmond, in Surrey. The prosecution was conducted by the Solicitor-General, with whom were Mr. Poland, and Mr. A. L. Smith, and the prisoner was defended by Mr. Warner Sleigh and Mr. Keith Frith; Mr. J. B. Brindly watched the case on behalf of the witness Church.

The prisoner was quite pale. She wore a black cloth jacket, which was thrown open at the top, disclosing a small white knitted shawl. Her hair neatly and carefully arranged. During the reading of the indictment, she stood at the bar, but afterwards at the suggestion of the learned judge, a chair was handed to her, and she sat down during the remainder of the hearing each day.

The Solicitor in stating the case for the prosecution, said the prisoner Webster, some time in the month of January or February, entered the service of Mrs. Thomas, the deceased, as general servant, leaving her son, a boy of five years of age, with a Mrs. Creavey, at Mitchell's-row, Hammersmith, with whom she had been living. Nothing more occurred to attract attention to the female prisoner until early in March, when the neighbours began to miss Mrs. Thomas, who had not been seen for some time. On March 4th, Webster went with a black bag to the house of a man named Porter, who lived a few doors from a quiet little beershop, and asked him to assist her in carrying it. As he should show, Porter and his young son then went with her to a beer-house in the Hammersmith Bridge-road. There Webster left them to go over the bridge, saying that she wanted to meet a friend. In a quarter of an hour she returned without the bag. She asked Porter to allow his son to go

with her to Richmond, and he consented, on condition that she sent him back the same night by the last train. The boy accompanied her to Mrs. Thomas's house. Presently Webster brought a deal bonnet-box of foreign make. The prisoner asked him to assist her in carrying it over Richmond Bridge, which he did. On the bridge she asked him to leave her for a moment, as she expected to meet a friend, and she would rejoin him shortly. The boy left her, but the night being dark he did not go far, and before he had got a few yards he heard a splash in the water. Just at the moment a tall gentleman was said to have passed over the bridge; but at present the police have no clue to the person, although it is possible they might hear something about him on a future occasion. A few minutes after the splash, Webster rejoined the boy, and told him that as it was then so late, half-past eleven—she should not send him home that night. Accordingly, he went to sleep at 2, Vine-cottages. Owing to the publicity given by the press, the facts ultimately became known.

On March 18th, two men went to the house of the deceased with a van for the purpose of purchasing the goods, but one of the neighbours—Miss Ioes, seeing that the property was about to be removed, stepped out and made inquiries, which seemed to have put a stop to the proceedings, the men with the empty van went away. It also seems that Webster afterwards left the house, and was seen no more until she was brought back from Ireland. The same night she fetched her little boy and a black bag, and was driven in a cab to Hammersmith station, where she took a ticket for King's-cross, from there she went to Ireland.

The statement of Mr. Church is that he was at the Rising Sun on Monday evening, March 3rd, and that on Tuesday, the 4th, he was at the Kensington Licensing Sessions for the purpose of obtaining a renewal of his beer and wine license. After that he was at Sandown Races, and reached home from the races between six and seven

in the evening, and did not again leave his house. Webster stated that the crime was committed on March the 3rd.

Church says he never saw the woman until he was introduced to her to buy the furniture.

The elder Porter is very emphatic in his denial of Webster's allegations. In her confession the woman states that she had known the man for six years; but Porter points out that this is scarcely consistent with the fact that, when he took her to negotiate about the purchase of the furniture, he states he had no knowledge and was entire ignorance of her, and did not accept her assertion that they had known each other for the period mentioned. Another important statement by Webster is contradicted by Porter's son. The woman avers that on the night the box was thrown into the river, she met by arrangement, leaving the lad in the Road to wait. Young Porter now denies this.

On the sixth day of the trial, the jury retired at a quarter-past 5 to consider their verdict, and returned into court at twenty six minutes past 6 o'clock.

Mr. Avory, the Clerk of Arraigns, said, Gentlemen of the Jury, have you agreed upon your verdict?

The Foreman: We have.

Mr. Avory: Do you find the prisoner, Catherine Webster, Guilty or Not Guilty of the murder of Julia Martha Thomas?

The Foreman: We find her GUILTY.

Mr. Avory: You say she is Guilty, and that is the verdict of you all?

The Foreman: Yes.

The prisoner then expressed her regret for implicating Church and Porter, and stated that the crime had been instigated by someone who had been her ruin. Sentence of death having been passed, the prisoner pleaded that her execution should be respited.

One of many anonymous Kate Webster broadsides.

The 'From Hell' letter. Was this one written by the killer?

A haunting image of Catherine Eddowes (1842–88), showing a hard-edged, working-class woman who liked a drink and dipped in and out of prostitution to survive. The kidney that accompanied the 'From Hell' letter might have belonged to Eddowes, while the shawl that Russell Edwards claims proves the killer was Aaron Kosminski was allegedly her property.

KATE EDDOWES THE MITRE SQUARE VICTIM

NO. 2 GRATIS WITH NO. 1. ONE PENNY.

SPRING-HEEL'D JACK,
THE TERROR OF LONDON.

SPRING-HEEL'D JACK'S DARING LEAP.

Spring-Heeled Jack will, in type, perform over again his midnight freaks and daring adventures.

WITH ILLUSTRATIONS EVERY WEEK OF HIS DOINGS.

NEWSAGENTS' PUBLISHING COMPANY, 147, FLEET STREET, LONDON, E.C.

'Spring-heel'd Jack: The Terror of London', urban legend turned penny dreadful, revived in 1885. A model for the press's creation of 'Jack the Ripper'?

Mary Kelly goes to her doom, from *The Penny Illustrated Paper*, 17 November 1888. Note the killer is already being depicted as a melodramatic villain with a top hat and a Gladstone bag, suggesting a gentleman and a medical man, the common conception of 'Jack the Ripper' to this day.

Victorian Secrets

But despite the celebrations of the SSV and the many prosecutions, searches, seizures and destruction orders that followed, Holywell Street did not fall. In fact, in the 1860s, the trade appeared to flourish in the rebellious Bohemian climate that had grown out of the Pre-Raphaelite Brotherhood. And although bawdy penny magazines like *Paul Pry* and its successors circulated among the street folk, customers and, indeed, writers were predominantly educated, professional and posh. The decadent poet Algernon Charles Swinburne, for example, liked to be flogged, and several panegyrics on the subject in poetry and prose have been attributed to him after being quietly overlooked by his Edwardian biographer, Edmund Gosse. These include *The Flogging Block* 'by Rufus Rodworthy, annotated by Barebum Birchingly', a mock-heroic tribute comprising a prologue and twelve eclogues (written between 1862 and 1881), *Arthur's Flogging*, an epic poem contributed to *The Whippingham Papers* by 'St George Stock' (1887), and, possibly, the erotic novel *Sadopaideia: Being the Experiences of Cecil Prendergast Undergraduate of the University of Oxford Shewing How he was Led Through the Pleasant Paths of Masochism to the Supreme joys of Sadism* (1907). Swinburne's *Poems and Ballads* (1866) had been withdrawn by their original publisher, Moxon, after a *Times* review had denounced the work – which included poems on lesbianism, sadomasochism, atheism and transgendered bodies – as 'obscene'. These were picked up by the publisher and lexicographer John Camden Hotten, whose Piccadilly premises were a long way from Holywell Street, but not so far that he didn't also publish (and probably write) a comic opera called *Lady Bumtickler's Revels* (1872). Hotten, who had compiled *A Dictionary of Modern Slang, Cant, and Vulgar Words* in 1859, also published reprints of Egan's *Life in London* and the anonymous *Exhibition of Female Flagellants* (originally published in 1830), and *The Romance of Chastisement* (another 'St George Stock' project) in 1866. The journalist George Augustus Henry Sala, who wrote for Dickens in *Household Words* and *All the Year Round*, Thackeray in the *Cornhill Magazine*, contributed regularly to the *Daily Telegraph* and ended up editing *Temple Bar*, also dabbled, co-authoring, under the pseudonym 'Etonensis', *The Mysteries of Verbena House, or, Miss Bellasis Birched for Thieving*, an erotic novel set in a girls' school. The book was completed by Dugdale-collaborator James Campbell Reddie, who may have also co-written *The Sins of the Cities of the Plain* (1882), regarded as the first wholly gay pornographic novel published in English. Miss Bellasis's adventures were also published in 1882, in a limited edition of 150 copies at four guineas a pop.

Edward Sellon was a particularly colourful public school Dugdale writer. A subaltern in the 4th Regiment of the East India Company Madras Infantry and a libertine of the old school, Sellon could have been a character in one of George MacDonald Fraser's 'Flashman' novels, perhaps even the hero. Born in Brighton in 1818, 'the son of a gentleman of moderate fortune, whom I lost when quite a child', Sellon enlisted at sixteen and spent several years in India.[25] There he developed a taste for prostitutes and the bored wives of officers and diplomats, thus embarking on a series of sexual adventures and at least one duel of which he wrote with wit and candour in his autobiography *The Ups and Downs of Life*, published posthumously in 1867. As a product of the Regency, Sellon was probably unaware of how out of step he was with the early Victorian England to which he returned in the early 1840s. While he continued to dally with Society hostesses – gaming, drinking and whoring – industry, trade and sobriety were swinging into fashion. Though they didn't yet realise it, Corinthians, plungers, and dandies like him were becoming extinct.

Prolonged mismanagement of his late father's estate by the family lawyers had left Sellon in need of an income. He tried his hand at novel writing with *Herbert Breakspear: A Legend of the Mahratta War* in 1848, a Kiplingesque adventure that, had it been published either earlier or later in the century, might have done quite well, but which was buried by a new generation of literary novelists that included Disraeli, Mrs Gaskell, the Brontë sisters, and Dickens and Thackeray at the height of their powers. His marriage was a disappointment, as both parties believed the other to be rich, and with an impoverished mother and a growing family he was reduced to driving the mail between London and Cambridge, under an assumed name to protect what was left of his family's reputation. The railway forced him out of business, and his next venture was a fencing school in London like that of the old soldier Mr George in Dickens's *Bleak House*. But Sellon's brand of swordsmanship was falling out of fashion too, and his school did not prosper. By the 1860s, drifting into middle age, his marriage and continuing affairs alternately running hot and cold, Sellon's wicked ways and his literary background led him to start penny-a-lining for William Dugdale.

Sellon was an educated man, and while he wrote for Dugdale he was also working on scholarly projects, most notably 'The Monolithic Temples of India' and 'On the Phallic Worship of India', papers presented before the

Anthropological Society of London, *Annotations on the Sacred Writings of the Hindus* (privately published in 1865), translations of Boccaccio and the *Bhagavad-Gita*, and the posthumously published *Ophiolatreia: an account of the rites and mysteries connected with the origin, rise, and development of serpent worship in various parts of the world* (1889). His erotica, meanwhile, seemed to reflect both spirit and experience, being by turns bawdy, funny, cultivated and elegant. Sellon wrote about what he knew: army life, the sexual intrigues of the gentry, and the exotic otherness of the colonies. His first outing was *The New Epicurean: The Delights of Sex, Facetiously and Philosophically Considered, in Graphic Letters Addressed to Young Ladies of Quality* in 1865. The book begins, 'I am a man who, having passed the Rubicon of youth, has arrived at that age when the passions require a more stimulating diet than is to be found in the arms of every painted courtesan.'[26] *The New Epicurean* is a Georgian pastiche, documenting the exploits of the debauched aristocratic couple Sir Charles and Lady Celia, both of whom have a predilection for young girls which they procure from poor families and a local orphanage. The action takes place in an Elysium villa in a fashionable suburb with extensive and beautiful grounds behind walls high enough to guarantee privacy, which the author describes as their 'happy valley'. The language is pastoral and classical, revealing the cultured and conflicted soul of the luckless author. Henry Spencer Ashbee wrote of it that 'The scenes depicted, many of which are doubtless from the author's own experience, and may be to a certain extent autobiographical, are remarkable for an ultra-lasciviousness, and a cynicism worthy of the Marquis de Sade.'[27]

The following year, Sellon worked on three books for Dugdale. He illustrated *The Adventures of a Schoolboy*, a queer novel (apparently censored by Dugdale) written by James Campbell Reddie, and wrote both the *The New Ladies' Tickler, or Adventures of Lady Lovesport and the Audacious Harry* (fladge), and *Phoebe Kissagen; or the Remarkable Adventures, Schemes, Wiles and Devilries of une Maquerelle*, billed as a sequel to *The New Epicurean*. Once more estranged from his wife and children, and having flogged Dugdale the manuscript of his thinly veiled autobiography, Sellon agreed to act as the companion to another 'Epicurean' called Scarsdale on a tour of Egypt. The trip, however, came to grief on the boat train to Vienna, when Sellon was caught seducing Scarsdale's underage mistress while his employer was asleep in the same carriage. 'I made a desperate effort to throw her on the opposite seat,' he later wrote to Dugdale, 'but it was no go, he had seen us. A row of course ensued.'[28]

Sellon was dismissed with fifteen quid in his pocket; he remained in Vienna until the money ran out, returning to London destitute. He took a room at Webb's in Piccadilly, where he shot himself with his service revolver. His suicide note, addressed to his latest mistress, was a short poem entitled 'No More', which concluded '*Vivat Lingam/Non Resurgam*' – 'Long live cock, I shall not rise again.' To those that knew only the brash, ebullient and rakish old soldier this was a shock, but Ashbee's final word on the subject could be the epitaph for all disappointed men who, through want of luck or money, fail to achieve their full potential and finally tire of repeated defeat: 'Here then is the melancholy career, terminating in suicide at the age of 48 years, of a man by no means devoid of talent, and undoubtedly capable of better things.'[29]

Whether or not Ashbee knew Sellon personally, he was a close friend of James Campbell Reddie. Unlike Ashbee, Reddie was not a wealthy man, and he wrote pornography for Dugdale under the name of 'James Campbell', some of it, as noted, illustrated by Sellon. Like Ashbee, however, he was an obsessive collector and bibliophile. When his eyesight began to fail in 1877, he sold his collection to Ashbee for £300 and made a gift of his ongoing research. He died the following year. Ashbee acknowledged that these bibliographical notes had been 'of great service' in the preparation of the third and final volume of his bibliography of erotica, *Catena Librorum Tacendorum*, published privately in 1885. 'Without the advantage of a university education, James Campbell's acquirements were considerable,' he wrote affectionately in his preliminary remarks, continuing:

> He read with ease Latin, French and Italian, and although not familiar with German, few erotic books in that language were unknown to him. So thorough indeed was his knowledge of this particular branch, that hardly an obscene book in any language had escaped his attention ... His enthusiasm for the bibliography of erotic literature was so great that, had his funds been sufficient to warrant his incurring the risk which such an undertaking must always involve, he would probably have given to the world a compilation of his own, which could not have failed to be a masterpiece of exact and comprehensive research.[30]

Reddie was a gay man, a fact he did not conceal from his friends and which apparently bothered Ashbee not at all. Through their friendship, and the other collectors Ashbee cites by name, William Simpson Potter – 'the shrewd business man, the ardent collector, and the enthusiastic traveller' – who collected mostly erotic photographs and engravings and is widely believed to have been the author of *The Romance of Lust* (the other contender being Sellon), and Frederick Hankey, a rich Englishman in Paris who fancied himself another Marquis de Sade and whose 'collection was small, but most choice', can be glimpsed the exclusive world of the upper-class eroticists, whose rank and privilege nonetheless led straight back to Dugdale and the traders of Holywell Street.[31] This intellectual underground included men like Swinburne and Sala, George Witt, the famous explorer and scholar Richard Francis Burton (publisher of the first English translation of the *Kama Sutra* and Ashbee's hero), and Richard Monckton Milnes, 1st Baron Houghton, Conservative member for Pontefract, who, like Witt and later Ashbee, awkwardly bequeathed a large collection of erotic literature to the British Museum. These were the kind of gentlemen scholars who the secret museums served, while they themselves also contributed to the collections.

Clandestine networks and the circulation of material is apparent in these artefacts, as signalled by Ashbee's remarks about collaborative research, and the drawings and annotations in the nine designated 'scrapbooks' of the Witt collection at the British Museum, which offers a direct line back to the secret museum in Naples, with detailed illustrations and descriptions of many of the erotic artefacts of Pompeii and Herculaneum, including the statue of Pan and the goat. The scrapbooks are comprised of sketches that are both drawn onto the page and pasted in, with accompanying notes in French and English. The museum catalogue attributes everything to Witt, but they are obviously the work of several different hands. When I examined them, I was reminded of the French bookseller Charles Hirsch's description of the ensemble writing of the erotic novel *Teleny, or The Reverse of the Medal* (1893), which is often erroneously attributed to Oscar Wilde:

> One day towards the end of 1890 I believe, he [Wilde] brought me a thin notebook, with a commercial format, tied up and carefully stamped with a wax seal. He told me: 'One of my friends will come round to fetch this manuscript. He will show you my calling card,' and he mentioned a name which I have forgotten. And just as he had said, a few days later, one of the young gentlemen I had seen with him came to take possession of the package. He kept it for a while and then brought it

back saying in turn: 'Would you kindly give this to one of our friends who will come and fetch it in the same person's name.'

The identical ceremony took place three more times. But the last time, the reader of the manuscript, less discreet and less conscientious than the others, brought me the package unsealed, tied with just a simple ribbon, barely closed.

It was a very strong temptation. I confess that I succumbed to it. I opened the package and on the grayish paper cover which held the bundle of handwritten pages I read the simple title written in large capital letters: TELENY. However, since I wasn't yet familiar with English penmanship, I took the 'T' for an 'F' and read: FELENY.

That very night I satisfied my curiosity by deciphering the two hundred pages of the manuscript. What an odd mixture of different handwritings, of scratched out, omitted, corrected or added to passages by various hands! It was obvious to me that several unequally talented writers had collaborated on this anonymous but profoundly interesting work.[32]

Hirsch ran the *Librairie Parisienne* bookshop on Coventry Street, and the above is taken from his introduction to his 1934 French translation of *Teleny* entitled *Souvenirs d'un vieux bibliopole* or 'Notes and Souvenirs from an old Biblioprick'.

The infamous *Teleny* had originally been published in 1893 as part of Harry Sidney Nichols and Leonard Smithers' 'Erotika Biblion Society' imprint out of Bond Street. Nichols and Smithers were associated with the Decadent movement and published work by Wilde, Richard Burton, Aubrey Beardsley, Max Beerbohm, Ernest Dowson, and Aleister Crowley. Like many high-class English erotic publishers, they eventually decamped to Paris. To avoid extradition, Nichols then moved to New York where he continued to publish pornography until he was committed to the Bellevue Mental Hospital in 1939, where he died soon after. Smithers went bankrupt in 1900. He died of an overdose in 1907, his naked body found on his 46th birthday, surrounded by empty bottles of Dr J. Collis Browne's *Chlorodyne*, a popular patent medicine composed of chloroform, hemp oil, morphine and peppermint. Wilde's former lover, Lord Alfred Douglas, paid for his funeral.[33]

Teleny's principle story arc involves the tragic pursuit of the bisexual and sexually magnetic pianist René Teleny by the young Frenchman Camille de

Grieux in *fin-de-siècle* Paris (altered from the original setting of London by the nervous publishers). 'The reverse of the medal' is a reference to sodomy:

> 'Then it must have been *le revers de la médaille* – the back side,' quoth the lawyer, laughing; 'that is, two snowclad lovely hillocks and deep in the valley below, a well, a tiny hole with a dark margin…'[34]

The narrative is interspersed with anecdotes that reflect the tropes of more conventional Victorian pornography, such as seduction and deflowerment, orgies, older women, golden showers and flagellation, which are written in very different styles, supporting Hirsch's claim of multiple authors. Literary historians disagree wildly about the authorship of *Teleny*, with some, like Justin O'Hearn and Gregory Mackie, actively pursuing a connection with Wilde (and some reprints citing Wilde as the sole author), and others, like Jason Boyd, arguing strongly against it on the grounds that old Bibliopricks are not to be trusted. 'There is no justification for taking at face value the 1934 account of publisher Charles Hirsch,' wrote Boyd, 'a shadowy figure about whom very little is known.'[35] Boyd argues that the Hirsch legend is opportunistic and apocryphal, but that the novel remains an important historical document because of what it reveals about the homosexual underworld a century before legalisation, gay bars, clubs, and dating sites.

Leaving Wilde aside, this is the legacy of *Teleny*, and the earlier *The Sins of the Cities of the Plain; or, The Recollections of a Mary-Ann, with Short Essays on Sodomy and Tribadism* (published by William Lazenby, who was connected with Swinburne, in 1881), another work that's difficult to assign. The author is given as 'Jack Saul', the name of a real gay prostitute known as 'Dublin Jack' who was implicated in the Cleveland Street scandal of 1889, when a homosexual male brothel was discovered by police and the Government was accused of covering up their findings to protect the aristocratic patrons. (A 'Mary-Ann' is slang for a rent boy.) It has been attributed to James Campbell Reddie in partnership with the disgraced Pre-Raphaelite painter Simeon Solomon, arrested in 1873 for attempting to commit sodomy in a public urinal. *The Sins of the Cities of the Plain* is cited several times by the author/s of *Teleny*, and the fear engendered by the Criminal Law Amendment Act reverberates through the text alongside the 'love that dare not speak its name', a phrase from the poem 'Two Loves' by Lord Alfred Douglas (1894) that was quoted at length during Wilde's trial for gross indecency under Section 11 of the Act. 'Going to my office, I heard a man walking behind me,' Camille tells his lover, fearful after a note suggesting blackmail arrives. 'I went on quickly; he hastened his step. I almost began to run. All at once a hand was laid on my shoulder. I was about to faint with terror. At that moment I almost expected to hear the awful words – "In the name of the law, I arrest you, sodomite!"'[36] But much as Boyd wants to disassociate his hero from the vulgarity of the erotic publishing scene and erratic writing, it is the clandestine nature of Victorian homosexuality, crossed with the tight huddle of specialist printers and booksellers, that gives Hirsch's account the ring of truth. Anyone familiar with Wilde's work can see that *Teleny* did not originate from his pen – his version of this world is *The Picture of Dorian Gray* (1891) – but that is not what Hirsch claimed. His story was simply that *Teleny* originated somewhere in Wilde's circle; probably, we might conjecture, through Lord Alfred Douglas, 'Bosie' himself, who also wrote and bore a marked resemblance to Camille de Grieux. Both were highly strung young men in reckless pursuit of brilliant artists, and both destroyed their lovers.

Although it is in the nature of Victorian pornographers to remain anonymous, the other contended authorship of the period again hurls us down the rabbit hole of covert networks, collectors and publishers. It concerns the identity of 'Walter', the author of the rambling and unrepentant eleven-volume confession, *My Secret Life*, a man whose prodigious sexual appetites were matched only by his propensity for writing about them. *My Secret Life* is a carnal epic, ranging from the 'amorous amusements' of youth through the 'gallant intrigues and adventures of a frisky order' of middle age to, finally, 'tastes and letches which years ago I thought were the dreams of erotic mad-men'.[37] The series is the work of a lifetime, chronicling the thoughts and experiences of an anonymous Victorian gentleman whose principle preoccupation was sex – mostly with prostitutes, sometimes with relatives, servants or working-class girls he picked up off the street, like 'Yellow-haired Kitty'. It is a huge and remarkable document. The text is over one million words long, which is twice the length of *The Lord of the Rings*.

The original publication is obscure, with the author himself offering a framing narration in the first volume suggesting that he is literary executor of a third party, an old friend, and has decided to have it printed as 'a contribution to psychology'. This awkward attempt at misdirection then gives way to a preface that starts, 'I began these memoirs when about twenty-five years old, having from youth kept a diary of some sort, which perhaps from habit made me think of recording my inner and secret life.'[38] The official, or at least frequently cited version of its publication comes from the pornographer Charles Carrington, who started out selling books from a barrow in Farrington Market and ended up with a shop in Montmartre. His account is reminiscent of Hirsch's remarks on *Teleny*:

> About the year 1888, a well-known bookseller and publisher of Amsterdam, whose speciality was literature of an incandescent kind, was summoned to London by one of his customers, a rich old Englishman, who desired to have privately printed for his own enjoyment an enormous MSS.; containing in the fullest detail all the secret venereal thoughts of his existence. He defrayed all costs of printing, on condition that no more than six copies should be struck off. A few years afterwards, this eccentric amateur shuffled off the mortal coil; and a few copies of the extraordinary work made a timid appearance on the market.[39]

The 'publisher of Amsterdam' is believed to be the Belgium pornographer Auguste Brancart, who also had ties to the Decadent movement. Carrington's account comes from an obscure publication called *Forbidden Books* (1902), which is a catalogue masquerading as an autobiography. As Steven Marcus noted, his description, which goes on to suggest that there were 'about twenty-five' copies of 'Walter's' memoir printed, is actually the prelude to a pitch, where he might be able to obtain a set. This follows an earlier advertisement in which he had claimed that the project took seven years to complete, costing the anonymous author £1,110, and that there were only six copies, four of which were for sale at £100 each. Apparently, he had found a few more. Yet there is likely still some truth to all this. Despite the introduction to the first volume, the author was very much alive when the series was printed, which he refers to in the eleventh and final volume, and he specifically mentions the six copies, after which the type, he claimed, was broken up. Although his identity was kept secret, and there are theories that Ashbee helped him get the series published, it is not surprising, given the nature of the trade, that his wishes concerning the limited edition were not respected.

The author's original preface is an interesting manifesto of intent and process. He was, he states, inspired by *Fanny Hill*, which he erroneously attributes to a real woman, only his intention was to use more authentic, and therefore obscene language:

> That book has no baudy [*sic*] word in it; but baudy acts need the baudy ejaculations; the erotic, full flavored expressions,

which even the chastest indulge in when lust, or love, is in its full tide of performance. So I determined to write my private life freely as to fact, and in the spirit of the lustful acts done by me, or witnessed; it is written therefore with absolute truth and without any regard whatever for what the world calls decency.[40]

'I began it for my amusement,' he continues, before noting the project was abandoned in his twenties until a decade later an unnamed lover convinced him to revisit and update it. He then again laid it aside for a while before recommencing his chronicle of 'early middle age', until 'a mess caused me to think seriously of burning the whole.' (Later remarks suggest this refers to a period of illness.) 'Not liking to destroy my labor,' he kept the manuscript, returning to it when 'another illness gave me long uninterrupted leisure'. Being an avid diarist who prided himself on his recall, *My Secret Life* was an attempt at a more detailed prose narrative, using the journal as a resource, with the voice of the text mediating between that of his younger self and the more reflective memoirist: 'I read my manuscript and filled in some occurrences which I had forgotten but which my diary enabled me to place in their proper order … I had from youth an excellent memory, but about sexual matters a wonderful one.' At this point, he notes, he began to consider publication, while describing both his obsession and his compositional method:

I then had entered my maturity, and on to the most lascivious portion of my life, the events were disjointed, and fragmentary and my amusement was to describe them just after they occurred. Most frequently the next day I wrote all down with much prolixity; since, I have much abbreviated it … Women were the pleasure of my life. I loved cunt, but also who had it, I like the woman I fucked and not simply the cunt I fucked, and therein is a great difference. I recollect even now in a degree which astonishes me, the face, colour, stature, thighs, backside, and cunt of well nigh every woman I have had, who was not a mere casual, and even of some who were. The clothes they wore, the houses and rooms in which I had them, were before me mentally as I wrote … I have one fear about publicity, it is that of having done a few things by curiosity and impulse (temporary aberrations) which even professed libertines may cry fie on ... Yet from that cause perhaps no mortal eye but mine will see this history.[41]

The method, then, was to have the sexual encounter, then write it up quickly in as much detail as possible in the diary, later revising, thereby reliving the experience, a carnal version of what Wordsworth called 'emotion recollected in tranquillity'.[42] In the third volume, he notes that, 'The narratives were written in the present tense, but in print have been altered to the past, which gives them an air of a studied composition, written as a man might write a novel.'[43] The original intention was purely narcissistic; he was writing for his eyes only, although the six copies suggests they were intended for close members of his circle. This is a fascinating conflation of sex and writing, in which the author is the protagonist of his own pornographic novel, having the experience and then transcribing it for his own titillation in an audacious piece of creative non-fiction.

He then goes on to explain that some names (though not those of servants) have been changed, while many of the places of which he wrote are now gone, a reference to the slum clearances at the end of the century, while he has 'mystified family affairs', however:

> If I say I had ten cousins when I had but six, or that one aunt's house was in Surrey instead of Kent, or in Lancashire, it breaks the due and cannot matter to the reader. But my doings with man and woman are as true as gospel. If I say that I saw, or did, that with a cousin, male or female, it was with a cousin and no mere acquaintance; if with a servant, it was with a servant; if with a casual acquaintance, it is equally true. Nor if I say I had that woman, and did this or that with her, or felt or did aught else with a man, be there a word of untruth, excepting as to the place at which the incidents occurred. But even those are mostly correctly given; this is intended to be a true history, and not a lie.[44]

All the clues to authorial intention and narrative function are in this preface, even if the author remains obscure. 'I like the woman I fucked' is a prelude to friendships and long, natural dialogues with working girls that bring colour and insight to the casually sexist and quickly repetitive cavalcade of creative shags that make up the main body of the text. This is alongside the most detailed first-hand description of the vanished world of low lodging houses and high-class brothels that proliferated in the era of Dickens and Mayhew, and priceless insights into the mind of the writer himself: on one hand a remarkably obsessive sex tourist and pornographer, but on the other probably a fairly representative example of the middle-class, mid-Victorian brothel creeper.

Any example can reflect the whole, and Steven Marcus identifies a startling episode in which the young 'Walter' spots a couple of working-class women nipping into a graveyard, obviously to pee, and uses his social rank to force himself on them in conversation. Money is soon mentioned, and one of the women accepts:

> The instant she had gone round the corner the selected one laid hold of my prick. 'Do it quick, someone may come,' said she as she grasped it. 'Lie down.' 'No I won't, it's dirty.' 'No it's dry, the grass is quite hay.' I stripped off my coat, made it into a bundle, and placed it for her head. 'There, there,' I said, and pulled her down. She made no resistance. I saw white thighs and belly, black hair on her cunt; and the next minute I was spending up her.
>
> 'Shove on,' said she, 'I was just coming,' and she was wriggling and heaving, 'go on.' I could always go on pushing after a spend in those days, my prick would not lose its stiffness for minutes afterwards; so I pushed till I thought of doing her a second time; but her pleasure came on, her cunt contracted, and with the usual wriggle and sigh she was over, and there were we laying in copulation, with the dead all around us; another living creature might that moment have been begotten, in its turn to eat, drink, fuck, die, be buried and rot.[45]

'The meaning, if it has one, escapes him,' wrote Marcus. [46] But perhaps it did not. This could equally be a moment of dark epiphany, in which the writer glimpses, while rutting like an animal amongst the dead, the true nature of the human condition. This cynicism is underpinned by the lack of coherent narrative across all eleven volumes, detailing fuck after fuck after meaningless fuck. There is no story arc, no sense of dramatic pacing, and all that happens is the protagonist grows older and less potent. The eleventh volume simply stops, with neither climax, denouement nor epilogue. It ends with the bittersweet memory of taking advantage of the drunken and married sister of an acquaintance at an inn where 'Walter', then aged twenty-three, was having a business meeting:

> I find from subsequent memoranda, that this amour of twenty minutes filled my brain long afterwards, and that at times I shut my eyes whilst fucking and thought of Mrs. * * * *. Idealities have always helped me in sexual enjoyments. When poor and I had women for five shillings, I used to close my eyes and fancy I was enjoying females of higher class. I saw Mrs. * * * * for the first time about six months afterwards. She always avoided me. Nevertheless I once alluded to it, tho I knew I ought not. 'Do you re-member being at * * * *,' I began, naming the place. 'You ought never to refer to it,' said she, getting up and leaving me on some pretext. I noticed that when afterwards we met in society she was always in a furtive way looking at me. — She died two or three years after of typhoid fever.

THE END[47]

Perhaps, like the beautiful Garance in Marcel Carné *Les Enfants du Paradis*, Mrs * * * * was the one that got away, the unattainable love object embellished by memory that 2,000 lovers – 'Walter's' estimate of his conquests over a forty-odd-year period – could not replace. Or perhaps, and more probably, it was simply the elderly man recalling his lost youth, the old memories now much more vivid than the new. Nothing has been learned of life except how to make it and that it ends. The hero's journey has been pointless.

But this structural and dramatic lack should not detract from 'Walter's' almost certainly unconscious contribution to the historical record. Though the subject is limited to say the least, defamiliar almost – when he tours Europe it is reported almost entirely through brothels, while his memory of the Great Exhibition was that he shagged a French girl there – there is an undoubted authenticity to the narrative. To return to the conversation with 'Yellow-haired Kitty', which was by no means an unusual dialogue scene in the vast text, it is difficult to imagine an amateur novelist, especially a pornographer, taking the time to create such a detailed character and give her such a distinct voice. Similarly, the author does not present himself in a particularly noble or heroic light. Many times, he shows himself being duped; he despised his first wife, describes, at one point raping her in a

129

particularly repellent episode, and celebrates her death. (There is also an appalling scene in which he tries unsuccessfully to drag a little girl into his carriage.) But though the descriptions of sex are samey and mechanical, settings and characters are not, and some, like the prostitutes Sarah and Camille, stay in his life for years, coming as close to love as he seems capable:

> To their class I owe a debt of gratitude, and say again what
> I think I have said elsewhere: that they have been my refuge
> in sorrow, an unfailing relief in all my miseries, have saved
> me from drinking, gambling, and perhaps worse. I shall never
> throw stones at them, nor speak harshly to them, nor of them.[48]

In this simple, almost tragic statement, rests a counterpoint to the scientific pragmatism of Dr Acton and the moralising of Dickens and Bracebridge Hemyng. Though these women deserved a better champion than 'Walter', at least through him we know who they were and how they truly lived.

What is not known, however, is who wrote *My Secret Life*. The hunt for the identity of the man the American sexologists Eberhard and Phyllis Kronhausen called the 'English Casanova' is not quite in the same league as the search for Jack the Ripper, but as unknown Victorians go, he is one of the biggest. As with the Whitechapel killer, there are many theories, all of which are notionally plausible but ultimately circumstantial. Gordon Grimley, the author of *Wicked Victorians: Clandestine Literature of the 19th Century* (1970), for example, in his introduction to the 1972 Granada reprint of *My Secret Life*, put forward Ashbee's associate William Simpson Potter, largely on the grounds of his assumed authorship of *The Romance of Lust*. (The other possible author of this work, Edward Sellon, has also been suggested as 'Walter', which is unlikely given his early death.) Potter died in Sicily in 1879, however, so his dates don't really match up either, unless the original introduction about the dead friend was actually true, a device that unravels as the author repeatedly refers to seeing the later printed editions in the text. Working with the editor of the *American Rationalist*, Gordon Stein, the historian and sexologist Vern Bullough made a case for the barrister Charles Stanley. This was based on a reference 'Walter' makes to a rape trial in Vol. II, saying he knew the defendant's barrister well. From the details, Stein and Bullough were convinced this was Regina v. Richard Clarke (1854), the counsel for the defence being William Overend QC, a childhood friend of Stanley's. Other clues matched up, for example periods spent abroad, while some dates did not. Stein died of cancer before he could complete his research.[49] John Patrick Pattinson, meanwhile, has put forward a strong argument for Joseph Bazalgette's colleague William J. Haywood, architect, surveyor and engineer to the City of London Commissioners of Sewers.[50] Pattinson's archive work was impressive, but at the end of the day, as David Monaghan and Nigel Cawthorne have argued, it's difficult to reconcile the productive, driven and highly organised professional life of Haywood with the 'obsessive, tormented, sometimes demented' voice of 'Walter', but then, they reckon 'Walter' was Jack the Ripper. He almost certainly wasn't; but *Jack the Ripper's Secret Confession: The Hidden Testimony of Britain's First Serial Killer* (2010) is still a reasonable contextual close reading of *My Secret Life*, as well as a summary of the contenders for authorship. The irony, of course, being that even if you accept Monaghan and Cawthorne's tenuous thesis, they still don't know who 'Walter' was.

But all these contenders are in the second eleven at best. Even though he was born about fourteen years after 'Walter', the name most commonly associated with him is that of the obsessive bibliographer Henry Spencer Ashbee, 'Pisanus Fraxi' himself, the man Steven Marcus dubbed 'Pornographer Royal'.

This all stems from the work of the independent American scholar Gershon Legman. He initially made the connection in the introduction to a reprint of Ashbee's bibliographies in 1962, which he formalised in his book *The Horn Book: Studies in Erotic Folklore and Bibliography* (1964) and then restated in the introduction to the Grove Press edition of *My Secret Life* in 1966. In his seminal work, *The Other Victorians*, Steven Marcus describes this as a 'shrewd and ingenious guess', noting that:

> There are a number of facts which Legman marshals in support of this bold stab in the dark, and it is possible that he may be right. There are, however, many more facts that seem to me to controvert this argument. In addition, Legman's essay is marred by a number of careless errors in scholarship and above all by the fact that he writes about *My Secret Life* without, apparently, having read more than three or four volumes.[51]

Legman was an autodidact, having dropped out of the University of Michigan after one semester in 1935. Marcus – a graduate of Cambridge and Columbia – often judges the academic rigour of other researchers in his book and finds it wanting. Nonetheless, this theory has stuck, with Channel Four's 2000 documentary *Walter: The Secret Life of a Victorian Pornographer* taking the connection for granted, and Ashbee's biographer, Ian Gibson, backing it up the following year in his book *The Erotomaniac: The secret life of Henry Spencer Ashbee*, further muddying the waters by arguing that although Ashbee was, indeed, 'Walter', *My Secret Life* was a work of fiction – an assertion that I'm inclined to dispute based on the written style (which is much less pompous) and amount of mundane detail in the narrative. Also, Ashbee would never attribute *Fanny Hill* to a female author, unless that was another sleight of hand.

Trying to pin 'Walter' on Ashbee rather misses the point. The two *are connected*, but by virtue of their magnificent obsessions, both of which produced voluminous and transgressive texts which between them give us an unparalleled insight into the real world of phallocentric Victorian sexuality. Ashbee, like 'Walter', was what we might deem a 'typical' Victorian gentleman. The only child of Kentish yeoman stock, he went into the textile trade, later marrying the boss's daughter and becoming a senior partner at Charles Lavy and Co. He worked hard and travelled extensively in an age when it was not safe to do so, wrote eloquently of his experiences, and amassed an impressive collection of fine art and antique first editions. He was a member of the Royal Geographical Society, the Royal Historical Society, and the Society of Arts; regular guests at the family home in Bloomsbury included such lions of the age as Sir Richard Burton and George Cruikshank. He voted Conservative, hated Catholics, looked down on foreigners, loathed suffragists, socialists and Pre-Raphaelites, and was possessed of that particular blend of arrogance and energy that characterised the late Victorian psyche. He also compiled and privately published a scholarly bibliography of erotic literature of such monumental detail that it remains the primary source of information on the subject to this day.

Ashbee had built up a huge collection of pornography alongside the European literature, his Cervantic library, for example, being unrivalled outside Spain. As a bibliographer, he approached dirty books with the same level of meticulous scholarship as any other printed work. His first bibliography, *Index Librorum Prohibitorum: being Notes Bio- Biblio- Iconographical and Critical, on Curious and Uncommon Books*, by 'Pisanus Fraxi', was printed privately in a large quarto single volume in 1877, limited to 250 copies. The title satirises the Catholic Church's *List of Prohibited Books*, while 'Fraxi' is taken from the Latin *fraxinus*, 'ash' or 'ash tree'. 'Pisanus' is a scatological pun that also includes an anagram of *apis*, the Latin for 'bee'. (Ashbee had been using the pseudonym 'Fraxinus' in contributions to *Notes and Queries*, so the subterfuge was not great.) It is a complex academic text in multiple languages, using different coloured inks and typefaces, and it took the long-suffering printers two years to proof, block and set, after which the author still had to append seven pages of errata. Pornographic books are listed alphabetically and cross-referenced, with full publication histories, different editions and physical descriptions (a typical entry is quoted above); a synopsis and critique of each book is also provided, and there are billowing footnotes. The entries themselves comprise 436 pages, with a 76-page introduction, a 38-page list of 'Authorities Consulted' and a 58-page index. As the work of the bibliographer is never done, a second volume, *Centuria Librorum Absconditorum: being Notes Bio- Icono- graphical and Critical, on Curious and Uncommon Books*[52] followed in 1879; with *Catena Librorum Tacendorum: being Notes Bio- Icono- graphical and Critical, on Curious and Uncommon Books*[53] completing the trilogy in 1885. The author's original introduction strikes a rebellious as well as a scholarly tone, his apparent plea for permissiveness at odds with his otherwise very conventional Victorian politics:

> That English erotic literature should never have had its bibliographer is not difficult to understand. First and foremost the English nation possesses an ultra-squeamishness and hyper-prudery peculiar to itself, sufficient alone to deter any author of position and talent from taking in hand so tabooed a subject; and secondly English books of that class have generally been written with so little talent, delicacy or art, that, in addition to the objectionableness of the subject itself, they would undoubtedly be considered by most bibliographers as totally unworthy of any consideration whatever.[54]

Step forward, Pisanus Fraxi: 'The object of the present work is to catalogue, as thoroughly, and at the same time, as tersely as possible, books which, as a rule, have not been mentioned but superficially by former bibliographers, and to notice them in such a way that the student or collector may be able to form a pretty just estimate of their value of purport.'[55]

While 'Walter' strove to hide his identity for fear of scandal, Ashbee seemed to flaunt his, but as Peter Fryer argued, the surprise is not that he got away with it; it's that Ashbee 'defied convention in one field alone, while being ultra-conventional in all the others'.[56] If we look beyond the superficial eccentricity of otherwise respectable Victorians like Ashbee and his mysterious double, 'Walter', however, there is a darker logic that Ian Gibson gets to in *The Erotomaniac*. There was nothing subversive about Ashbee's project, or, by extension, 'Walter's'; he was merely applying the ideals of imperial Victorian capitalism to sexuality. Ashbee was a very successful businessman, and his approach to pornography shows the same entrepreneurial spirit that drove the engine of free trade and British influence across the globe, just as 'Walter's' world is one of maximum profit at minimum expense and the exploitation of the working classes. And in the industry of pornography, it was the luckless proletarian publishers and printers that suffered, while collectors like Ashbee and his circle lived safely, well beyond the reach of the Obscene Publications Act.

Ashbee died in the summer of 1900. His last laugh was to leave his entire collection to the British Museum, while disinheriting a family from whom he had grown increasingly estranged, largely because of his intractable conservatism in an age of increasing social change. Like George Witt's bequest, the offer was predicated on the pornography being accepted as well. As the trustees wanted Ashbee's library of Spanish literature, they had no choice but to take the erotica, which became the main body of the 'Private Case'. This Janus-faced collection is yet another symbol of the extreme contrasts of Victorian culture, a gothic double that is as once fractured yet oddly holistic, in the same way that Stevenson's Dr Jekyll ultimately starts to describe both himself and Mr Hyde in the third person, unifying the alien creature he had become.[57] In the end, rich men like Henry Spencer Ashbee and rogues like William Dugdale were not so different. They were all, in a sense, 'Walter'.

Chapter 8

The Death Hunters

The other type of pornography the Victorians craved was murder. The drug-addled journalist Thomas De Quincey was way ahead of the curve in this regard, and his Swiftian treatise 'On Murder Considered as One of the Fine Arts' did as much, if not more, to create the concept of the modern 'serial killer' as did the Ratcliffe Highway murderer or murderers who formed the substance of the original essay. De Quincey loved a good homicide, and in his brief tenure as the editor of the *Westmorland Gazette*, a provincial newspaper with Tory affiliations, he reported murder trials in all their gory detail alongside the general news, until the owners forced him out in 1819. By then, his opium habit was already ingrained and severe, making his working practices erratic.

Written originally for *Blackwood's Edinburgh Magazine* in 1827, 'On Murder Considered as One of the Fine Arts' is presented as a lecture to 'The Society of Connoisseurs in Murder' – a club 'curious in homicide; amateurs and dilettanti in the various modes of bloodshed; and, in short, Murder-Fanciers'. In an elegant and lengthy discourse, the humour strictly gallows and the irony savage, De Quincey gleefully analyses violent crime as Burke had considered the sublime and Aristotle tragedy:

> Everything in this world has two handles. Murder, for instance, may be laid hold of by its moral handle, (as it generally is in the pulpit and at the Old Bailey); and *that*, I confess, is its weak side; or it may also be treated *aesthetically*, as the Germans call it, that is, in relation to good taste.

The voyeuristic connection between true crime stories and pornography is implicit in an opening satire of the Society for the Suppression of Vice. The murder society, De Quincey explains, is 'of a character still more atrocious' than the 'Society for the Promotion of Vice' and another 'formed for the Suppression of Virtue'. Moving from the theory to the practice, De Quincey dismisses the Thurtell case – 'his principle performance as an artist has been much overrated' – in favour of Williams's (presumed) murders of the Marr and Williamson families on the Ratcliffe Highway:

> People begin to see that something more goes to the composition of a fine murder than two blockheads to kill and be killed – a knife – a purse – and a dark lane. Design, gentlemen, grouping, light and shade, poetry, sentiment, are now deemed indispensable to attempts of this nature. Mr Williams has exalted the ideal of murder to all of us ... Like Æschylus or Milton in poetry, like Michael Angelo in painting, he has carried his art to a point of colossal sublimity, and, as Mr Wordsworth observes, has in a manner 'created the taste by which he is to be enjoyed.'[1]

The sordid and sketchy nature of the actual crime – it being far from certain that Williams even was the killer – is presented in epic terms, with Williams more like Milton's Satan, a glamorous, fallen angel, than a violent, drunken sailor with a grudge. De Quincey even dresses him in the clothes of a gentleman, in black silk with a long dark coat. There are parallels with Dr John Polidori's Lord Ruthven in 'The Vampyre' (1819), which transformed the zombie-like ghoul of medieval European folklore into the aristocratic and sexually magnetic modern vampire.[2] Emotional depth was added to the character, as well as creative motive; the murdered families were largely ignored. Murder was art, murder was performance, and Williams was the author of a play that, like *MacBeth*, was about the killer not his victims, a production that had commanded a huge audience. The truth was that the seedy and brutal version was much more common than De Quincey's idealised and gothic figure, yet it was in this theatrical interpretation that murder became a subject of mass and popular entertainment across social classes. Like Cain, De Quincey, channelling the Ratcliffe Highway fiend, had become 'the inventor of murder'.[3]

Brides of Death

This is not to suggest that crime, catastrophe, misery and violence were not already a staple of British newspapers and magazines, modern journalism having emerged in a recognisable form from the eight-page 'weekly newsbooks' of the seventeenth century, the playwright Ben Jonson complaining that the news was a 'dereliction' and 'a degradation of the proper function of a writer'.[4] Similarly, 'Newgate Calendars' were nothing new. These lurid collections of criminal biographies, passed off as 'improving' literature, had grown out of the Keeper's lists of prisoners scheduled for trial at an assize, often wrapped around the indictments, and accounts of trials and executions by the Ordinaries of Newgate, the practice being adopted in parallel by numerous entrepreneurial printers in the early eighteenth century. There is consequently no definitive Newgate Calendar, but most have the same *dramatis personae*, including Captain Kidd, Jack Sheppard, Jonathan Wild, Joseph Blake ('Blueskin'), Dick Turpin, Catherine Hayes and Eugene Aram. The fact that many of these criminals never went anywhere near Newgate did not seem to matter – the name sold copy. Even Defoe produced a few.[5] The commonality of entries in Newgate Calendars, often going back to Elizabethan criminals like the mythical cannibal Sawney Bean and Mary Frith (AKA 'Moll Cutpurse'), are indicative of the sluggish nature of information in the preceding century, with criminal trials rarely dominating the national press. Also, there simply weren't that many murders. In 1810, the year before the Ratcliffe Highway killings, only fifteen people were convicted of murder out of the entire population of England and Wales.[6]

The modern magazine, meanwhile, had been around since Edward Cave founded the monthly digest the *Gentleman's Magazine* in 1731, applying the term 'magazine' (a military storehouse) to publishing for the first time. Cave's format included serial fiction, literary criticism, illustrations, news and commentary, combining original copy by regular contributors – Dr Johnson's first full-time job as a writer was on the *Gentleman's Magazine* – with extracts from other publications. A new generation of monthly magazines had risen in the Regency, with *Blackwood's Edinburgh Magazine* blazing a trail that the *London Magazine* and the *New Monthly Magazine* soon followed. These magazines were highly partisan, and dealt mostly with politics and high culture, the target audience being middle and upper class. Newspapers remained small, and outside London there were no daily editions. Again, politics dominated the news, with regional papers often reproducing stories from their London counterparts. Circulation was relatively small, with profits largely coming from advertising. There was therefore little incentive to increase sales, and not much content likely to interest working-class readers. Crime reporting was negligible, and left to the broadsides and pamphlets, a broadside being a single printed sheet sold for a penny that usually offered an account of the crime, a morbid woodcut and a song. A pamphlet, such as Egan's interview with Thurtell, was longer and cost about fivepence.

The writers, printers and sellers at the lower end were known as 'Death Hunters', originally an old Flash term for an undertaker, who kept up a steady stream of news on the subject of 'orrible murder for the masses. And if it was a slow day, they'd simply make something up. As Mayhew explained:

> I have described the particular business of the running patterer, who is known by another and a very expressive cognonmen — as a 'Death Hunter'. This title refers not only to his vending accounts of all the murders that become topics of public conversation, but to his being a 'murderer' on his own account, as in the sale of 'cocks' mentioned incidentally in this narrative. If the truth be saleable, a running patterer prefers selling the truth, for then — as one man told me — he can 'go the same round comfortably another day.' If there be no truths for sale — no stories of criminals' lives and loves to be condensed from the diffusive biographies in the newspapers — no 'helegy' for a great man gone — no prophecy and no crim. con. — the death hunter invents, or rather announces, them. He puts someone to death for the occasion, which is called 'a cock'. The paper he sells may give the dreadful details, or it may be a religious tract, 'brought out in mistake,' should the vendor be questioned on the subject; or else the poor fellow puts on a bewildered look and murmurs, 'O, it's shocking to be done this way — but I can't read.' The patterers pass along so rapidly that this detection rarely happens.[7]

The master of this trade was James Catnach, an enterprising Geordie who set up as a printer in Seven Dials in 1813 or thereabouts. He retained a small group of alcoholic hacks known locally as the 'Seven Bards of Seven Dials' who could bang out a broadside to order for a penny a line.[8] The brother of the Death Hunter was the 'Fire Hunter'.

While the slaughter on the Ratcliffe Highway set something of a precedent, it was the Battle of Waterloo that marked the sea change in reporting, the French Wars having provided a steady stream of copy since 1793. As nature abhors a vacuum, many saw the connection between this sudden lack and the enthusiasm with which the Radlett murder was reported and consumed. 'No public news,' wrote Sir Walter Scott to a friend in 1824, 'except the more last words of Mr Thurtell, whose tale seems to interest the public as long as that of Waterloo, showing that a bloody murther will do the business of the newspapers when a bloody battle is not to be heard.'[9] The end of the war had also coincided with the coming of cheap pulp paper, and steam-powered presses accelerating print runs from 250 per hour in 1814 to 4,000 by 1827.[10] The repressive laws that had hammered the radical press and turned the Holywell Street printers to pornography, meanwhile, had done nothing to suppress an increasingly literate working-class desire for the printed word, creating an ideal environment for newspapers to thrive. The market grew, and the middle-class papers at last faced competition. Increasingly desperate for copy, editors were quick to realise that unlike an execution, a criminal trial was a gift that kept on giving.

After the Ratcliffe Highway and Radlett murders (although not, oddly, the assassination of the Tory Prime Minister Spencer Perceval in 1812), and just before the Burke and Hare scandal broke, the next murder to really capture the pre-Victorian public imagination occurred in April 1828, when Thomas Marten, a mole-catcher from Suffolk, found his daughter's remains buried in a barn, eleven months after she had supposedly married and settled in the Isle of Wight.

The 'Red Barn' sat on Barnfield Hill, just outside the small rural village of Polstead, about half a mile from Thomas Marten's cottage. It was so called because of the red clay of the roof tiles, a feature common to the area – all barns were red, but not like this one. There, on a warm evening in May 1827, 25-year-old local beauty Maria Marten had met her lover, William Corder, who was a year younger than her and whose family rented the barn. Corder had originally been keen to keep their relationship secret, but Maria had fallen pregnant. The baby died, but Maria was set on marriage. That night, she was expecting to travel to Ipswich to tie the knot. That was as far as she got. Corder kept in touch with her family, telling them that their daughter was in Yarmouth, until he left Polstead for good after the harvest. He sent the news that they had married and gone west, but that an injury to her hand prevented his new bride from writing herself. In fact, he was living in Brentwood, where he had married the proprietress of a girls' boarding school.

Broadside legend has it that his crime was exposed after Maria's stepmother, Ann, became plagued with nightmare visions of Maria's murder and convinced her husband to investigate the barn. Although her dreams were raised at the inquest, they were prudently omitted from the trial in favour of a neighbour testifying that he had remembered Corder borrowing a spade on the day of Maria's disappearance, a fact he communicated to her increasingly worried parents. That labourers had complained about an unpleasant odour in the barn, which was initially ascribed to rats, is another more likely reason. Either way, her badly decomposed and mutilated body was discovered, identified by a missing tooth and some clothing, including a handkerchief that had belonged to Corder around her neck. Cause of death was difficult to determine, and some injuries may have been caused post-mortem by her father's shovel, but she appeared to have been shot, strangled and stabbed in the eye. One thing was certain: she'd put up a fight.

The story was gold dust to journalists of all classes, from newspapermen all the way down to the Death Hunters and street balladeers. A narrative was quickly created, that of the innocent country girl seduced, ruined and murdered by a local squire. She was 'the innocent nymph of her native village' wrote J. Curtis in his hastily composed book *An authentic and faithful history of the mysterious murder of Maria Marten.*[11] In reality, her reluctant fiancé was an unremarkable farmer; and, not that it justified her appalling fate, before Maria had fallen pregnant by Corder, she had already had two illegitimate children by different fathers, including, Curtis wrote, Corder's older brother, Thomas, who had recently drowned. As Maria's sins became as white as snow, Corder's were reported as scarlet. He was accused in the press of attempting to poison his lover's second child (the first had died in infancy); he was presented as a forger, and a pig and horse thief. Worse – and this was actually true – he had persuaded Maria to dress in male attire to throw any possible witnesses off the scent, by convincing her that the local constable was after her over her care of her surviving child. Readers were further scandalised by the revelation that in London Corder had advertised for a wife in the *Morning Herald* and *Sunday Times* and had received over forty proposals. Along with the supernatural dimension, this was a sensational story.

Although there was never really any doubt of Corder's guilt – he had wanted Maria out of his life and he went to great lengths to convince her family she was still alive – it was nonetheless a trial by media. He had been arrested quickly and returned to Suffolk. The crowd at that year's Polstead Cherry Fair broke all previous records, as an estimated 200,000 sightseers descended on the now famous 'Red Barn' to grab a souvenir such as a nail, a broken tile or a piece of wooden siding, until guards were posted to stop the building being completely dismantled, and to lay siege to the inns of Bury St Edmunds and the surrounding villages in anticipation of Corder's trial. Methodists preached in the open air about the wages of sin, their voices vying for attention with street theatre, Punch and Judy shows, and camera obscura displays depicting the murder, much to the chagrin of Corder's lawyers, while his likeness could be purchased in local shops for sixpence. Like John Thurtell before him, Corder recklessly chose to defend himself, appearing throughout the trial in blue-tinted French eyeglasses. His defence was that he had left Maria at the barn in good health after they had argued, and then heard a shot. Running back, he found her dead by her own hand, having used one of his pistols. Panicking, he had concealed the body. Several witnesses, however, painted a picture of a man being forced into marriage by blackmail, Maria having knowledge of some of his shadier activities. The two also often apparently fought over Maria's connection to the father of her other child, Peter Matthews, and Corder had exacerbated the issue by taking money that Matthews had sent for child support. Maria was not letting this go. George Marten, Maria's younger brother, testified that he had seen Corder around the barn on the fatal day, once with a pistol, and later returning with a pickaxe. Most damning of all were Corder's letters to Maria's family, which were read out in court. According to coverage in the *Gentleman's Magazine*, it only took the jury thirty-five minutes to convict him.

Corder was hanged in Bury St Edmunds before a huge crowd just before midday on 11 August 1828. Workmen in the surrounding fields downed tools to attend the event. After initially continuing to claim his innocence, he had finally confessed for the sake of his immortal soul when it became clear all hope of reprieve was lost. He claimed they had argued and he had accidently discharged a pistol, shooting his lover in the eye. He did not die well. He required physical support on the scaffold, and as he was a slight man, the drop did not kill him. John Foxton, the Newgate hangman who had also done for Thurtell as well as the Cato Street Conspirators, had to pull down on Corder's legs for an agonising eight minutes until he finally stopped moving, after which the body was partially flayed, taken back to the courtroom and displayed to the public, being dissected the following day. Curtis reported that it was wired to a galvanic battery brought down from Cambridge University and seen to twitch. After his relics were distributed to several local hospitals and museums, the Red Barn was once again stripped, much of its wood becoming toothpicks, pipe stoppers and snuff boxes. For many years after, the village of Polstead became a popular tourist destination, and W.T. Moncrieff's theatrical version of the story, *The Red Farm, or, The Well of St Marie* (1842), itself an amalgam of previous tales and dramas, was revived throughout the century. It was filmed by George King as *Maria Marten, or The Murder in the Red Barn* in 1935, starring the king of pre-war melodramatic English villains, Tod Slaughter, as 'Squire' William Corder: 'Don't be afraid, Maria. You shall be a bride – a bride of Death!'

Although not, alas, immortalised on the screen by the wonderful Tod Slaughter, another crime that shook Britain was discovered in the last days of 1836, the year preceding the accession of Victoria. On 28 December, a brickie working on the Edgware Road found a sack tucked behind a leaning flagstone containing the headless upper body of a middle-aged woman, wrapped in some gory clothing. The exposed spine and femurs looked to have been sawn about halfway through and then snapped off. It was a cold day, and the blood around the sack had frozen. An inquest at the White Lion Inn on Edgware Road took place on the last day of the year, and a verdict of 'Wilful murder against some person or persons unknown' was returned. A week later, a head was found, jammed in the 'Ben Jonson' sluice of the Regent's Canal in Stepney, its earlobes split, the skull fractured and missing an eye. A parish surgeon declared the parts to be a match, and, as was common practice, they were preserved in spirits for the purposes of possible identification. His opinion was that the eye had been removed prior to the victim's death. The legs turned up in early February, in a ditch near Coldharbour Lane in Brixton. Like the torso, they were in a sack; some maker's letters were still discernible, and the local constable traced it to a shop in Camberwell. Nothing much came of this until the next month, when a man called William Gay tentatively identified the head as that of his missing sister, a widowed washerwoman called Hannah Brown. She had disappeared on Christmas Eve, having sold her mangle and left to marry a Camberwell cabinetmaker named James Greenacre on Christmas Day. Greenacre had subsequently told friends and family that the wedding was cancelled when it became apparent that his betrothed had misrepresented her financial condition. Her people had initially thought she had gone to ground out of shame.

Greenacre was arrested at his lodgings along with his lover, Sarah Gale, the day before the couple had intended to ship for America. At first, he denied all knowledge of the unfortunate Mrs Brown, but Gale was found to be hiding a pair of earrings belonging to the deceased and a pawn ticket for two silk dresses also identified as the victim's property. At his hearing, Greenacre claimed that they had argued over money on the eve of their wedding while drunk. She had laughed at him, he said, when he raised her promised dowry. He had hit her in the heat of the moment; she had fallen, struck her head and died. He then walked this back, claiming instead that she had arrived drunk and belligerent, tripped and hit her head. He had

142

panicked and disposed of the body, keeping the clothes and jewellery in payment for a debt. Miss Gale, he stressed, had nothing to do with the 'accident' or its concealment. Greenacre was charged with murder and Gale as an accessory after the fact. The press had a field day. Greenacre was rumoured, like Corder, to have advertised for a wife after Hannah's death; he was also, said *The Times*, an abortionist, a child killer, and a rapist, as well as a miser, a fraud, and a dangerous radical who was involved in the Cato Street Conspiracy and had plotted to assassinate the Duke of Wellington.

At his trial, a surgeon testified that in his opinion all the victim's injuries occurred 'before life was extinct', including, by implication, the decapitation, and that there was no evidence that she had been drinking. As forensic science was in its absolute infancy, there was no way to determine the truth of such a terrible statement, but it was generally accepted as fact at the time. After a two-day trial, the jury deliberated for fifteen minutes before finding both defendants guilty.[12] Gale was transported for life, and Greenacre was hanged in front of a vast mob outside Newgate by Foxton's successor, William Calcraft, who was known for favouring a short drop, thereby entertaining the crowds with a slower death.

After his conviction, Greenacre had finally confessed to 'accidently' putting Hannah's eye out with a rolling pin, after which she fell and died of her injuries and he dismembered her using the tools of his trade. But it was not the gristly murder so much as the details of the disposal of the body that really captured the public imagination. His confession had suggested a kind of macabre day trip, in which he took two omnibuses to the canal, the head wrapped in a silk handkerchief and sitting on his lap. The torso he carried in a pack on his back until a passing carter let him rest his burden on the tailboard. Once they parted company, he hired a cab, lamenting the time wasted and the expenses incurred. As the legs were dumped in a local marsh, he just walked. The first London buses had only appeared in 1829, and their use in a homicide tickled journalists and readers alike, leading to numerous jokes about the fare, which was 'sixpence a head', and the fact that Greenacre really should have bought two tickets.

The Chamber of Horrors

And so began the Victorian epoch, bathed in blood by Williams, Thurtell, Corder, Greenacre, and Burke and Hare. And as the century progressed, the violence, as it does, continued, enthusiastically reported by both street and mainstream press to the point of cliché, and consumed with a ghoulish relish by working- and middle-class readers, as gently satirised by Dickens in *Great Expectations*:

> It was in the fourth year of my apprenticeship to Joe, and it was a Saturday night. There was a group assembled round the fire at the Three Jolly Bargemen, attentive to Mr. Wopsle as he read the newspaper aloud. Of that group I was one.
>
> A highly popular murder had been committed, and Mr. Wopsle was imbrued in blood to the eyebrows. He gloated over every abhorrent adjective in the description, and identified himself with every witness at the Inquest. He faintly moaned, 'I am done for,' as the victim, and he barbarously bellowed, 'I'll serve you out,' as the murderer. He gave the medical testimony, in pointed imitation of our local practitioner; and he piped and shook, as the aged turnpike-keeper who had heard blows, to an extent so very paralytic as to suggest a doubt regarding the mental competency of that witness. The coroner, in Mr. Wopsle's hands, became Timon of Athens; the beadle, Coriolanus. He enjoyed himself thoroughly, and we all enjoyed ourselves, and were delightfully comfortable. In this cozy state of mind we came to the verdict of Wilful Murder.[13]

Apart from the obvious one, the majority of the famous Victorian murderers have been forgotten now, the subject of history rather than popular culture, although they occasionally resurface in film and television. Their names were, however, common currency throughout the century, their notoriety confirmed by inclusion in Madame Tussaud's 'Chamber of Horrors', a separate room in the permanent exhibition established in London in 1835 – an ever-changing cavalcade of cruelty that remained open until April 2016, when it was replaced by the 'Sherlock Holmes Experience' after an increasing number of complaints from the parents of young children.

Thurtell, Corder, Burke and Hare were among the first of these eerie wax effigies. As the century progressed, there was also:

- James Bloomfield Rush, the 'Stanfield Hall murderer', a delinquent tenant farmer who shot his landlords near Norwich in 1849.
- Maria Manning who, with her husband Frederick, murdered her lover, Patrick O'Connor, and buried him under the flagstones in their kitchen in the 'Bermondsey Horror' (also 1849).

- William Palmer, the Rugeley Poisoner.
- Franz Müller, a German tailor hanged for the murder of Thomas Briggs in 1864, the first person to be killed on a British train.
- Mary Ann Cotton, hanged for poisoning her stepson, Charles Edward Cotton, in 1873, but who may also have murdered three of her four husbands for the insurance, and eleven of her thirteen children.
- Charles Peace, a cat burglar and master of disguise who had killed PC Nicholas Cock in Manchester in 1876, gotten away with, it but was later hanged for the murder of Arthur Dyson, the husband of a woman with whom he was obsessed.
- Percy Lefroy Mapleton, the 'Railway Murderer' of 1881, who had shot and stabbed the coin dealer Isaac Frederick Gold on the London to Brighton express and was the first subject of a police facial composite.
- Israel Lipski, a Polish Jew, who forced his pregnant landlady, Miriam Angel, to drink nitric acid in 1887 and for whose reprieve W.T. Stead unsuccessfully campaigned on the grounds that the trial was racially prejudiced.

There was also Mary Pearcey, who killed her lover's wife and 18-month-old daughter in 1890 and was erroneously connected with the 'Jill the Ripper' theory owing to the savagery of the crime – Mrs Phoebe Hogg's throat had been cut with such violence that she was virtually decapitated. As *The Graphic* enthusiastically announced on the discovery of her body in the Crossfield Road in Hampstead:

> Great excitement was aroused last Saturday when it became known that a crime had been committed which seemed to indicate that the mysterious 'Jack the Ripper' had recommenced his atrocities in a new neighbourhood; but the tide of curiosity rose far higher on Monday, when it was discovered that the horror was not of the 'Ripper' type, but was even more complicated and puzzling in its surroundings.[14]

A bloodstained pram was soon found nearby, as was the body of the child, apparently suffocated. Notionally a friend of the family, Pearcey had gone to the police with Phoebe's sister-in-law, Clara, who feared the dead woman might be her brother's wife, who had gone missing the day before. Her demeanour in the mortuary where the body was identified was suspicious enough to justify a search of her lodgings. The sitting room was positively painted with blood; there were also bloodstained knives in the kitchen and blood and hair on a poker. Pearcey claimed that she had been killing mice. It later emerged that she had invited the young mother over for tea. The scandalous nature of the story (Pearcey had been having an affair with Phoebe's husband before and after their marriage), the fact that the murderer was a young woman, which was unusual, and the sheer horror of the crime caused a public sensation. After her conviction, Madame Tussaud's purchased the furniture from Pearcey's lodgings to create an authentic tableau. The company even bought the victim's clothes and the fatal pram, which had been used to dump the bodies, from the traumatised Mr Hogg. As many as 75,000 people visited the 'Hampstead Tragedy' display in the first three days alone. As Judith Flanders wrote, 'Madame Tussaud's knew its audience.'[15]

Another particularly sinister waxwork bore the likeness of Kate Webster, an Irish maid servant and petty thief who murdered her mistress, Julia Thomas, in her Richmond home in 1879. Webster had pushed Mrs Thomas down the stairs and then strangled her, after a fractious professional relationship that the unfortunate widow had been unable to control. (It's likely she was killed when she tried to dismiss her servant.) She then dismembered the body, boiled the flesh off the bones and gradually disposed of most of it in the Thames. Legend had it that she had offered the fat to neighbours as lard. A foot was found at Twickenham, and her torso was washed ashore in a hatbox at Barnes. The head was not found, and its absence led to the case becoming known as the 'Barnes Mystery'.

In a shocking affront to social class, when tradesmen came to the house, Webster assumed Mrs Thomas's identity, and started to sell her possessions. Neighbours became suspicious when removal vans arrived to collect furniture Webster had sold to a local publican and she fled to Ireland. The house was searched, and bloodstains were discovered, along with burnt finger bones in a fireplace and fatty deposits in a copper pot used for laundry. Webster was traced to a relative's farm in County Wexford and returned to London where she stood trial. In an indication of the public interest in the case and the general sense of media frenzy, the prosecution was conducted by the Solicitor General himself, Hardinge Stanley Giffard, 1st Earl of Halsbury. Huge crowds flocked around the Old Bailey and the trial was attended by men and women of all classes, the *Manchester Guardian* reporting that on the fourth day the Crown Prince of Sweden was observed in the gallery.[16] Although Webster pleaded her belly in an attempt to avoid the death penalty, a jury of matrons did not concur that she was pregnant and neither did the Home Secretary. She was hanged at Wandsworth Prison on 29 July, the hangman, William Marwood, using his newly developed 'long drop' technique for a quick and supposedly painless death. In a strange coda, Mrs Thomas's skull was found by workman in Richmond in 2010, in the foundations of what had been the Hole in the Wall pub in the back garden of the naturalist and broadcaster Sir David Attenborough.[17]

By the time Kate Webster was active, death hunting of the old school had evolved into the emergent tabloid press, in the form of the *Illustrated Police News*, the dark reflection of the more wholesome *Illustrated London News*, the first illustrated weekly news magazine, established in 1842 by the journalist and Liberal politician Herbert Ingram. The *Illustrated London News* was very much an organ of empire, reporting on politics at home and abroad, military campaigns, the royal family, culture and technology. It radiated the confidence of the most powerful country in the world. The *Illustrated Police News*, on the other hand, was predominantly murder porn. True crime met real life horror, and death in all its myriad and macabre forms was reported each week, from murders and executions to suicides, found bodies, natural and man-made disasters, freak accidents and animal attacks, plundered from newspapers from all over the world. Domestic horrors were preferred, with an emphasis on violent crime and punishment, but in a slow week the editors would throw in industrial accidents in America, shipwrecks and shark attacks, or atrocities from Asia, adding to the sense of oriental otherness that pervaded the outer reaches of the globe in the minds of Victorian readers; there be monsters. The headlines were sensational and the reports melodramatic, accompanied by theatrical woodcut illustrations in the tradition of the broadside and the penny dreadful.

To give a flavour of the content, headlines included: 'Double Murder and Suicide at Kennington'; 'Death of a Somnambulist'; 'Fatal Case of Elephant Teasing'; 'Killed by a Bicycle'; 'Killed by a Cricket Ball'; 'Five Children Thrown into a Well'; 'Flogging Garrotters at Leeds'; 'Horrible Discovery of a Girl Eaten by Rats'; 'Shocking Murder Near Grimsby'; 'Fearful Struggle on the Scaffold'; 'Murderous Attack by a Gorilla'; 'A Man Crucifying Himself'; 'Japanese Punishment for Adultery'; 'Mysterious Death at Penge'; 'A Burglar Bitten by a Skeleton'; 'Dreadful Child Murder at Hull'; 'An Encounter with a Mad Dog at a Post Office'; 'Baby Farming at Brixton'; 'Strange Discovery of a Woman Dressed in Male Attire'; 'Death in a Bathing Machine'; 'Six Nuns Buried Alive'; 'Burned to Death through Reading in Bed'; and 'A Wife Driven Insane by a Husband Tickling her Feet'. Kate Webster's execution warranted a souvenir edition.

The *Illustrated Police News, Law Courts and Weekly Record* was a product of the Purkess publishing dynasty out of Dean Street, Soho. George Purkess Senior (1801–59) was an associate of William Dugdale's partner in crime William Strange, as well as Edward Lloyd, the king of the penny dreadful, famous for publishing *Varney the Vampire* and *The String of Pearls*, which unleashed Sweeney Todd upon the world, and George Vickers, who published *The Mysteries of London*. Purkess had dozens of penny serials to his name and had worked with Lloyd on the Newgate calendar *The History and Lives of the Most Notorious Pirates of All Nations*. His son, George Junior (1839–92), continued the family business, establishing the *Illustrated Police News* in 1864, starting out with four pages (three of text and a pictorial front page), price one penny, later expanding to twelve pages in 1897. Primarily pitched at a mass working-class audience, the paper was enormously successful, early editions shifting 175,000 copies a week.[18]

The paper's unique selling point was the use of striking and detailed illustration, delivering what no twentieth-century photojournalist could – a graphic recreation of the moment of death, the victim's eyes wide in terror and agony, blood spraying from the wounds. In his offices in the Strand, Purkess had six artists permanently on his staff with almost a hundred regional freelancers on his books, who could be quickly deployed to a crime scene anywhere in the country, against only an editor and subeditor collating and summarising the text. And just as the pictures sold the paper, they also attracted the most criticism, readers of W.T. Stead's *Pall Mall Gazette* voting it the 'Worst Newspaper in England' in 1886. 'I acknowledge it to be a sensational newspaper,' said Purkess, in a good-natured interview with the *Gazette* in which he denied that his paper incited crime and suggested that criticism of his artwork from the *Illustrated London News* and *The Graphic* amounted to jealousy. He had concluded, 'I know what people say, but as I replied to a friend who asked me why I did not produce some other paper than the *Police News*, "We can't all have *Timeses* and *Telegraphs*, and if we can't have the *Telegraph* or *The Times*, we must put up with the *Police News*."' He could, after all, laugh all the way to the bank, having a weekly circulation, he claimed, of 150,000 at its lowest, rising to as much as 600,000 during a particularly sensational case.[19]

While Purkess had explained that, 'Should a terrible murder or extraordinary incident be reported from the country we would at once despatch a telegram to an artist,' the case with which his paper remains most associated to this day quite literally occurred on its doorstep, when the body of Mary Ann 'Polly' Nichols was discovered in the small hours of the last day of August 1888, in front of a stable entrance in Buck's Row, Whitechapel, her throat cut and her abdomen torn open. She was identified by the laundry mark on her petticoats: Lambeth Workhouse. Sketch artists were dispatched, and the now iconic *Illustrated Police News* cover showing Nichols's corpse – immediately familiar from hundreds of books, articles and websites – is so close to the equally famous mortuary photograph of the unfortunate woman that the artist almost certainly viewed her body. The accompanying report had the same sense of atmospheric immediacy, beginning:

> At a quarter to four on Friday morning Police-constable Neil was on his beat in Buck's-row, Thomas-street, Whitechapel, when his attention was attracted to the body of a woman lying on the pavement close to the door of the stable-yard in connection with Essex Wharf. Buck's-row, like many other miser thoroughfares in this and similar neighbourhoods, is not overburdened with gas lamps, and in the dim light the constable at first thought that the woman had fallen down in a drunken stupor and was sleeping off the effects of a night's debauch. With the aid of the light from his bullseye lantern Neil at once perceived that the woman had been the victim of some horrible outrage. Her livid face was stained with blood and her throat cut from ear to ear.[20]

Murders in Whitechapel were nothing new. Already that year, two other prostitutes had been brutally killed in the dark streets off the Whitechapel Road. Emma Elizabeth Smith, aged forty-five or thereabouts, a well-spoken woman about whom little is known, was robbed and viciously assaulted by a gang on Osborn Street at about 1.30 am on Tuesday, 3 April. She survived the attack and made it to the London Hospital, where she died the following morning. Her injuries were horrific. 'A portion of the right ear was torn,' the attending surgeon had reported, 'and there was a rupture of the peritoneum and other internal organs, caused by some blunt instrument.'[21] Emma could not describe her assailants, but had told the doctor it had been three men, one of whom looked like a teenager. In a case that the newspapers at once connected, the body of Martha Tabram was next found at dawn on 7 August, the day after a Bank Holiday, on a landing in a tenement in George Yard, an alley running between Wentworth Street and Whitechapel High Street. She had been stabbed thirty-nine times and, like Smith, sexually mutilated.

She was discovered by a docker who lived in the building leaving for work. A soldier was initially suspected, the fatal injury to the heart being ascribed to a bayonet by surgeons, but no one was ultimately charged. Whether or not she was killed by the same man or men, Polly Nichols was actually the third name to go into the Metropolitan Police files designated 'Whitechapel Murders'.

This was the start of what the press dubbed the 'autumn of terror', in which four more prostitutes were killed and mutilated after Nichols, all within a quarter of a mile in Whitechapel bar one, Catherine Eddowes, who died in Mitre Square, just within the boundary of the City of London. On 8 September, the day after Nichols's funeral, Annie Chapman, a widow and mother of three known locally as 'Dark Annie'[22] was found dead in a back yard in Hanbury Street, having gone out the night before in the hope of earning enough money for a night's lodgings. 'The body was terribly mutilated,' the police surgeon Mr George Bagster Phillips told the coroner at her inquest, though, reported *The Times*, 'he thought he had better not go into further details of the mutilations, which could only be painful to the feelings of the jury and the public.'[23] Her throat had been cut and there were signs that she might have been suffocated first. She'd also been disembowelled, and her intestines draped over her shoulder; a post-mortem later revealed that part of her uterus had been removed. Struggling to find some sort of context for a crime that was appalling even by East End standards, *The Times* went straight to gothic fiction:

> One may search the ghastliest efforts of fiction and fail to find anything to surpass these crimes in diabolical audacity. The mind travels back to the pages of De Quincey for an equal display of scientific delight in the details of butchery; or Edgar Allan Poe's 'Murders in the Rue Morgue' recur in the endeavour to conjure up some parallel for this murderer's brutish savagery. But, so far as we know, nothing in fact or fiction equals these outrages at once in their horrible nature and in the effect which they have produced upon the popular imagination.

In the same piece, the paper also made the connection with the earlier killings, concluding that, 'Probably Smith's assailants did not mean to kill her outright. But there is no room for doubt that the slayer of Tabram, Nichols, and Chapman meant murder, and nothing else but murder.'[24]

Things went quiet for a couple weeks, and then, on 27 September, the Central News Agency received the following letter:

Dear Boss,

I keep on hearing the police have caught me but they wont fix me just yet. I have laughed when they look so clever and talk about being on the right track. That joke about Leather Apron gave me real fits. I am down on whores and I shant quit ripping them till I do get buckled. Grand work the last job was. I gave the lady no time to squeal. How can they catch me now. I love my work and want to start again. You will soon hear of me with my funny little games. I saved some of the proper red stuff in a ginger beer bottle over the last job to write with but it went thick like glue and I cant use it. Red ink is fit enough I hope *ha ha*. The next job I do I shall clip the ladys ears off and send to the police officers just for jolly wouldnt you. Keep this letter back till I do a bit more work, then give it out straight. My knife's so nice and sharp I want to get to work right away if I get a chance. Good Luck.

Yours truly

Jack the Ripper

Dont mind me giving the trade name

wasnt good enough to post this before I got all the red ink off my hands curse it.

No luck yet. They say I am a doctor now *ha ha*.

The Central News Agency was a rival of the Press Association and Reuters known for distributing sensational and often questionable stories. The letter was passed on to Scotland Yard on 29 September, and initially dismissed as a hoax, of which there had already been many.

September ended with the so-called 'double event'. Elizabeth Stride (née Gustafsdotter – 'Long Liz' to her mates), who came from Sweden and once ran a coffee shop with her husband in Poplar, was found with her throat cut in Dutfield's Yard on Berner Street, over the road from the Working Men's International Club, at about 1.00 am on Sunday, 30 September. The wound was fresh and still bleeding when Louis Diemschutz, a club steward, found her. Evidently, he had disturbed the killer. At 1.45 am, Catherine Eddowes, a mother of three and another middle-aged casual prostitute, was found in a corner of Mitre Square by a police constable called Edward Watkins. She'd spent Saturday night in Bishopgate nick, having been found dead drunk in Aldgate High Street, but this time she was just dead. Her left carotid artery had been cut, and although, like Stride, not yet cold, her killer had had time to mutilate her face and remove her left kidney. Thankfully after death, Catherine had been cut across the bridge of the nose, on both cheeks, and both eyelids; the tip of her nose and part of an ear had been sliced off. Because of the location of Mitre Square, the City of London Police joined the investigation alongside the Metropolitan Police. At about 3.00 am, a fragment of her apron stained with blood and excrement was found in a passage in Goulston Street, Whitechapel. 'The Juwes are the men that Will not be Blamed for nothing' was reportedly written in chalk on the wall above it, but the graffiti was quickly washed away at the orders of Sir Charles Warren, Metropolitan Police Commissioner, for fear it would incite race riots.

As Eddowes had lost part of an ear, the 'Dear Boss' letter suddenly became interesting, and the next day, the Central News Agency received another message, this time on a postcard, which read:

> I wasnt codding dear old Boss when I gave you the tip. youll hear about saucy Jackys work tomorrow double event this time number one squealed a bit couldnt finish straight off. had not got time to get ears off for police thanks for keeping last letter back till I got to work again.
>
> Jack the Ripper

The card was postmarked and delivered 1 October, which meant whoever wrote it could have heard about the murders the night before, but as it referenced the 'Dear Boss' letter and contained what might have still been privileged information, the Met decided to go public in the hope of tracing the correspondent. Facsimile posters were put up around the East End on 3 October, and the following day the full text of both letters appeared in several newspapers. This shifted a lot of papers and resulted in a deluge of copycat letters, but otherwise achieved very little of practical use. As Charles Warren suspected at the time, the original 'Jack the Ripper' letters were almost certainly the work of a canny journalist trying to keep the story alive during a slow period after Annie Chapman's murder. 'I think the whole thing a hoax,' Warren wrote to Godfrey Lushington, Permanent Under-Secretary at the Home Office, on 10 October 1888, 'but we are bound to try and ascertain the writer in any case.'[25] Sir Robert Anderson, the Assistant

Commissioner, went further in his 1910 memoir, *The Lighter Side of My Official Life*, claiming that he knew exactly who'd written the letters but that he thought it prudent not to name names for legal reasons. 'Scotland Yard can boast that not even the subordinate officers of the department will tell tales out of school,' he wrote, 'and it would ill become me to violate the unwritten rule of the service. So I will only add here that the "Jack-the-Ripper" letter which is preserved in the Police Museum at New Scotland Yard is the creation of an enterprising London journalist.'[26] What these letters achieved had nothing to do with apprehending a sadistic killer cutting up women in the East End. They simply gave him a memorable *nom de guerre* and the identity of a penny dreadful villain.

Of all the hoax letters that muddied the waters that autumn, the most haunting was sent directly to the builder George Lusk, the chairman of the Whitechapel Vigilance Committee, a volunteer group that patrolled the area at night set up by local businessmen:

> From hell
>
> Mr Lusk
>
> Sor
>
> I send you half the Kidne I took from one woman and prasarved it for you tother piece I fried and ate it was very nise I may send you the bloody knif that took it out if you only wate a whil longer
>
> signed
>
> Catch me when you can Mishter Lusk

The note arrived in the evening on 16 October, accompanied by a small cardboard box wrapped in brown paper containing half a kidney badly preserved in wine. Lusk made light of this, but he was shaken. He wanted to throw the stinking thing away but the committee treasurer, Joseph Aarons, was suspicious enough to take it to a local doctor who passed it to Dr Thomas Openshaw, the Curator of the Pathological Museum at the Royal London Hospital. Openshaw pronounced it part of a middle-aged woman's left kidney, about three weeks dead, adding that it was 'ginny', meaning it came from a hard drinker, although he later retracted much of his original analysis, stating that as the organ had been preserved in alcohol it was impossible to ascertain age or gender.[27] This raised the tantalising possibility that the letter was genuine, and that the kidney could have come from Catherine Eddowes. Or it was just another hoax, this time probably from a medical student, or a journalist who knew a medical student, because the story had gone quiet again. But there's still something chilling about that letter. The handwriting is untidy, and spelling and grammar is primitive, suggesting someone unaccustomed to writing, and it doesn't match the 'Dear Boss' and 'Saucy Jack' letters; neither does it reference them or use the popular epithet. Then there is the return address, 'From hell'. It could all have been another misdirection, or a message from a very damaged mind.

Nothing happened in October, then, on 9 November, hell came to Miller's Court.

Dorset Street, Spitalfields was mostly made up of cheap lodging houses, offering a bed for around a shilling a night, interspersed with stables and the odd chandler's shop. It was close to Hanbury Street, where Annie Chapman had been found, and several small courts led off it, largely occupied by prostitutes. It was locally referred to as 'Do as You Please Street'. As Chief Inspector Walter Dew later recalled, after each murder the community of Whitechapel prostitutes would react in horror, staying indoors or travelling in groups, but as the weeks passed without incident these groups became pairs until, finally, financial necessity drove them back out onto the streets alone. Dew was then a CID detective constable based at Commercial Street (H Division) who went on to arrest Dr Crippen. As an officer in the Met investigation he was well known around Whitechapel, and with a stoic gallows humour working girls would often call out, 'I'm the next for Jack!' when they saw him.[28]

One of these girls was Mary Jane Kelly, an Irish woman in her mid-twenties with good looks and a big personality. Mary liked a drink, and was apt to belt out songs from the emerald isle when tipsy. Descriptions from her neighbours paint a vivid picture of a pretty girl who was generous and warm-hearted but also a mean drunk. She was 'tall and pretty, as fair as a lily', said Elizabeth Prater, who lived above her, and 'seemed to be on good terms with everybody'. She was 'of rather stout build', said Elizabeth Phoenix, the sister of a previous landlady, 'with blue eyes and a very fine head of hair, which reached nearly to her waist'.[29] Mary lived at 13 Miller's Court, a partitioned, ground floor room at the back of 26 Dorset Street, accessed by a low, flagstoned passage at the entrance of which was posted a flyer, which read, 'The Proprietor of the *Illustrated Police News* Offers £100 Reward for the Capture of the Whitechapel Murderer.' Until recently, she'd cohabited with her lover, Joe Barnett, but the couple had quarrelled over the presence of a homeless prostitute that Mary had taken in and Joe had left her at the end of October.

She was found, horribly mutilated, on her bed, on the morning of 9 November, by her landlord's assistant, Thomas Bowyer, who was chasing her for 29s rent arrears. Receiving no answer, Bowyer had looked through a broken window pane and seen unidentified body parts on a bedside table. Dew was one of the first police officers at the scene – unbeknown to him at the time, Sir Charles Warren had just resigned:

> I tried the door. It would not yield. So I moved to the window, over which, on the inside, an old coat was hanging to act as a curtain and to block the draught from the hole in the glass. Inspector Beck pushed the coat to one side and peered through the aperture. A moment later he staggered back with his face as white as a sheet. 'For God's sake, Dew,' he cried. 'Don't look.' I ignored the order, and took my place at the window. When my eyes became accustomed to the dim light I saw a sight which I shall never forget to my dying day.'[30]

The killer had taken his time. It was only through her blue eyes and fine head of hair that Joe Barnett was later able to identify what was left of pretty Mary Jane Kelly. The police surgeon, Dr Thomas Bond, who was already profiling the killer at the request of Sir Robert Anderson, examined the body at the scene:

> The whole of the surface of the abdomen and thighs was removed and the abdominal cavity emptied of its viscera. The breasts were cut off, the arms mutilated by several jagged wounds and the face hacked beyond recognition of the features. The tissues of the neck were severed all round down to the bone.
>
>   The viscera were found in various parts viz: the uterus and kidneys with one breast under the head, the other breast by the right foot, the liver between the feet, the intestines by the right side and the spleen by the left side of the body. The flaps removed from the abdomen and thighs were on a table.[31]

In the subsequent post-mortem examination conducted by Bond and Dr George Bagster Phillips, Mary's heart was found to be missing.

Bond estimated that death had occurred sometime between 2.00 am and 8.00 am. Phillips believed the mutilations were done after Mary's throat had been cut, and suggested that it would have taken at least two hours to perform them. In a later report to the Home Office, Bond wrote that 'In each case the mutilation was inflicted by a person who had no scientific nor anatomical knowledge. In my opinion he does not even possess the technical knowledge of a butcher or horse slaughterer or a person accustomed to cut up dead animals.'[32]

After this brutal escalation, the killings abruptly stopped, and the killer faded into the shadows from which he'd come. There were no reliable witnesses beyond the women he had murdered, and no rational motive. Evidence was collated, theories abounded, and the myth grew, but the Whitechapel Murderer had vanished; either incarcerated, physically or mentally incapacitated, abroad or dead. His identity remains a mystery that self-styled 'Ripperologists' have been trying to solve ever since. He is everyone and no one, 'Leather Apron', 'Saucy Jacky', and 'Catch me when you can'. He is the Invisible Man. But once the passage of time precluded the possibility of justice, chasing the killer became largely redundant, yet still he endures in the popular imagination. In truth, 'Jack the Ripper' never existed in the first place, beyond the bleak reality of an anonymous psychopath who achieved some sort of gratification from carving up women. 'Jack the Ripper', on the other hand, was always a fictional construct, a character from a continuing gothic melodrama that was already being written before Mary Kelly met her horrific death, and which would appear to have no end.

Chapter 9

A Highly Popular Murder

The ongoing public fascination with Jack the Ripper is all about genre, setting, and the lack of a third act. But the recognisable shape of the character as perceived in modern film, fiction, popular history and tourism was initially created during the media frenzy of 1888. The press understood the Whitechapel killings were a genre piece from the start – *The Times* immediately making a connection with De Quincey's essay on murder and Poe's 'The Murders in the Rue Morgue' (1841), a short story in which two women are brutally murdered by a razor-wielding ape in Paris. Similarly, the *Daily Telegraph*, in an editorial following a report on the inquest of Elizabeth Stride, lamenting a lack of obvious motive upon which the Government might act (their example being Burking in Edinburgh and London and the subsequent Anatomy Act), ended up hinting at werewolves:

> we are thus left to weave the merest figments of fancy, and to form unpleasant visions of roving lunatics distraught with homicidal mania or bloodthirsty lust; of abandoned desperadoes wreaking their thirst for slaughter on forlorn and hopeless women, the wretchedest and most pitiable of their sex, to satisfy some inscrutably foul and crapulous vendetta; or, finally, we may dream of monsters, or ogres, and chimeras in the shape of wretched beings who catch from each awful story the contagion of senseless crime, and, out of a horrid imitativeness, repeat the abominable acts which they have seen described.[1]

Walter Dew even recalled that 'People allowed their imagination to run riot. There was talk of black magic and vampires.'[2]

Portrait of a Serial Killer

Most influentially of all, in an article in the *Pall Mall Gazette* called 'Another Murder – And More to Follow?' which ran on the day of Chapman's murder, W.T. Stead made the connection with Robert Louis Stevenson's *The Strange Case of Dr Jekyll and Mr Hyde* (first published in 1886), giving the reading public a recognisable correlative for the killer:

> There certainly seems to be a tolerably realistic impersonification of Mr Hyde at large in Whitechapel. The Savage of Civilisation whom we are raising by the hundred thousand in our slums is quite as capable of bathing his hands in blood as any Sioux who ever scalped a foe. But we should not be surprised if the murderer in the present case should not turn out to be slum bred. The nature of the outrages and the calling of the victims suggests that we have to look out for a man who is animated by that mania of bloodthirsty cruelty which sometimes springs from the unbridled indulgence of the worst passions. We may have a plebeian Marquis DE SADE at large in Whitechapel. If so, and if he is not promptly apprehended, we shall not have long to wait for another addition to the ghastly catalogue of murder.[3]

Other journalists were glad to pick this up and run with it, and the split personality thesis quickly became the dominate, the *East London Advertiser* reporting in October that:

> Among the theories as to the Whitechapel murders, which start up one day and vanish the next, the one which is most in favour is the Jekyll and Hyde theory, namely, that the murderer is a man living a dual life, one respectable and even religious, and the other lawless and brutal; that he has two sets of chambers, and is probably a married man, and in every way a person whom you would not for a moment suspect.[4]

Some concerned members of the public even wrote in suggesting that the actor Richard Mansfield, then playing Jekyll and Hyde at the Lyceum, might be the murderer, on account of the disturbing authenticity of his performance. Steering well clear of horror stories, Mansfield responded with a special benefit performance of the comedy *Prince Karl* as a goodwill gesture in aid of the Suffragan Bishop of London's Home and Refuge Fund, which was raising money to open a laundry for the employment of reformed prostitutes. The Ripper publicity proved to be a poison chalice, and his *Jekyll and Hyde* closed due to the falling box office.

Fiction soon followed what passed for fact with *The Curse Upon Mitre Square* by John Francis Brewer, a little gothic number published in October 1888 – before the final murder – in which the Whitechapel killer is possessed by an ancient curse that hangs over Mitre Square, where Catherine Eddowes had been found the previous month. The short novel is a story of vengeful revenants and a transgenerational curse that began on the steps of the high altar of the Holy Trinity Church in Aldgate, where a mad monk murdered his sister in 1530. The original killer had committed suicide, but his ghost still appears, pointing at the spot and prognosticating murder: 'Who is there so bold as to say that the one bit of ground that has sustained the weight of countless lifeless bodies, during more than three centuries, is not accursed — that there is no Curse upon Mitre Square?'[5]

Then there were the original 'Jack the Ripper' letters. Written in red ink in lieu of blood, and in a confident and literate hand that was ill-disguised by a few deliberate grammatical lapses, the killer, whose lack of identity separated him from all the rest, was christened by the press. 'Jack' was a good name, recalling the Newgate anti-hero Jack Sheppard and probably inspired by the urban legend of 'Spring-heeled Jack', a Batman-like apparition reportedly sighted across Britain and immortalised in John Thomas Haines' 1840 play *Spring-Heeled Jack, the Terror of London* as a brigand who attacks women after he was betrayed by his lover. Spring-heeled Jack was the subject of several penny serials, one of which had been running in the *Boy's Standard* in 1885. The tone of the letters is reminiscent of the confessional tales of terror that Poe had refined and perfected in the 1840s, like the *doppelgänger* story 'William Wilson' (1839), which Stevenson had tapped into in *Dr Jekyll and Mr Hyde*, and the language of the penny dreadful: 'I am down on whores and I shant quit ripping them till I do get buckled.' This is a long way from the chilling, semi-literate note subsequently sent to George Lusk, along with the human kidney. Perhaps that one was real, the infernal return address indicating the waking nightmare of a disintegrating mind, or maybe it was a medical student having a laugh. Either way, it's not so much a piece of the puzzle as it is part of the legend, the backdrop; another genre device. While Mary Kelly was still going about her business, tragically unaware of the ghastly fate that was to befall her in

November, the penny and popular press had placed the killer firmly in the tradition of the literary gothic, where he has remained ever since.

The setting was similarly sensational. With its proximity to the City, Whitechapel had always been the *other* of bourgeois London: a dark hinterland a few streets over from the financial district, on the edge of the sprawling East End, an alien world of 900,000 lost souls that had come to epitomise sex and violence in the minds of middle-class Victorians. To the social explorers and reformers, Whitechapel was a symbol of urban deprivation, with poor, overcrowded housing, high rents, sweatshops, rising unemployment, crime, epidemic disease and prostitution. But to rich young bucks going back to the days of Tom and Jerry, it had always been something of a playground, a place where one might have a bit of a spree, slumming it in the music halls and the low taverns, and then sampling the girls on offer in the courts and alleys off Whitechapel Road, one of the last of the old London rookeries. This was 'Outcast London', as captivating as it was appalling, its impoverished communities as remote and unknowable as those at the far reaches of the empire, a bleak, infernal place, where coppers travelled in pairs, if they ventured there at all. 'Whitechapel and Spitalfields are always interesting neighbourhoods,' wrote the anonymous author of 'An Autumn Evening in Whitechapel' in the *Daily News*, 'and recent events have made them decidedly more interesting,' continuing:

> They have afforded startling illustrations of the dreadful possibilities of life down in the unfathomable depths of these vast human warrens. At all times one who strolls through this quarter of town, especially by night, must feel that below his ken are the awful deeps of an ocean teeming with life, but enshrouded in impenetrable mystery ... A momentary sense of what human nature may become may here and there flash in upon one as he gazes out upon the dark waters, but it is only when the human monster actually rises for a moment to the surface and disappears again, leaving a victim dead and disembowelled, that one quite realizes that that momentary scene is a dread reality.[6]

Like a favourite subject of the *Illustrated Police News*, the controlling metaphor invites an association between the murders and a shark attack – swift, arbitrary, and catastrophically violent. And onto this dimly lit stage – a space that anticipates the expressionist horror films of the early part of the next century – steps the nameless assassin and his victims. As Peter Ackroyd has written, 'All the anxieties about the city in general then became attached to the East End in particular, as if in some peculiar sense it had become a microcosm of London's own dark life,' while modern urban life felt as suddenly fragmented and incoherent as the killings themselves.[7]

Not only did Whitechapel project class anxiety, there was also racism. The statement of the unemployed labourer, George Hutchinson, marked another significant character development. Hutchinson had come forward after Kelly's murder and told police that he'd seen her on Commercial Street at about 2.00 am on 9 November, and exchanged a few words (she tried to borrow sixpence). 'A man coming in the opposite direction to Kelly tapped her on the shoulder and said something to her,' he said. 'They both burst out laughing.' The couple passed him and 'the man hid down his head with his hat over his eyes. I stooped down and looked him in the face. He looked at me stern. They both went into Dorset Street.' As his 'suspicions were aroused by seeing the man so well-dressed,' Hutchinson decided to follow them, but he lost sight of them in the court, and after hanging around for three quarters of an hour he returned to the Victoria Working Men's Home where he lived. His description of the well-dressed man was unusually precise: 'age about 34 or 35. height 5ft 6 complexion pale, dark eyes and eye lashes slight moustache, curled up each end, and hair dark, very surley [sic] looking dress long dark coat, collar and cuffs trimmed astracan [sic]. And a dark jacket under. Light waistcoat dark trousers dark felt hat turned down in the middle. Button boots and gaiters with white buttons. Wore a very thick gold chain white linen collar. Black tie with horse shoe pin. Respectable appearance walked very sharp. Jewish appearance.' Chief Inspector Frederick Abberline, a leading detective on the case, interrogated Hutchinson and reported that 'I am of the opinion that his statement is true,'[8] although it cannot be overlooked that the description recalls the look and demeanour of the archetypal melodramatic villain: dressed in black, rakish, affluent, swarthy and sinister, twirling a moustache with a bejewelled finger and forcing himself on the innocent heroine.

As for the mystery man looking 'Jewish', anti-Semitism had played a role in the public perception of the event since the beginning, Whitechapel then being an area beset with racial tension between the Irish and the immigrant Jewish community escaping persecution in Eastern Europe, all poor and competing for dwindling resources. After Polly Nicholls was killed, the *Star* was quick to finger a suspect, 'Leather Apron', who: 'by himself is quite an unpleasant character. If, as many of the people suspect, he is the real author of the three murders which, in everybody's judgement, were done by the same person, he is a more ghoulish and devilish brute than can be found in all the pages of shocking fiction. He has ranged Whitechapel for a long time. He exercises over the unfortunates who ply their trade after twelve o'clock at night, a sway that is BASED ON UNIVERSAL TERROR.'[9] The leather apron was a cultural code that readers would immediately recognise as signifying Jewish artisans, and *Lloyd's Weekly Newspaper* had helpfully chipped in that 'His name nobody knows, but all are united in the belief that he is a Jew, or of Jewish parentage, his face being of a marked Hebrew type.'[10] Local Police Sergeant William Thick knew that the man described was a Polish Jew called John Pizer, who worked in Whitechapel as a bootmaker and who Thick suspected of shaking down prostitutes. Pizer knew it too, and kept his head down for fear of being mobbed on the street. He was briefly arrested after Annie Chapman's murder, but his alibi was cast iron on both fatal nights, and he subsequently sued several newspapers for gross libel. But this didn't stop the rumours, following a general line that no Englishman could commit such atrocities. On 2 October, for instance, *The Times* suggested the killer might be enacting an ancient Talmudic ritual, citing a recent case in Vienna:

> A Galician Jew named Ritter was accused in 1884 of having murdered and mutilated a Christian woman in a village near Cracow. The mutilation was like that perpetrated on the body of the woman Chapman, and at the trial numbers of witnesses deposed that among certain fanatical Jews there existed a superstition to the effect that if a Jew became intimate with a Christian woman he would atone for his offence by slaying and mutilating the object of his passion. Sundry passages of the Talmud were quoted which, according to the witnesses, expressly sanctioned this form of atonement. The trial caused an immense sensation, and Ritter, being found guilty, was sentenced to death.[11]

This is the first suggestion of ritualistic killing to enter the narrative, foreshadowing Stephen Knight's famous royal/masonic conspiracy theory, set out in his influential book *Jack the Ripper: The Final Solution* (1976).

Xenophobia was already rife in Whitechapel, and the papers were far from averse to stoking it. Jews were regarded as either religious enthusiasts like Ritter or as socialists and revolutionaries, and this was not helped when

Elizabeth Stride was found dead in a yard opposite the International Working Men's Educational Club, a socialist and predominantly Jewish social club where, that night, the subject of the evening's lecture had been 'The Necessity of Socialism amongst Jews'. It was against this charged backdrop that Sir Charles Warren felt it prudent to remove the graffiti on Goulston Street that implicated local Jews in Stride's murder, a move that infuriated the press and some of his own detectives, but which was praised by London's Chief Rabbi.[12] This act also spawned one of the most enduring modern conspiracy theories connected with the case, the journalist Stephen Knight claiming that 'Juwes' was not a misspelling of 'Jews' but a reference to three apprentice masons named Jubela, Jubelo, and Jubelum, collectively known as the 'Juwes', who, in masonic lore, were hunted down and ritually executed, 'by the breast being torn open and the heart and vitals taken out and thrown over the left shoulder'.[13] Knight wove an elaborate plot in which the five canonical victims were both punished and silenced by physician-in-ordinary to Queen Victoria, the mad freemason Dr William Withey Gull, to cover the birth of an illegitimate child to Prince Albert Victor, Duke of Clarence and Avondale, and second in succession to the throne. This is unlikely, as Gull was over seventy and had recently suffered a stroke. The prince was also implicated in the Cleveland Street Scandal, again without a shred of evidence.

But the masonic theories were a while away yet, although many contemporary commentators were scrutinising the growing body of secondary evidence in exactly the same way as future 'Ripperologists', looking for a deeper meaning within such apparently random, insane and motiveless slaughter. Minute particulars were studied with microscopic intensity, artefacts, fragments of information, anything whereby a pattern might be discerned, a semiology of murder. And hand in hand with the reading of the entrails came the theories and the social agendas. Commissioner Warren, a military man, was not popular, and Tory and Liberal papers alike attacked perceived police incompetence during the investigation. Many reformers had turned against him after 'Bloody Sunday' the previous November, when an Irish Nationalist demonstration was violently dispersed by the Metropolitan Police and the British Army, leading to 400 arrests, and over seventy serious injuries on both sides, including one protester bayonetted. Stead, among many others, was quick to conflate the two events. 'The triumphant success with which the metropolitan police have suppressed all political meetings in Trafalgar-square,' he wrote, 'contrasts strangely with their absolute failure to prevent the most brutal kind of murder in Whitechapel. The Criminal Investigation Department under Mr MONRO was so pre-occupied in tracking out the men suspected of meditating political crimes that the ordinary vulgar assassin has a free field in which to indulge his propensities.'[14] Amateur detectives like the psychiatrist L. Forbes Winslow also invaded the pitch. Everyone loves a good mystery, and the first Sherlock Holmes novel, *A Study in Scarlet*, had been published in *Beeton's Christmas Annual* the previous year. Winslow was convinced the killer was a Canadian called G. Wentworth Smith, a religious enthusiast who was, according to his landlords, Mr and Mrs Callaghan, obsessed with prostitutes, and was allegedly out late the night Martha Tabram was murdered. There were reports of bloodstained linen and recently washed cuffs, and he may well have been the origin of the 'lodger' myth, made famous by Marie Belloc Lowndes in her 1913 novel of the same name. Dates turned out not to match up and the police quickly discounted Smith, but Winslow's desire to insert himself into the investigation made him briefly a suspect.

Locals, meanwhile, formed 'vigilance committees', including Lusk's group, the Toynbee Hall Settlement reformists, and Jewish, socialist and radical workingmen's clubs, all patrolling the streets at night and collecting data on the most notorious red light areas, like Flower and Dean Street. Several vigilance committees, such as the Toynbee Hall group, shared a moral agenda with the social purity organisations already operating in the Borough, who had been instrumental in closing down brothels, thereby forcing hundreds of women back out onto the street.

The status of the victims themselves also led to darker social and erotic interpretations. As Judith Walkowitz writes, 'Because they were committed on female bodies, particularly on the bodies of prostitutes, the mutilations carried especially transgressive associations.'[15] And these were not the threatened innocents that Stead had sought to publicise and protect in the 'Maiden Tribute' articles, but middle-aged women with children, estranged from their husbands, intemperate, and dipping in and out of prostitution to survive. Only Mary Kelly bucked the trend, but her lover's description of her life during the inquest made her sound like a modern Fanny Hill. Images of grotesque female body parts yawned wetly from newspaper illustrations based on police mortuary photographs, as immodest as the 'French' postcards of Holywell Street, symbolic of the kind of vice and physical corruption that had motivated the passing of the Contagious Diseases Acts, repealed only two years previously. This was an era in which the emergent science of Criminology and Lombroso's theory of 'criminal atavism' vied with 'de-moralising' social theorists like Charles Booth, who argued that criminals, including prostitutes, did not act out of deliberate depravity but in response to environmental factors, most notably poverty resulting from low-paid and irregular employment. Arguments therefore abounded in the press regarding the need for social improvement, the *Daily Telegraph* suggesting, for example, that the 'one main lesson' that 'Dark Annie's Spirit' was trying to impart was, 'When it is possible for the poor of London to live and sleep in decency you will not pick up from backyards so many corpses like mine.'[16] *Punch*, meanwhile, captured the essence of the faceless killer and the relationship between poverty and violent crime in an emotive poem entitled the 'Nemesis of Neglect'. The final stanza reads:

> Dank roofs, dark entries, closely-clustered walls,
> Murder-inviting nooks, death-reeking gutters,
> A boding voice from your foul chaos calls,
> When will men heed the warning that it utters?
> There floats a phantom on the slum's foul air,
> Shaping, to eyes which have the gift of seeing,
> Into the Spectre of that loathly lair.
> Face it—for vain is fleeing!
> Red-handed, ruthless, furtive, unerect,
> 'Tis murderous Crime—the Nemesis of Neglect![17]

The poem was accompanied by a powerful illustration by *Alice in Wonderland* artist John Tenniel depicting a shrouded, ape-like phantom with hollow eyes wielding a butcher's knife and drifting through the East End slums, the word 'crime' scrawled across its forehead. The piece bore an epigraph quoting a recent letter to *The Times* from the philanthropist Lord Sydney Godolphin Osborne: 'Just as long as the dwellings of this race continue in their present condition, their whole surroundings a sort of warren of foul alleys garnished with the flaring lamps of the gin-shops, and offering to all sorts of lodgers, for all conceivable wicked purposes, every possible accommodation to further brutalise, we shall have still to go on—affecting astonishment that in such a state of things we have outbreaks, from time to time, of the horrors of the present day.'[18] Engels had called this 'social murder':

> when society places hundreds of proletarians in such a position
> that they inevitably meet a too early and an unnatural death, one
> which is quite as much a death by violence as that by the sword
> or bullet ... and yet permits these conditions to remain, its deed
> is murder just as surely as the deed of the single individual.[19]

But for every letter or article on the 'Nemesis of Neglect', there was another on the wages of sin.

The continuing suspicion that the victims might have been asking for it is apparent in one of the most enduring of the urban myths connected with the case. Richard Jones, who began the original East End Jack the Ripper tour in 1982, relates the following anecdote:

> The number of times that I would be sitting in an East End pub and an elderly lady would come over to me and tell me how her mother had been walking home one night when she had been stopped by Jack the Ripper.
>
> However, on learning that she was a 'good girl' and so not one of the prostitutes, as all his victims were, the ripper allowed her to live and, in several cases, even told her to be careful as she made her way home![20]

The truth was probably much more quotidian. As Donald Rumbelow noted regarding *My Secret Life*, 'Walter's' memoirs 'give us a chance to grasp how easy it was for a man to pick up a woman in any slum area of Victorian London.' Rumbelow did not see 'Walter' as a sadist – and neither do I – but he is, he concludes, 'a coarse brute who stalks around the East End like a tiger looking for prey. Add a sadistic obsession with slashing bellies, and you have an accurate notion of the kind of man the Ripper *could* have been, and probably was.'[21] In short, sex workers have always been, and remain, easy prey for psychopaths.

Nonetheless, such polarised versions of female virtue and female vice also bled into continuing anxiety about venereal disease and lobbying from the medical profession, publicly initiated by doctors of the previous generation, most notably William Acton, for state regulation, social hygiene and prevention, generally targeted at the women rather than their male clients. But there were several ways to clean the streets, and the Jekyll and Hyde theory crossed with conjecture among some police surgeons that the killer possessed 'medical knowledge' (a fact later disputed by Dr Thomas Bond, who profiled the killer), led to the formation of another common archetype, the mad doctor. Burke and Hare were not so long ago, and Wynne Baxter, the coroner who conducted the inquests of Emma Smith, Polly Nichols, Annie Chapman, and Elizabeth Stride, suggested with relation to the removal of body parts during the Chapman inquest that the market for medical specimens might have been a motive, discounting the theory put forward by Winslow that the killer was a 'homicidal maniac'.[22] At the time of Chapman's murder, Winslow had also gone against the 'Leather Apron' theory, suggesting, as had Stead, that, 'I think that the murderer is not of the class of which "Leather Apron" belongs, but is of the upper class of society, and … that the murders have been committed by a lunatic lately discharged from some asylum, or by one who has escaped.'[23] That such madness might be syphilitic was raised by the foreign correspondent Archibald Forbes in a letter to the *Daily News*:

> Suppose his lunacy is the lunacy of revenge, possibly complicated by physical disease … Probably, a dissolute man, he fell a victim to a specific contagion, and so seriously that in the sequel he lost his career. What shape the deterioration may have taken, yet left him with a strong, steady hand, a brain of devilish coolness, and an active step, is not to be defined. Medical men know how varied, how penetrating, how obstinate are its phases … Let it be noted, finally, that his work with the knife proves him to possess some knowledge of anatomy. The medical schools of the hospitals have a large attendance, and perhaps it would be futile to inquire whether any one connected with these beneficent institutions may have a vague memory of an excitable, impressionable student whose career had been arrested and whose hopes had been blighted by such a misadventure as I have referred to, whose reason had given way, and in whose mania was the crave that he might have revenge for the mischief that had destroyed him.[24]

A few years later, in April 1895, a largely unfounded story surfaced in the *Chicago Sunday Times Herald* that the Spiritualist Robert James Lees had had visions of the killer, tracking him to the fashionable home of a well-known but unnamed physician.

Alice in Ripperland

To pursue all the theories of the true identity of the killer is to enter the Ripperologist labyrinth. In his 2005 book, *Jack the Ripper: A Suspect Guide*, Christopher J. Morley lists over 200 suspects, and it's grown since then. As Abberline lamented, 'Theories! We were almost lost in theories, there were so many of them.'[25] The narratology of the murders, however, is less mysterious.

During the 'autumn of terror', the character study of 'Jack the Ripper' came together from the originally protean list of archetypal suspects. The options explored by the press, the police and the armchair detectives included:

- A street gang (the 'Old Nichol Gang' – named for the street, their turf at the top of Brick Lane – were suspected of killing Emma Smith and, probably, Martha Tabram).
- A seaman (whose comings and goings would explain the irregular cycle of murders).
- A woman or a cross-dressing man. ('Jill the Ripper').
- A Whitechapel artisan who was good with a knife, such as a butcher or a shoemaker, or one of the many itinerant local denizens. ('Leather Apron').
- A foreigner, such as a 'Red Indian' from a Wild West show.
- A Jew; An anarchist; A Jewish anarchist.
- A large ape that had escaped from a travelling circus. (Essentially the plot of Poe's 'The Murders in the Rue Morgue').
- A policeman (Sergeant Thick was at one point maliciously accused).
- A religious fanatic.
- A social reformer drawing attention to the cause (sardonically suggested by George Bernard Shaw in a letter to the editor of the *Star* and taken at face value).
- A mad doctor, or a Jekyll and Hyde figure (an upper-class 'erotic maniac') – the latter in reality impossible to apprehend because of the reticence on the part of the police to interfere with posh punters – with a wry sense of humour thrown in care of the 'Dear Boss' letters.

The Metropolitan Police's Whitechapel Murders file remained open until the murder of the prostitute Frances Coles on Friday, 13 February 1891, although the hysteria had reached its peak with the murder of Mary Kelly and the subsequent unsolved murders in the district did not match the Ripper's MO or garner the same level of press. The other cases in the file, which opened with Emma Smith, are Rose Mylett, found strangled on Thursday, 20 December 1888, in Clarke's Yard, off Poplar High Street; Alice McKenzie, whose throat was cut sometime after midnight on Wednesday, 17 July 1889 in Castle Alley; and the unidentified female 'Pinchin Street torso' found under a railway arch on Tuesday, 10 September 1889. McKenzie's wounds bore some resemblance to the earlier killings. Her left carotid artery was severed from left to right and there were also abdominal wounds although not on the scale of the earlier mutilations. It was also believed by police pathologists that the murder weapon was not the same, the blade being shorter. Monro and Bond considered this to be a Ripper murder, although Phillips, Anderson and Abberline did not. In the inquest, Baxter acknowledged both possibilities, suggesting it might be the work of a copycat.[26] The 'autumn of terror' had passed and the furore began to die down. By the following spring most of the vigilante groups had disbanded, and by the end of the century slum clearance programmes had all but demolished the last of the late Victorian rookeries.

The hunt for 'Jack the Ripper', however, is as active now as it was in 1888 – over a century of what Alan Moore described in an appendix to his seminal graphic novel *From Hell* as 'dodgy pseudo-history'.[27] The analogy for 'Ripperology' that Moore chooses is Koch's fractal snowflake, which 'begins with an equilateral triangle, which can be contained within a circle, just as the murders are constrained to Whitechapel and autumn, 1888':

> Next, half-sized triangles are added to the triangle's three sides. Quarter-sized triangles are added to the new shape's twelves sides and so on. Eventually, the snowflake edge becomes so crinkly and complex that its length, theoretically, is INFINITE. Its AREA, however, never exceeds the initial circle. Likewise, each new book provides fresh details, finer crenulations of the subject's edge. Its area, however, can't extend past the initial circle: autumn, 1888. Whitechapel.[28]

At time of writing, the latest significant crenulation arrived in a *Mail on Sunday* 'world exclusive' in September 2014, heralding the launch of *Naming Jack the Ripper: New Crime Scene Evidence, A Stunning Forensic Breakthrough, The Killer Revealed* by Russell Edwards. 'The landmark discovery,' said the leader, 'was made after businessman Russell Edwards, 48, bought the shawl [of Catherine Eddowes] at auction and enlisted the help of Dr Jari Louhelainen, a world-renowned expert in analysing genetic evidence from historical crime scenes.'[29] Based on mitochondrial DNA taken from the shawl that matches the female descendants of Eddowes and, supposedly, her killer, Edwards and Louhelainen present Aaron Kosminski, a mad Polish hairdresser based in Whitechapel, as Britain's favourite serial killer. Kosminski had also been named as a suspect in 1894 by Sir Melville Leslie Macnaghten, then Assistant Commissioner of the Met, but this seems to hark back to the prejudicial 'Leather Apron' theory, with no real evidence to support the claim.

Reviews remain mixed, ranging from very positive – it's a page-turner – to sceptical – it's popular history and science, rather than a well referenced and peer-reviewed piece of research. The provenance of the shawl has also been questioned. Similarly, mitochondrial DNA evidence cited by the crime writer Patricia Cornwell in her 2002 book *Portrait of a Killer: Jack the Ripper Case Closed* allegedly pointed to the English Post-Impressionist Walter Sickert as the killer. And so, as Moore notes, the infuriating fractal continues, travelling back past the *The Diary of Jack the Ripper: The Discovery, The Investigation, The Authentication* edited by Shirley Harrison (1993), the fake memoir of James Maybrick, a Liverpool cotton merchant poisoned by his wife in a sensational murder case in 1889;[30] Stephen Knight's *Jack the Ripper: The Final Solution*; all the way back to Sickert himself, dining out on the original killings by spinning the yarn of Winslow's mysterious lodger; Dr Neill Cream, the 'Lambeth Poisoner', claiming the killings on the gallows in 1892; and Samuel E. Hudson's gothic account, *Leather Apron; or, the Horrors of Whitechapel, London*, published in December 1888. There are far too many to enumerate, although Moore's book offers a concise and considered overview. You've read one of these things, and you've essentially read them all. There are sensational retellings of the original murders, pseudo-science and conjecture wrapped in history; new artefacts are discovered, and there's generally an evangelical level of epistemological certainty. That said, it probably was Kosminski, or someone very much like him: an anonymous local psycho who knew the back alleys and rat runs and could thus strike fast and disappear, his frenzy escalating to two victims in one night and, finally, spending hours playing with a body; socially alienated and otherwise powerless, and forced to stop by external circumstances. Kosminski, who had shown signs of serious mental illness from at least 1885, was committed to Colney Hatch Lunatic Asylum in 1891 for paranoia, obsessive compulsive behaviour, auditory hallucinations, 'self-abuse' and allegedly threatening a female relative with a knife. He was never released, and died in the Leavesden Metropolitan Asylum for Chronic Imbeciles in 1919 at the age of fifty-three.[31] You pay your money and you takes your choice, although, as the historian Julia Laite pointed out in the *Guardian*'s response to the *Mail*, while each 'Ripperologist' claims to have solved the crime, as a body of armchair detectives, amateur historians and tour guides they also have a vested interest in maintaining the mystery.[32]

Equally, there are so many suspects and conspiracy theories surrounding the case, regenerating and expanding all the time, that in the unlikely event that new evidence came to light revealing the identity of the killer it would immediately get lost in the crowd. Nowadays, any historical figure is fair game. In his 1996 book *Jack the Ripper, Light-Hearted Friend*, for example, Richard Wallace claimed that Lewis Carroll was Jack the Ripper using anagrams from Carroll's writing as a confession. As Charles Dodgson's biographer Karoline Leach notes, the theory 'is only an extreme expression of the existing trend. There is no evidence at all – anywhere – to support Wallace's claim. But then there is no evidence at all – anywhere – to support the story of Dodgson's marriage proposal to child-Alice – and that has never stopped anyone believing in it.'[33]

This mystery now constitutes one of the last thriving British industries, with endless books, movies, documentaries, exhibits, and tours perpetuating the story and presenting it as part of our cultural heritage. In narratological terms, it is the 'high concept' simplicity of the story that makes it so versatile, a kind of *Jaws* meets *Oliver Twist*, in which the lack of historical closure offers a multiplicity of possible solutions and interpretations. As Moore notes, there is just Whitechapel in 1888, the five women, and a man with a knife. The literary benchmark is the novel *The Lodger* by Marie Belloc Lowndes (1913), which has been filmed five times, most notably by Hitchcock in 1927 as *The Lodger: A Story of the London Fog* starring Ivor Novello. A century later, the novels are still coming, the most recent being *The Heart Absent* by Carla E. Anderton (2013), Mark R. Vogel's *The Ripper Times* (2016), and *Jack the Ripper: Case Closed* by Gyles Brandreth (2017).

These are mostly gothic stories and whodunits (including the non-fiction). The most interesting follow a symbolic line started during the murders with Osborne's letters to *The Times* and *Punch's* 'Nemesis of Neglect', in which the faceless Ripper comes to personify some sort of malevolent manifestation of the city itself. Although first seen in terms of social depravation, this presence has grown into something much more ancient and terrible in the works of Iain Sinclair (*Lud Heat*, 1975, and *White Chappell, Scarlet Tracings*, 1987), Peter Ackroyd (*Hawksmoor*, 1985, and *Dan Leno and the Limehouse Golem*, 1994), and Moore and Campbell's *From Hell*, supposedly channelled by the mystic geometry of 'The Devil's Architect', Nicholas Hawksmoor.

There was a memorable variant of this concept in *Star Trek*, in an episode entitled 'Wolf in the Fold' (1967), written by Robert Bloch, the author of the original *Psycho*. In this version of the story, the Ripper is a vicious alien consciousness possessing beings across the universe and killing through them. (In a particularly traumatic piece of casting, the latest

Ripper incarnation, 'Administrator Hengist', was portrayed by the actor John Fiedler, whose distinctive voice was also that of Piglet in the Disney *Winnie the Pooh* movies.) This was not Bloch's first Ripper story either, and his *Star Trek* screenplay was based on his short story 'Yours Truly, Jack the Ripper' (first published in the pulp magazine *Weird Tales* in 1943), in which the killer was a gothic immortal who had to sacrifice human beings to prolong his own existence.

That Captain Kirk matched wits with the Ripper really demonstrates the unlimited narrative possibilities. Like the DC and Marvel universes, crossovers are positively *de rigueur* in popular fiction, so, for example, Batman fought the Ripper in the graphic novel *Gotham by Gaslight* by Brian Augustyn and Mike Mignola (1989), while Sherlock Holmes was inevitably cast in the ultimate Victorian team-up. In *A Study in Terror* (1966), the great detective was beautifully played by John Neville, while Christopher Plummer took the lead in *Murder by Decree* (1979), which used Stephen Knight's masonic theory as its frame. The most recent Sherlock Holmes/Ripper bout occurs in the novel *Dust and Shadow: An Account of the Ripper Killings by Dr John H. Watson* by Lyndsay Faye (2009), while Gyles Brandreth's recent novel has Sir Arthur Conan Doyle himself cracking the case. Another period piece frequently plundered in popular culture is Nicholas Meyer's film *Time After Time* (1979), in which H.G. Wells (Malcolm MacDowell) pursues the Ripper (David Warner) across time like Dr Who. More recently, the ITV series *Whitechapel* (2009–13) was a police procedural in which historical crimes were being recreated, starting, obviously, with a Jack the Ripper copycat, while the BBC's *Ripper Street* (2012–16) is set in the East End six months after the original murders.

As far as the actual writing of all this material goes, whether fiction or speculative non-fiction, it's always an interesting case study in the adaptation of the historical record as historical fiction, with chronological events reordered, reinterpreted, and reimagined as the plot of a prose or film narrative. The difference with Ripperology is that the authors insist on pretending that it's all real. If you write historical fiction, it's always important to remember the golden rule that novels are novels and history is history. They are different forms of narrative, and although historians interpret the raw data as much as novelists, imposing order on the facts, such as they are, to create meaning, they're usually less bothered by story arcs, tragedy, and dramatic expediency. The writer of historical fiction tries to keep to the essence of the story, while being mindful always of dramatic pacing and the perils of information dumping. But in Ripperology it all crosses over. Russell Edwards, for example, cites seeing the film version of *From Hell* (2001), a loose adaptation of Moore's graphic novel starring Johnny Depp as a psychic Fred Abberline, as his primary influence in pursuing the case. This is a stylish thriller, but denuded of Moore's elegant and deeper symbolism, it is essentially a retelling of *Murder by Decree*, but without Sherlock Holmes. Nonetheless, the latest collision in the narrative multiverse of 'Jack the Ripper' would no doubt appeal to Moore's sense of irony.

As the identity of the killer continues to expand and develop, it is worth noting, in conclusion, that the reverse is the case with his victims. The killer started the process himself, stealing their lives and physically obliterating their identities through grotesque mutilations that we can still see in the snuff Victorian autopsy images plastered all over the internet. Catherine Eddowes, for example, the penultimate victim whose shawl supposedly contains traces of Kosminski's DNA, is the naked woman without a face, emaciated by poverty and disease, and laid out and stitched together like some obscene mummy. Until it was replaced in 2003, her grave in the City of London Cemetery at Manor Park bore the inscription 'Victim of Jack the Ripper'. (She now has a 'Heritage Trail' plaque.) There's a bitter, gallows irony here, because the level of investigation during the murders means that there are very detailed portraits of the lives of the victims available in a story that is, apparently, not considered to be worth telling. Coroners' reports are scrutinised by generations of Ripperologists looking for clues, and missing the point when it comes to the real narrative of these women's lives, their relationships, and their living conditions. Final movements were reconstructed, regular haunts listed, incomes assessed, and friends and families investigated; while every pathetic little personal possession was itemised and catalogued. Funnily enough, there's no official record of Catherine Eddowes wearing a shawl at the time of her murder – it was supposedly pinched by a policeman called Amos Simpson and passed down through his family, unwashed, until it was loaned to Scotland Yard's Black Museum in 1991, Edwards buying it at auction in 2007.

As the dead recede further into the past it is easy to forget that they were once as we are now, living, feeling, loving, and easier still to turn them into characters in an entertaining fiction. (Perhaps they went to Jack the Ripper heaven, a bit like the one at the end of James Cameron's 1997 film *Titanic*.) But Polly Nichols, Annie Chapman, Elizabeth Stride, Catharine Eddowes, and Mary Jane Kelly are all secondary characters in this long running melodrama, nowhere near as well realised, for example, as Dickens's Nancy in *Oliver Twist*. As with any slasher movie, it is the killer who's the star of the show, equally fictionalised to the extent that, just as many tourists supposedly believe Sherlock Holmes was a real person, Jack the Ripper has become a fantasy. Stead was right, he is Mr Hyde: a gothic icon, in the nineteenth-century pantheon with Count Dracula, Frankenstein, and the Invisible Man. The London Dungeon, for example, presently has two shows devoted to him – the 'Whitechapel Labyrinth' and 'Jack the Ripper' – in a programme that muddles fact with fiction, including Sweeney Todd with historical figures such as Guy Fawkes, with the Ripper bridging the gap: he is at once a historical figure and a fictional character. Who he really was remains of no account in the continuing chronicles of a cultural obsession, in which history is fictionalised and fiction is historicised, until what Dickens called the 'miserable reality' of Victorian poverty, crime and violence becomes a ripping yarn and a hyper-real media event. But then, wasn't it always?

Notes

CHAPTER 1

1 Beames, Thomas, *The Rookeries of London: Past, Present, and Prospective*, 2nd ed, Thomas Bosworth, London, 1852, p.4.

2 Reynolds, G.W.M., *The Mysteries of London*, Vol. I, George Vickers, London, 1848, p.43.

3 Reynolds, pp.1–2.

4 Reynolds, p.3.

5 Colquhoun, Patrick, *A Treatise on the Police of the Metropolis*, C. Dilly, London, 1796, p.vi.

6 Quoted in Low, Donald A., *The Regency Underworld*, Sutton, London, 1999, p.19.

7 Colquhoun, pp.vii–xi.

8 Anon ('A Student of the Inner Temple'), *The Criminal Recorder; Or, Biographical Sketches of Notorious Public Characters*, James Cundee, London, 1804, p.348.

9 Stow, John, *A Survey of London*, William. J. Thoms (ed), Whittaker & Co, London, 1848 (original work published 1598), p.167.

10 De Quincey, Thomas, 'On Murder Considered as One of the Fine Arts', 1854 postscript in *The Collected Writings of Thomas De Quincey*, David Masson (ed), 14 vols, A. & C. Black, Edinburgh, 1889, XIII, p.76.

11 Borrow, George, *Celebrated Trials and Remarkable Cases*, 6 vols, Knight & Lacy, London, 1825, VI, p.90.

12 De Quincey, Works XIII, p.74.

13 Borrow, VI, p.94.

14 De Quincey, Works XIII, p.124.

15 Ackroyd, Peter, *London: The Biography*, Vintage, London, 2001, p.274.

16 James, P.D. & Critchley, T.A., *The Maul and the Pear Tree*, Faber & Faber, London, 2010 (original work published 1971), pp.xviii–xix.

CHAPTER 2

1 Hazlitt, William, 'The Fight', *The New Monthly Magazine*, IV (14), January 1822, p.107.

2 Egan, Pierce, *Boxiana; or Sketches of Ancient and Modern Pugilism*, G. Smeeton, London, 1812, p.341.
3 Hazlitt, p.107.
4 Hazlitt, p.108.
5 East, Edward, *A Treatise of the Pleas of the Crown*, A. Strahan for J. Butterworth, London, 1803, p.270.
6 Anon (ed), *The Annual Register, Or A View of the History and Politics of the Year 1838*, J.G. & F. Rivington, London, 1839, p.41.
7 The name of the organiser or promoter would be substituted here.
8 Egan, 1812, pp.51–2.
9 Hazlitt, pp.109–10.
10 Egan, Pierce, *Recollections of John Thurtell, who was executed at Hertford on Friday, the 9th of January, 1824; For murdering Mr W. Weare*, Knight & Lacey, London, 1824, p.27.
11 Reid, J.C., *Bucks and Bruisers: Pierce Egan and Regency England*, Routledge & Kegan Paul, London, 1971, p.5.
12 Egan, 1812, pp.455–6.
13 Labourers, gypsies, gentlemen, not-quite-gentlemen, army officers on half-pay, prostitutes and beggars, professional gamblers, pickpockets, dissolute rakes and rowdy drunks.
14 Egan, Pierce, *Life in London or The Day and Night Scenes of Jerry Hawthorn, ESQ. and his elegant friend Corinthian Tom in their Rambles and Sprees through the Metropolis*, John Camden Hotten, London, 1896 (original work published 1821), p.46.
15 Egan, 1896, pp.110–11.
16 'Blue Ruin' remains a familiar name for gin to this day. A 'sluicery' was a gin shop, of which there were many in the East End, and the 'Spell' was the saloon at the Covent Garden Theatre (a public space of note in a notoriously bad area), where Tom and Jerry had failed to find women. 'So termed for its attraction,' wrote Egan, referring to the proliferation of prostitutes and courtesans: 'A species of enchantment!'
17 Whetting the whistle. (*See also*: to sluice one's gob.)
18 In funds, flush. This is as opposed to being in 'Bushy Park', meaning broke.
19 A woman, especially a prostitute. Not to be confused with a 'moll buzzer', a buzgloak who only picks the pockets of women.
20 'Very fond.' (Egan's original note.)
21 'Pockets full of money.' (Egan's original note.) A Swell was a well-dressed gentleman.
22 To get, or make, the gate is to be released from prison.
23 Prostitute.
24 A victim of crime, or a prostitute's client, usually both.
25 To buzz, to pick a pocket.

NOTES

26 Gin.
27 To toddle, to walk away, presumably from her patch and/or last unruly customer.
28 A glass of gin.
29 A euphemism for prostitute, rather than a Flash term.
30 Unable to keep a secret – Egan also double-punning on the amount of gin the ladies contain, and the other bodily fluids associated with their profession.
31 Talking and teasing, although 'chaffing' could also mean deceiving, while to 'chafe' was to beat up.
32 Whatever the mixer accompanying the spirit.
33 Queer suck, or queer booze, was bad drink, often poisonous.
34 A beggar, a thief of the lowest order.
35 'Thieves that, just as day begins to break, *sneak* into the passages of houses, if the servant maid has left the door open by accident, and take anything within their reach.' (Egan's original note.)
36 'It is a very common practice in London for women to borrow young children to go out begging with.' (Egan's original note.)
37 'The master and mistress of the house, &c.' (Egan's original note.)
38 Gammon had several meanings: insincerity, knowing the Flash tongue, and being a criminal's accomplice. Egan was probably thinking of all three here.
39 Money. (See also: to flash the screens; sport the rhino; show the needful; post the pony; nap the rent; stump the pewter; tip the brads; be down with the dust; get into Tip Street.)
40 'A cobbler that can *vamp* up old shoes to look like new. A *prime* piece of deception; and those persons who purchase second hand shoes soon find it out on a wet day.' (Egan's original note.)
41 Bender, to drink oneself stupid.
42 A tavern, but not necessarily a sluicery.
43 'Twopence.' (Egan's original note.)
44 Kit is a costermonger who sells fish from a barrow.
45 High, rotten.
46 An Irish expression for strong drink.
47 Egan, 1896, pp.217–19.
48 Egan, 1896, pp.51–2.
49 Egan, 1896, p.321.
50 Egan, 1896, p.317.
51 Egan, 1896, p.320.
52 Egan, 1896, p.324.
53 Thackeray, W.M., *Roundabout Papers*, Smith, Elder & Co, London, 1863, p.124.

CHAPTER 3

1 Dickens, Charles, *Sketches by Boz*, Penguin, London, 1995 (original work published in one volume in 1839), p.7. The pseudonym 'Boz' was a family nickname.

2   Forster, John, *The Life of Charles Dickens*, Cecil Palmer, London, 1928 (original work published 1872), pp.76–7.

3   Bagehot, Walter, *Literary Studies,* 2 vols, Dent, London, 1911, II, p.176.

4   Dickens, 1995, 'A Visit to Newgate', p.136.

5   Dickens, 1995, 'Criminal Courts', p.233.

6   Quoted in Andrews, Malcolm, *Dickensian Laughter*, Oxford University Press, 2013, p.2.

7   Lytton, Edward George Earle Bulwer-Lytton, *Paul Clifford*, George Routledge & Sons, London, 1863 (original work published 1830), p.200. In 1793, Godwin had similarly written, 'The superiority of the rich, being thus unmercifully exercised, must inevitably expose them to reprisals; and the poor man will be induced to regard the state of society as a state of war.'

8   Ainsworth, William Harrison, *Rookwood: A Romance*, George Barrie & Sons, Philadelphia, 1900 (original work published 1834), p.xx.

9   Ainsworth, 1900, p.xxi.

10 Ainsworth, 1900, p.253.

11 Quoted in Ellis, S.M., *William Harrison Ainsworth and His Friends*, 2 vols, John Lane, London, 1911, I, p.254.

12 Anon, 'High Ways and Low Ways; or Ainsworth's Dictionary, with Notes by Turpin', *Fraser's Magazine*, IX, June 1834, p.274.

13 Forster, John, '*Rookwood. A Romance.* By William Harrison Ainsworth, Esq', *Examiner*, Sunday, 18 May 1834, p.308.

14 Ainsworth, 1900, pp.xxii–xxiii.

15 Quoted in Ellis, I, p.366.

16 Forster, John, '*Jack Sheppard. A Romance.* By William Harrison Ainsworth, Esq', *Examiner*, Sunday, 3 November 1839, p.691.

17 Thackeray, W.M., *Catherine: A Story*, Caxton, London, 1920 (original work published 1840), p.24.

18 Anon, '*Jack Sheppard: A Romance* by W. Harrison Ainsworth Esq', *Athenaeum*, Saturday, 26 October 1839, p.803.

19 Anon, *Athenaeum*, p.804.

20 Ainsworth, William Harrison, *Jack Sheppard: A Romance*, George Routledge & Sons, London, 1881 (original work published 1839), p.17.

21 Anon, *Athenaeum*, p.805. As this was effectively an editorial within a literary review, it is possible that the author may have been the critic Charles Wentworth Dilke, then editor of the *Athenaeum*.

22 Forster, 1839, p.691.

23 Quoted in Hollingsworth, Keith, *The Newgate Novel*, Wayne State University Press, Detroit, 1963, pp.145–6.

24 Thackeray, W.M., 'Going to see a man hanged', *Fraser's Magazine*, Vol. 22, No. 128, August 1840, pp.154–5.

25 Thackeray, W.M., *Literary Essays*, Thomas Y. Crowell & Co, New York, 1904, p.233.

26 Thackeray, 1904, p.239.
27 Horne, R.H., *A New Spirit of the Age*, 2 vols, Smith, Elder & Co, London, 1844, I, p.13.
28 Horne, I, p.14.
29 Dickens, Charles, *Oliver Twist*, Penguin, London, 1978 (original work published 1839), p.34.
30 Dickens, 1978, p.36.
31 Dickens, 1978, p.137.
32 Dickens, 1978, pp.36–7.
33 Thackeray, W.M., *Vanity Fair*, Collins, London, 1949 (original work published 1848), p.59.

CHAPTER 4

 1 Quoted in Richardson, Ruth, *Death, Dissection and the Destitute*, Penguin, London, 1988, p.41.
 2 Levin, John, '1751: 25 George 2 c.37: The Murder Act', *The Statutes Project*, 2017, available at: http://statutes.org.uk/site/the-statutes/eighteenth-century/1751-25-geo2-c37-murder-act/ (accessed 19 May 2017).
 3 Southey, Robert, *Poems*, 2 vols, Bristol, 1799, II, 'The Surgeon's Warning', lines 41–8.
 4 Southey, II, lines 161–8.
 5 Cooper, Bransby Blake, *The Life of Sir Astley Cooper*, 2 vols, John W. Parker, London, 1843, I, p.339.
 6 Cooper, I, pp.340–1.
 7 Cooper, I, p.344.
 8 Cooper, I, p.359.
 9 Cooper, I, p.361.
10 Low, p.88.
11 A burial ground attached to a hospital.
12 Bailey conjectures that Harper was probably the keeper of a burial ground.
13 This turns up a lot in the diary, and was obviously a favourite meeting place. Bailey notes that it was 'doubtless, the entrance to some burial-ground' but he was unable to precisely locate it.
14 'Opened' meant a body that had had a post-mortem performed on it, which would have been worth less than an intact corpse. This one was exhumed from the St Bartholomew's Hospital burial ground.
15 Henry Cline was the surgeon at St Thomas' and a teacher of Astley Cooper, becoming President of the Royal College of Surgeons in 1823.
16 Meaning the whole gang gathered intelligence on local funerals, an essential part of the job.
17 Michael Mordecai was a well-known fence.
18 The whole gang.
19 An addition to the St Giles churchyard, Cripplegate.

20 J.C. Carpue was the founder of the Dean Street Anatomical School.

21 Dr Frampton, London Hospital.

22 James Wilson, Great Windmill Street School.

23 Joshua Brookes studied under William Hunter. He was the founder of the Brookesian Museum of Comparative Anatomy.

24 Bailey, James Blake, *The Diary of a Resurrectionist 1811–1812*, S. Sonnenschien & Co, London, 1896, pp.139–41.

25 Dickens, Charles, *Bleak House*, Penguin, London, 2003 (original work published 1853), pp.262–3.

26 Arnold, Catherine, *Necropolis: London and its Dead*, Simon & Schuster, London, 2006, pp.104–105.

27 Quoted in Bailey, p.76.

28 Quoted in Bailey, pp.73–5.

29 South-East History Boards, 'Vaughan – A Resurrectionist', *KSH History Forum*, 2017, available at: http://sussexhistoryforum.co.uk/index. php?topic=12032.0 (accessed 27 May 2017).

30 Select Committee on Anatomy, *Report and Evidence of the Select Committee on Anatomy*, House of Commons, London, 1828, p.2.

31 Bentham, Jeremy: Burns, J.H. & Hart, H.L.A., eds, *A Comment on the Commentaries and A Fragment on Government*, The Athlone Press, London, 1977, p.393.

32 Richardson, pp.108–109.

33 Select Committee on Anatomy, p.14.

34 Select Committee on Anatomy, p.23.

35 Select Committee on Anatomy, pp.15–16.

36 Select Committee on Anatomy, p.18.

37 Select Committee on Anatomy, pp.70–2.

38 Select Committee on Anatomy, p.119.

39 Select Committee on Anatomy, p.20.

40 Select Committee on Anatomy, p.24.

41 Select Committee on Anatomy, p.119.

42 Select Committee on Anatomy, p.19.

43 Select Committee on Anatomy, p.24.

44 Select Committee on Anatomy, p.9.

45 Anon, *The Official Confessions of William Burke, Executed at Edinburgh for Murder, on Wednesday, the 28th of January 1829*, Stillie's Library, Edinburgh, 1829, p.6.

46 Anon, *Confessions made by William Burke. Now under Sentence of Death, in the Calton Jail, for the Horrid Murder of Mrs Campbell, frankly detailing several other atrocious Murders, in which he was concerned along with Hare ... Extracted from the Caledonian Mercury, 5th January, 1829*, Edinburgh, 1829, p.1.

47 Flanders, Judith, *The Invention of Murder*, Harper Press, London, 2011, p.64.

NOTES

48 Quoted in Ward, Jenny, *Crimebusting: Breakthroughs in Forensic Science*, Blandford, London, 1998, p.17.

49 'In and out.'

50 Cobbett, William, *Eleven Lectures on the French and Belgium Revolutions and the English Boroughmongering*, W. Strange, London, 1830, p.13.

CHAPTER 5

1 Forster, 1928, p.381.

2 Checkland, S.G. & E.O.A., *The Poor Law Report of 1834*, Penguin, London, 1974, p.395.

3 Quoted in Rose, Lionel, *The Massacre of Innocents: Infanticide in Britain 1800–1939*, Routledge & Kegan Paul, London, 1986, p.37.

4 See William Stewart, *Jack the Ripper: A New Theory*, Quality Press, London, 1939.

5 Anon, 'The Salford Tragedy', *Spectator*, Saturday, 11 February 1888, p.11.

6 Dickens, 1978, p.71.

7 Mayhew, Henry, *London Labour and the London Poor*, Vol. II, Griffin Bohn & Company, London, 1861, p.142.

8 Dickens, 1978, p.391.

9 Committee on the State of the Police of the Metropolis, *Report from the Committee on the state of the police of the metropolis with minutes of evidence*, William & Charles Clement, London, 1816, p.391.

10 Egan, Pierce, *Grose's Classical Dictionary of the Vulgar Tongue, Revised and Corrected*, printed for the editor, London, 1823, p.278.

11 Committee on the State of the Police, pp.85–6.

12 The mistress of a brothel, or 'Lady Abbess'.

13 Committee on the State of the Police, pp.217.

14 Quoted in Thomas, Donald, *The Victorian Underworld*, John Murray, London, 1998, p.115.

15 Committee on the State of the Police, p.225.

16 Dickens, 1978, p.237.

17 House, Humphry, *The Dickens World*, Oxford University Press, 1979, p.215.

18 Committee on the State of the Police, p.347.

19 Bedford, Peter & Crawford, William, *Report of the Committee Investigating the Causes of the Alarming Increase of Juvenile Delinquency in the Metropolis*, J.F. Dove, London, 1816, p.23.

20 Mayhew, Henry, *London Labour and the London Poor*, Vol. I, G. Woodfall & Son, London, 1851, p.477.

21 Dickens, 1978, p.190.

22 Bedford & Crawford, pp.29–31.

23 Collins, Philip, *Dickens and Crime*, 2nd ed, Macmillan & Co, London, 1964, p.262. Collins is here alluding to several respected studies, for example

L. Lane's 'Dickens' Archetypal Jew' in *PMLA* I.xxiii (1958) and 'Dickens and the Jews' by H. Stone, *Victorian Studies* II (1959), both of which sprang, in part, from the book *The Charles Dickens Originals* by E.W. Pugh (1913). For a more recent example, see *The First Fagin: The True Story of Ikey Solomon* by Judith Sackville-O'Donnell (2002), filmed in 2012.

24 Dickens, 1978, p.105.

25 Details of all these characters and more can be found in the Notebook of Sir John Silvester, Recorder of London (1803–22), held in the British Library.

26 Mayhew, Henry, *London Labour and the London Poor*, Vol. IV, Griffin Bohn & Company, London, 1862, p.274.

27 Solomon's exact date of birth is unknown, but assumed to be somewhere around 1785.

28 Solomon's name was often mistakenly spelt 'Solomons'.

29 Tobias, J.J., *Prince of Fences: The Life and Crimes of Ikey Solomons*, Vallentine, Mitchell, London, 1974, pp.43–9.

30 Smith, Alexander, *A History of the Lives and Robberies of the Most Notorious Highwaymen, Footpads, Shoplifts, and Cheats*, Routledge, London, 1926 (original work published 1714), p.108.

31 Quoted in Tobias, p.67.

32 We know this because he was berthed with chaplain on his way to work at the penal colony, who complained about his cabin mate.

33 Quoted in Tobias, pp.159–64.

34 Quoted in Tobias, p.151.

35 See 'Anti-Semitism and Social Critique in Dickens' *Oliver Twist*' by Susan Meyer, *Victorian Literature and Culture* (2005) 33, pp.239–52; 'Charles Dickens and Eliza Davis' by Israel Solomons, *Miscellanies (Jewish Historical Society of England)* Vol. 1 (1925), pp.iv–vi; '"The Other Woman" – Eliza Davis and Charles Dickens', *Dickens Quarterly*, Vol. 32, No. 1, March 2015, pp.44–7.

36 Ackroyd, Peter, *Dickens*, QPD, London, 1990, p.544.

CHAPTER 6

1 Quoted in Pearsall, Ronald, *The Worm in the Bud*, Penguin, London, 1971, p.333.

2 Egan, 1823, p.14.

3 'In a state of undress.'

4 A cigar bar, a mixture of tobacconist and lounge.

5 Mayhew, IV, p.219.

6 Not to be confused with the Hotel Café Royal in Regent's Street, founded by Daniel Nicholas Thévenon in the mid-1860s.

7 Newman, F. W., *The Cure of the Great Social Evil, With Special Reference to Recent Laws Delusively Called the Contagious Diseases' Acts*, Trübner & Co, London, 1869, p.3.

8   Acton, William, *Prostitution, Considered in Its Moral, Social, and Sanitary Aspects in London and Other Large Cities and Garrison Towns with Proposals for the Control and Prevention of its Attendant Evils*, 2nd ed, John Churchill & Sons, London, 1870 (original work published 1857), p.xi.

9   Quoted in Tristan, Flora, *London Journal, 1840*. Dennis Palmer & Giselle Pincetl, trans, Charles River Books, Charlestown, 1980 (original work – *Promenades dans Londres* – published 1840), p.v.

10 Tristan, pp.7–8.

11 Tristan, p.72.

12 Tait, William, *Magdalenism: An Inquiry into the extent causes and consequences of Prostitution in Edinburgh*, P. Rickard, Edinburgh, 1842, pp.235–6.

13 Stallybrass, Peter, & White, Allon, *The Politics and Poetics of Transgression*, Methuen, London, 1986, p.137.

14 Select Committee of the House of Lords on the Law Relating to the Protection of Young Girls, *Report from the Select Committee of the House of Lords on the Law Relating to the Protection of Young Girls; Together with the Proceedings of the Committee, Minutes of Evidence, and Appendix*, House of Commons, London, 1881, p.69.

15 Tristan, p.73, p.85.

16 Ryan, Michael, *Prostitution in London, with a Comparative View of that of Paris and New York*, H. Bailliere, London, 1839, p.v.

17 Tristan, pp.77–8.

18 Anon, *The New Swell's Night Guide to the Bowers of Venus*, J. Paul, London, c. 1847, p.27.

19 Tristan, pp.72–3.

20 Mayhew, IV, p.211.

21 Acton, William, *The Functions and Disorders of the Reproductive Organs in Childhood, Youth, Adult Age, and Advanced Life: Considered in Their Physiological, Social, and Moral Relations*, 3rd ed, John Churchill & Sons, London, 1862, pp.101–102.

22 Marcus, Steven, *The Other Victorians: A Study of Sexuality and Pornography in Mid-Nineteenth-Century England*, Book Club Association, London, 1970, p.23.

23 Acton, 1870, pp.1–2.

24 Acton, 1870, p.7.

25 Acton, 1870, pp.28–9.

26 Acton, 1870, p.2.

27 Acton, 1870, p.7.

28 Acton, 1870, p.x.

29 Acton, 1870, pp.301–302.

30 Mayhew, I, p.iii.

31 Mayhew, IV, p.232.

32 Mayhew, IV, p.219.

33 Acton, 1870, p.39.

34 For the sake of authenticity, I've retained the author's non-standard format for reported speech.

35 'Walter', *My Secret Life*. Vols III–XI. *The Jack Horntip Collection*, 1888, available at: http://www.horntip.com/html/books_&_MSS/1880s/1888_my_secret_life/vol_03/index.htm (accessed 2 October 2017), III, chapter 3. Although multiply reprinted, this is a very rare collection. I only have the first two volumes of the original series, after which it becomes a ragtag of different editions, for example the Arrow and Wordsworth reprints of the mid-90s. The entire series is now available online as part of the Jack Horntip Collection, so unless citing one of the original two volumes – in which I can give a page reference – I will just give the volume and chapter numbers in reference.

36 Chesney, Kellow, *The Victorian Underworld: A Fascinating Recreation*, Penguin, London, 1991 (original work published 1970), p.387.

37 Select Committee of the House of Lords, p.63.

38 Arnold, Matthew, 'Up to Easter', *The Nineteenth Century; A Monthly Review*, 21, (May 1887), p.629.

39 Quoted in Shannon, Richard, *Gladstone: Heroic minister, 1865–1898*, Allen Lane, London, 1999, 450n.

40 Quoted in Whyte, Frederick, *The Life of W.T. Stead*, 2 vols, Jonathan Cape, London, 1925, I, p.305.

41 Baylen, J.O., 'Swinburne and the Pall Mall Gazette', *Research Studies*, 36, 1968, p.326.

42 Stead, letter to Rev Henry Kendall, 11 April 1871.

43 Stead, W.T., 'The Maiden Tribute of the Modern Babylon', *W.T. Stead Resources Site*, 1885, available at: http://www.attackingthedevil.co.uk/pmg/tribute/mt1.php (accessed 14 September, 2017).

44 Stead, 1885.

45 Irwin, Mary Ann, 'White Slavery as Metaphor: Anatomy of a Moral Panic', *The History Journal*, V, 1996, available at: http://www.walnet.org/csis/papers/irwin-wslavery.html#text83 (accessed 15 September 2017).

46 'Gross indecency' was defined no further. Criminal Law Amendment Act 1885, Section 11: 'Outrages on Decency'.

47 Mr Justice Henry Charles Lopes' Sentence. The Old Bailey (10 November 1885).

48 Harris, Frank, *My Life and Loves*, Grove Press, New York, 1991 (original work published 1927), p.641.

CHAPTER 7

1 Thomas, p.123.

2 As described by the specialist publisher Charles Carrington in *Forbidden Books: Notes and Gossip on Tabooed Literature* (1902).

NOTES

3 Fanin, Colonel, *The Secret Erotic Paintings: Pictures and Descriptions of Classical Erotic Paintings, Bronzes and Statues*, London, 1871, p.22.

4 Quoted in Tang, Isabel, *Pornography: The Secret History of Civilisation*, Channel 4 Books, London, 1999, p.29.

5 Tang, p.29.

6 Foucault, Michel, *The History of Sexuality: An Introduction*, Robert Hurley, trans, Penguin, London, 1990 (original work, *La Volonté de savoir*, published 1976), pp.3–4.

7 Cleland, John, *Fanny Hill, or Memoirs of a Woman of Pleasure*, Peter Wagner, ed, Penguin, London, 1985 (original work published 1748), p.62.

8 The publisher and bookseller Samuel Drybutter took a turn in the pillory in 1757 for reprinting the original text, the charge specifically relating to a scene depicting sodomy. See Gladfelder, Hal, *Fanny Hill in Bombay*, John Hopkins University Press, Baltimore, 2012.

9 Quoted in Cleland, Introduction, p.14.

10 Central Criminal Court, *The Whole Proceedings on The Queen's Commission of the Peace for The City of London*, Tenth Session, George Hebert, London, 1846–47, pp.783–4.

11 Ashbee, Henry Spencer (as 'Pisamus Fraxi'), *Catena Librorum Tacendorum: Being Notes Bio-biblio-Icono-graphical and Critical, on Curious and Uncommon Books*, privately printed, London, 1885, pp.152–4.

12 Ashbee, p.310.

13 Anon, 'The Nuisances in St Clements Danes', *Morning Post*, Saturday, 6 September 1851, p.6.

14 'Verecundia', 'To the Editor of the *Times*', *The Times*, Saturday, 15 September 1849, from the Latin *verecundus*, meaning 'shamefaced', 'bashful', 'shy', or 'modest'.

15 Reynolds, p.319.

16 Mayhew, I, p.243.

17 Mayhew, I, p.240.

18 Quoted in Marcus, p.74.

19 Anon, *The Lustful Turk, or Lascivious Scenes from a Harem*, Read Books, London, 2016 (original work published 1828), p.11.

20 Nead, Lynda, *Victorian Babylon: People, Streets and Images in Nineteenth-Century London*, Yale University Press, New Haven, 2000, p.190.

21 Quoted in Thomas, p.139.

22 Quoted in Kendrick, Walter, *The Secret Museum: Pornography in Modern Culture*, University of California Press, Berkley, 1987, p.116.

23 Quoted in Kendrick, p.117.

24 Quoted in Nead, p.194.

25 Sellon, Edward, *The Ups and Downs of Life*, Wordsworth, London, 1996 (original work published 1867), p.17. In what few brief biographical accounts

of Sellon exist, all of which appear to be based on Henry Spencer Ashbee's remarks in the first volume of his *Index of Forbidden Books* (which is in turn largely based on Sellon's memoir), he is said to have spent ten years in India and risen to the rank of captain. Sheryl Straight, meanwhile, the 'Erotica Bibliophile', cites East India Company records that indicate Sellon left the army much earlier and at a much lower rank having been court-marshalled in 1836 for 'scandalous and infamous behaviour, unbecoming the character of an officer and a gentleman'. The charge was that Sellon had used 'grossly abusive and highly insulting language' towards Lieutenants Herbert William Wood and Henry Colheckat while at the same time threatening Wood with a loaded pistol. He was found guilty on both counts, but acquitted and discharged with a pension as 'the evidence afforded a strong presumption that Ens. Sellon was insane at the time' (qtd. in Straight, 2010). Although Ashbee had Sellon returning to England in 1844 – ten years after joining the military – parish records show him home in 1840, when he was married in Brighton, his first child being born there two years later. As the epithet 'Captain' was also a courtesy granted to dashing males in the period – W.H. Ainsworth was frequently accorded this honorary rank though he'd served in no army – it is possible that a certain amount of exaggeration crept into Sellon's CV over the years and much of his 'autobiography' is clearly fictionalised.

26 Sellon, Edward, *The New Epicurean. The Jack Horntip Collection*, 2017 (original work published 1865), available at: http://www.horntip.com/html/books_&_MSS/1860s/1865_the_new_epicurean/index.htm (accessed 29 September 2017).

27 Ashbee, Henry Spencer, *Index of Forbidden Books*, Sphere, London, 1969, p.416.

28 Quoted in Fryer, Peter, *Forbidden Books of the Victorians*, The Odyssey Press, London, 1969, p.203.

29 Ashbee, 1969, p.417.

30 Ashbee, 1885, p.xlix.

31 Ashbee, 1885, p.l.

32 Hirsch, Charles, 'Notes and Souvenirs from an old Biblioprick', in *Erotic Fantasies: A Study of the Sexual Imagination*, Phyllis & Eberhard Kronhausen (Noel Burch trans), Grove Press, New York, 1969 (original work published in 1934), p.114.

33 Sweet, Matthew, *Inventing the Victorians*, Faber & Faber, London, 2001, p.98.

34 Anon, *Teleny or The Reverse of the Medal*, Wordsworth, London, 1995 (original work published 1893), p.16.

35 Boyd, Jason, '*Teleny* and Wilde's Missing Gay Texts', *The Oscholars: Special Teleny Issue*, 2008, available at: http://www.oscholars.com/Teleny/boyd.htm#_edn2 (accessed 1 October 2017).

36 Anon, *Teleny*, p.105.

NOTES

37 'Walter', I, p.16. The 'dreams of erotic mad-men' is a phrase taken from the Second Preface, written some time later and not appended to the original set.
38 'Walter', I, p.11.
39 Quoted in Marcus, p.79.
40 'Walter', I, p.15.
41 'Walter', I, pp.16–18.
42 William Wordsworth, Preface to the 1800 edition of *Lyrical Ballads*.
43 'Walter', III, chapter 2.
44 'Walter', I, pp.18–19.
45 'Walter', III, chapter 2.
46 Marcus, p.102.
47 'Walter', XI, chapter 11.
48 'Walter', V, chapter 4.
49 Bullough published his findings in the article 'Who wrote *My Secret Life*? An evaluation of possibilities and a tentative suggestion' in *Sexuality and Culture*, March 2000, 4 (1) pp.37–60.
50 Pattinson, John Patrick, 'The Man Who Was Walter', *Victorian Literature and Culture*, 30 (1), 2002, pp.19–40.
51 Marcus, p.81.
52 'A Hundred Books that should be Hidden.'
53 'Further Books which should not be Mentioned.'
54 Quoted in Fryer, p.17.
55 Quoted in Fryer, p.26.
56 Fryer, p.13.
57 In the initially first person 'Henry Jekyll's Full statement of the Case', his point of view becomes more fluid as he writes: 'The powers of Hyde seemed to have grown with the sickliness of Jekyll. And certainly the hate that now divided them was equal on each side. With Jekyll, it was a thing of vital instinct. He had now seen the full deformity of that creature that shared with him some of the phenomena of consciousness ...' (Stevenson, 1979, p.95).

CHAPTER 8

1 De Quincey, Thomas, 'On Murder Considered as One of the Fine Arts', *Blackwood's Edinburgh Magazine*. XXI (122), February 1827, pp.199–200.
2 Originally published anonymously the *New Monthly Magazine* in April 1819.
3 De Quincey, 1827, p.202.
4 Quoted in Williams, Kevin, *Get Me a Murder a Day! A History of Mass Communication in Britain*, Arnold, London, 1998, p.18.
5 *The True and Genuine Account of The Life and Actions of The Late Jonathan Wild, Not made up of fiction and fable, but taken from his own mouth, and collected from papers of his own writing* (1725); and (probably but not definitely assigned), *A Narrative of All the Robberies, Escapes, etc. of*

John Sheppard, and *The History of the remarkable Life of John Sheppard, containing A particular account of his many Robberies and Escapes* (1724). *Moll Flanders* (1722) is also very much a Newgate narrative.

6   Flanders, p.1.

7   Mayhew, I, p.228.

8   Altick, Richard D., *Victorian Studies in Scarlet*, Norton, New York, 1970, p.44.

9   To Miss Clephane, Edinburgh, 23 January 1824, Grierson, Herbert, *Letters of Sir Walter Scott*, 12 vols., Constable, London, 1937, VIII, p.160.

10 Williams, p.18.

11 Curtis, J., *An authentic and faithful history of the mysterious murder of Maria Marten, with a full development of all the extraordinary circumstances which led to the discovery of her body in the Red barn; to which is added the trial of William Corder*, T. Kelly, London, 1828, p.55.

12 Anon, 'The trial of James Greenacre for the murder of Hannah Brown', *Spectator*, Saturday, 15 April 1837, p.9.

13 Dickens, Charles, *Great Expectations,* Collier, New York, 1890 (original work published 1861), pp.138–9.

14 Quoted in Jones, Richard, 'The Murder of Phoebe Hogg by Mary Pearcey', *Jack the Ripper Tour*, 2016, available at: https://www.jack-the-ripper-tour.com/generalnews/murder-of-phoebe-hogg/ (accessed 13 October 2017).

15 Flanders, p.412.

16 Anon, 'The Richmond Murder', *Manchester Guardian*, Sunday, 6 July 1879, p.6.

17 Anon, 'Head found in David Attenborough's garden was murder victim', *The Telegraph*, Tuesday, 5 July 2011, available at: http://www.telegraph.co.uk/news/newstopics/howaboutthat/8618240/Head-found-in-David-Attenboroughs-garden-was-murder-victim.html (accessed 10 October 2017).

18 BNA, 'The *Illustrated Police News*: "The worst newspaper in England"', *The British Newspaper Archive*, 2016, available at: https://blog.britishnewspaperarchive.co.uk/2016/04/19/the-illustrated-police-news-the-worst-newspaper-in-england/ (accessed 13 October 2017).

19 Anon, 'The Worst Newspaper in England. An Interview with the Proprietor of the *Police News*', *Pall Mall Gazette*, Tuesday, 23 November 1886, available at: http://john-adcock.blogspot.co.uk/2009/03/worst-newspaper-in-england.html (accessed 14 October 2017).

20 Anon, 'The Murder in Whitechapel', *Illustrated Police News*, Saturday, 8 September 1888, p.2.

21 Anon, 'The Horrible Murder in Whitechapel', *Morning Advertiser*, Monday, 9 April 1888, p.7.

22 Contemporary reports ascribe this to her dark brown hair, but friends' testimonies at her inquest suggest she was a depressive.

NOTES

23 Quoted in Evans, Stewart P. & Skinner, Keith, *The Ultimate Jack the Ripper Sourcebook*, Robinson, London, 2001, pp.96–7.

24 Anon, 'Another Murder at East End', *The Times*, 10 September 1888, available at: http://www.casebook.org/press_reports/times/18880910.html (accessed 15 October, 2017).

25 Quoted in Sugden, Philip, *The Complete History of Jack the Ripper*, Robinson, London, 2002, p.270.

26 Anderson, Sir Robert, *The Lighter Side of My Official Life*, Hodder & Stoughton, London, 1910, p.138.

27 Sugden, p.264.

28 Dew, Walter, *I Caught Crippen*, Blackie & Son, London, 1938, p.86.

29 Quoted in Sugden, p.310.

30 Dew, p.143.

31 Quoted in Evans, Stewart P. & Skinner, Keith, *The Ultimate Jack the Ripper Sourcebook*, Robinson, London, 2001, p.383.

32 Quoted in Evans & Skinner, p.401.

CHAPTER 9

1 Anon, 'It is time that her Majesty's Government awoke', *Daily Telegraph*, Tuesday, 2 October 1888, p.5.

2 Dew, p.125.

3 Stead, W.T., 'Another Murder – And More to Follow?', *Pall Mall Gazette*. Saturday, 8 September 1888, p.1.

4 Anon, 'Here and There', *East London Advertiser*, Saturday, 13 October 1888, available at: http://www.casebook.org/press_reports/east_london_advertiser/ela881013.html (accessed 21 October 2017).

5 Brewer, John Francis, *The Curse Upon Mitre Square*, J. W. Lovell Company, New York, 1899 (original work published 1888), p.71.

6 Anon, 'An Autumn Evening in Whitechapel', *Daily News*, in *Littell's Living Age* LXIV, October–December 1888, Littell & Co, Boston, p.313.

7 Ackroyd, 2001, p.678.

8 Quoted in Stewart & Evans, pp.419–20.

9 Anon, 'Leather Apron', *Star*, Wednesday, 5 September 1888, p.3.

10 Anon, 'Who is Leather Apron?', *Lloyd's Weekly Newspaper*. Sunday, 9 September 1888, available at: http://www.casebook.org/press_reports/lloyds_weekly_news/18880909.html (accessed 22 October 2017).

11 Anon, 'The Whitechapel Murders', *The Times*, Tuesday, 2 October 1888, available at: http://www.casebook.org/press_reports/times/18881002.html (accessed 22 October, 2017).

12 Walkowitz, Judith R., *City of Dreadful Delight: Narratives of Sexual Danger in Late-Victorian London*, Virago, London, 1992, p.204.

13 Knight, Stephen, *The Brotherhood: The Secret World of the Freemasons*, Panther, London, 1985, p.54.

14 Stead, 1888, p.1. James Monro (1838–1920) was then the Assistant Commissioner (Crime) of the London Metropolitan Police; he became Commissioner a month after this article, when Warren resigned.

15 Walkowitz, p.198.

16 Anon, 'DARK ANNIE'S spirit still walks Whitechapel', *Daily Telegraph*. Saturday, 22 September 1888, p.5.

17 Anon, 'The Nemesis of Neglect', *Punch, or the London Charivari,* Saturday, 29 September 1888, available at: https://www.bl.uk/collection-items/the-nemesis-of-neglect-from-punch (accessed 4 November 2017).

18 S.G.O. (Lord Sydney Godolphin Osborne), 'At Last. To the Editor of the *Times*', *The Times*, Tuesday, 18 September 1888, available at: http://www.casebook.org/press_reports/times/18880918.html (accessed 4 November 2017).

19 Engels, Frederick, *The Condition of the Working Class in England in 1844*, Florence Kelley Wischnewetzky trans, George Allen & Unwin, London, 1892 (original work, *Die Lage der arbeitenden Klasse in England*, published in Germany, 1845), p.96.

20 Jones, Richard, 'Jack the Ripper lived next door', *Jack the Ripper Tour*, 2014, available at: https://www.jack-the-ripper-tour.com/generalnews/jack-the-ripper-lived-next-door/ (accessed 24 October 2017).

21 Rumbelow, Donald, *The Complete Jack the Ripper*, Penguin, London, 1988 (original work published 1975), p.11.

22 Rumbelow, p.58.

23 Winslow, L. Forbes, 'To the Editor of the *Times*', *The Times*, Wednesday, 12 September 1888, available at: http://www.casebook.org/press_reports/times/18880912.html (accessed 24 October 2017).

24 Jones, Archibald, 'To the Editor of the *Daily News*', *Daily News*, Wednesday, 3 October 1888, available at: http://www.casebook.org/press_reports/daily_news/18881003.html (accessed 24 October 2017).

25 Fred Abberline, interviewed in *Cassell's Saturday Journal*, 22 May 1892, quoted in Moore, Alan & Campbell, Eddie, *From Hell*, Eddie Campbell Comics, Paddington, 1999, Chapter Six, p.1.

26 Sugden, pp.497–530.

27 Moore & Campbell, Appendix II, p.16.

28 Moore & Campbell, Appendix II, p.23.

29 Edwards, Russell, 'Jack the Ripper unmasked: How amateur sleuth used DNA breakthrough to identify Britain's most notorious criminal 126 years after string of terrible murders', *Mail on Sunday*, 6 September 2014, available at: http://www.dailymail.co.uk/news/article-2746321/Jack-Ripper-unmasked-How-amateur-sleuth-used-DNA-breakthrough-identify-Britains-notorious-criminal-126-years-string-terrible-murders.html (accessed 15 September, 2014).

NOTES

30 Although the perpetrator of the admittedly excellent forgery, Michael Barrett, confessed in a sworn affidavit dated 5 January 1995, the *Daily Mail* is still claiming the diary is real. See Spillett, Richard (2017), 'Does this diary prove Jack the Ripper was a Liverpool cotton merchant? Victorian journal found 25 years ago is the real deal, say experts,' *Daily Mail*, 7 August. Available at: http://www.dailymail.co.uk/news/article-4767434/Jack-Ripper-s-diaryauthentic-says-expert.html (accessed 25 October 2017).

On a similar tack, in his 2016 book *They All Love Jack: Busting the Ripper*, writer and film-maker Bruce Robinson makes a spirited case for James Maybrick's *brother*, Michael, as the killer, recycling Stephen Knight's thesis that the murders were based around the occult mythology of the Freemasons. Robinson sees an establishment conspiracy, with the main thrust of the police investigation at all senior levels being to conceal the masonic allusions in the crimes because the Victorian state was so reliant on the organisation that it could not survive without it. Under the pseudonym Stephen Adams, Michael Maybrick (1841–1913) was a popular singer and composer best known for his religious ballad *The Holy City*. He also wrote *They All Love Jack*, and became Masonic grand organist in 1889, taking over from Sir Arthur Sullivan. Reviewing for the *Guardian*, P.D. Smith praised Robinson's conviction but noted that his theory 'strains the limits of credibility'. See Smith, P.D. (2015), '*They All Love Jack: Busting the Ripper* by Bruce Robinson review – a huge establishment cover-up', *Guardian*, Saturday, 3 October. Available at: https://www.theguardian.com/books/2015/oct/03/they-all-love-jack-busting-ripper-bruce-robinson-review-withnail-i (accessed 30 March 2018).

31 Lekh, S.K., Langa, A., Begg, P. & Puri, B.K. 'Sketches from the History of Psychiatry. The case of Aaron Kosminski: was he Jack the Ripper?', *Psychiatric Bulletin*, 16 (12), December 1992, pp.786–8.

32 Laite, Julia, 'No "solving" of the Jack the Ripper case will satisfy our obsession', *Guardian*, Tuesday, 9 September 2014, available at: https://www.theguardian.com/commentisfree/2014/sep/09/solving-jack-the-ripper-case-dna (accessed 15 September 2014).

33 Leach, Karoline, 'Lewis Carroll', *Casebook: Jack the Ripper*, 1999, available at: http://www.casebook.org/suspects/carroll.html (accessed 26 October 2017).

Bibliography

Ackroyd, Peter, *Dickens*, QPD, London, 1990.

Ackroyd, Peter, *London: The Biography*, Vintage, London, 2001.

Acton, William, *The Functions and Disorders of the Reproductive Organs in Childhood, Youth, Adult Age, and Advanced Life: Considered in Their Physiological, Social, and Moral Relations,* 3rd ed, John Churchill & Sons, London, 1862.

Acton, William, *Prostitution, Considered in Its Moral, Social, and Sanitary Aspects in London and Other Large Cities and Garrison Towns with Proposals for the Control and Prevention of its Attendant Evils,* 2nd ed, John Churchill & Sons, London, 1870 (original work published 1857.)

Ainsworth, William Harrison, *Rookwood: A Romance,* George Barrie & Sons, Philadelphia, 1900 (original work published 1834).

Ainsworth, William Harrison, *Jack Sheppard: A Romance,* George Routledge & Sons, London, 1881 (original work published 1839).

Altick, Richard D., *Victorian Studies in Scarlet,* Norton, New York, 1970.

Anderson, Sir Robert, *The Lighter Side of My Official Life,* Hodder & Stoughton, London, 1910.

Andrews, Malcolm, *Dickensian Laughter,* Oxford University Press, 2013.

Anon ('A Student of the Inner Temple'), *The Criminal Recorder; Or, Biographical Sketches of Notorious Public Characters,* James Cundee, London, 1804.

Anon (ed), *The Annual Register, Or A View of the History and Politics of the Year 1838,* J.G. & F. Rivington, London, 1839.

Anon, 'Execution of William Burke', *Spectator,* Saturday, 31 January 1829, p.5.

Anon, *Confessions made by William Burke. Now under Sentence of Death, in the Calton Jail, for the Horrid Murder of Mrs Campbell, frankly detailing several other atrocious Murders, in which he was concerned along with Hare ... Extracted from the Caledonian Mercury, 5th January, 1829,* Edinburgh.

Anon, *The Official Confessions of William Burke, Executed at Edinburgh for Murder, on Wednesday, the 28th of January 1829,* Stillie's Library, Edinburgh.

Anon, 'High Ways and Low Ways; or Ainsworth's Dictionary, with Notes by Turpin', *Fraser's Magazine,* IX (June) 1834, pp.724–8.

Anon, 'The trial of James Greenacre for the murder of Hannah Brown', *Spectator*, Saturday, 15 April 1837, p.9.

Anon, '*Jack Sheppard. A Romance.* By William Harrison Ainsworth, Esq', *Athenaeum*, Saturday, 26 October 1839, pp.803–805.

Anon, 'The Nuisances in St Clements Danes', *Morning Post*, Saturday, 6 September 1851, p.6.

Anon, 'The Richmond Murder', *Manchester Guardian*, Sunday, 6 July 1879, p.6.

Anon, 'The Worst Newspaper in England. An Interview with the Proprietor of the *Police News*', *Pall Mall Gazette*, Tuesday, 23 November 1886, available at: http://john-adcock.blogspot.co.uk/2009/03/worst-newspaper-in-england.html (accessed 14 October 2017).

Anon, 'An Autumn Evening in Whitechapel', *Daily News*, in *Littell's Living Age* LXIV, October–December 1888, Littell & Co, Boston, pp.313–15.

Anon, 'Another Murder at East End', *The Times*, 10 September 1888, available at: http://www.casebook.org/press_reports/times/18880910.html (accessed 15 October 2017).

Anon, 'DARK ANNIE'S spirit still walks Whitechapel', *Daily Telegraph*, Saturday, 22 September 1888, p.5.

Anon, 'Here and There', *East London Advertiser*, Saturday, 13 October 1888, available at: http://www.casebook.org/press_reports/east_london_advertiser/ela881013.html (accessed 21 October 2017).

Anon, 'It is time that Her Majesty's Government awoke', *Daily Telegraph*, Tuesday, 2 October 1888, p.5.

Anon, 'Leather Apron', *Star*, Wednesday, 5 September 1888, p.3.

Anon, 'The Horrible Murder in Whitechapel', *Morning Advertiser*, Monday, 9 April 1888, p.7.

Anon, 'The Murder in Whitechapel', *Illustrated Police News*, Saturday, 8 September 1888, p.2.

Anon, 'The Nemesis of Neglect', *Punch, or the London Charivari*, Saturday, 29 September 1888, available at: https://www.bl.uk/collection-items/the-nemesis-of-neglect-from-punch (accessed 4 November 2017).

Anon, 'The Salford Tragedy', *Spectator*, Saturday, 11 February 1888, p.11.

Anon, 'The Whitechapel Murders', *The Times*, Tuesday, 2 October 1888, available at: http://www.casebook.org/press_reports/times/18881002.html (accessed 22 October 2017).

Anon, 'Who is Leather Apron?', *Lloyd's Weekly Newspaper*, Sunday, 9 September 1888, available at: http://www.casebook.org/press_reports/lloyds_weekly_news/18880909.html (accessed 22 October 2017).

Anon, *Teleny or The Reverse of the Medal*, Wordsworth, London, 1995 (original work published 1893).

Anon, 'Head found in David Attenborough's garden was murder victim', *Telegraph*, Tuesday, 5 July 2011, available at: http://www.telegraph.co.uk/news/newstopics/

THE 19TH CENTURY UNDERWORLD

howaboutthat/8618240/Head-found-in-David-Attenboroughs-garden-was-murder-victim.html (accessed 10 October 2017).

Anon, *The Lustful Turk, or Lascivious Scenes from a Harem*, Read Books, London, 2016 (original work published 1828).

South-East History Boards, 'Vaughan – A Resurrectionist', *KSH History Forum*, 2017, available at: http://sussexhistoryforum.co.uk/index.php?topic=12032.0 (accessed 27 May 2017).

Anon, *The New Swell's Night Guide to the Bowers of Venus*, J. Paul, London, c. 1847.

Arnold, Catherine, *Necropolis: London and its Dead*, Simon & Schuster, London, 2006.

Arnold, Matthew, 'Up to Easter', *The Nineteenth Century; A Monthly Review*, 21, (May), 1887, pp.629–43.

Ashbee, Henry Spencer (as 'Pisamus Fraxi'), *Catena Librorum Tacendorum: Being Notes Bio-biblio-Icono-graphical and Critical, on Curious and Uncommon Books*, privately printed, London, 1885.

Ashbee, Henry Spencer, *Index of Forbidden Books*, Sphere, London, 1969.

Bagehot, Walter, *Literary Studies,* 2 vols, Dent, London, 1911.

Bailey, James Blake, *The Diary of a Resurrectionist 1811–1812, to which are added an account of the resurrection men in London & a short history of the passing of the anatomy act*, S. Sonnenschien & Co, London, 1896.

Baylen, J.O., 'Swinburne and the Pall Mall Gazette', *Research Studies*, 36, 1968.

Beames, Thomas, *The Rookeries of London: Past, Present, and Prospective*, 2nd ed, Thomas Bosworth, London, 1852.

Bedford, Peter & Crawford, William, *Report of the Committee Investigating the Causes of the Alarming Increase of Juvenile Delinquency in the Metropolis*, J.F. Dove, London, 1816.

Bentham, Jeremy; Burns, J.H & Hart, H.L.A., eds., *A Comment on the Commentaries and A Fragment on Government*, The Athlone Press, London, 1977.

BNA, 'The *Illustrated Police News*: "The worst newspaper in England."', The British Newspaper Archive, 2016, available at: https://blog.britishnewspaperarchive.co.uk/2016/04/19/the-illustrated-police-news-the-worst-newspaper-in-england/ (accessed 13 October 2017).

Borrow, George, *Celebrated Trials and Remarkable Cases*, 6 vols, Knight & Lacy, London, 1825.

Boyd, Jason, '*Teleny* and Wilde's Missing Gay Texts', *The Oscholars: Special Teleny Issue*, 2008, available at: http://www.oscholars.com/Teleny/boyd.htm#_edn2 (accessed 1 October 2017).

Brewer, John Francis, *The Curse Upon Mitre Square*, J.W. Lovell Company, New York, 1899 (original work published 1888).

Central Criminal Court, *The Whole Proceedings on The Queen's Commission of the Peace for The City of London*, Tenth Session (1846–47), George Hebert, London.

BIBLIOGRAPHY

Checkland, S.G. & E.O.A., *The Poor Law Report of 1834*, Penguin, London, 1974.

Chesney, Kellow, *The Victorian Underworld: A Fascinating Recreation*, Penguin, London, 1991 (original work published 1970).

Cleland, John, *Fanny Hill, or Memoirs of a Woman of Pleasure*, Peter Wagner ed, Penguin, London, 1985 (original work published 1748).

Cobbett, William, *Eleven Lectures on the French and Belgium Revolutions and the English Boroughmongering*, W. Strange, London, 1830.

Collins, Philip, *Dickens and Crime*. 2nd ed, Macmillan & Co, London, 1964.

Colquhoun, Patrick, *A Treatise on the Police of the Metropolis*, C. Dilly, London, 1796.

Committee on the State of the Police of the Metropolis, *Report from the Committee on the state of the police of the metropolis with minutes of evidence*, William & Charles Clement, London, 1816.

Cooper, Bransby Blake, *The Life of Sir Astley Cooper*, 2 vols., John W. Parker, London, 1843.

Curtis, J., *An authentic and faithful history of the mysterious murder of Maria Marten, with a full development of all the extraordinary circumstances which led to the discovery of her body in the Red barn; to which is added the trial of William Corder*, T. Kelly, London, 1828.

De Quincey, Thomas, 'On Murder Considered as One of the Fine Arts', *Blackwood's Edinburgh Magazine*, XXI (122), February 1827, pp.199–213.

De Quincey, Thomas, *The Collected Writings of Thomas De Quincey*, David Masson (ed), 14 vols, A. & C. Black, Edinburgh, 1889.

Dew, Walter, *I Caught Crippen*, Blackie & Son, London, 1938.

Dickens, Charles, *Great Expectations*, Collier, New York, 1890 (original work published 1861).

Dickens, Charles, *Oliver Twist*, Penguin, London, 1978 (original work published 1839).

Dickens, Charles, *Sketches by Boz*, Penguin, London, 1995 (original work published in one volume in 1839).

Dickens, Charles, *Bleak House*, Penguin, London, 2003 (original work published 1853).

East, Edward, *A Treatise of the Pleas of the Crown*, A. Strahan for J. Butterworth, London, 1803.

Edwards, Russell, 'Jack the Ripper unmasked: How amateur sleuth used DNA breakthrough to identify Britain's most notorious criminal 126 years after string of terrible murders', *Mail on Sunday*, 6 September 2014, available at: http://www.dailymail.co.uk/news/article-2746321/Jack-Ripper-unmasked-How-amateur-sleuth-used-DNA-breakthrough-identify-Britains-notorious-criminal-126-years-string-terrible-murders.html (accessed 15 September 2014).

Egan, Pierce, *Boxiana; or Sketches of Ancient and Modern Pugilism*, G. Smeeton, London, 1812.

Egan, Pierce, *Grose's Classical Dictionary of the Vulgar Tongue, Revised and Corrected*, Printed for the Editor, London, 1823.

Egan, Pierce, *Recollections of John Thurtell, who was executed at Hertford on Friday, the 9th of January, 1824; For murdering Mr W. Weare*, Knight & Lacey, London, 1824.

Egan, Pierce, *Life in London or The Day and Night Scenes of Jerry Hawthorn, ESQ. and his elegant friend Corinthian Tom in their Rambles and Sprees through the Metropolis*, John Camden Hotten, London, 1896 (original work published 1821).

Ellis, S.M., *William Harrison Ainsworth and His Friends*, 2 vols, John Lane, London, 1911.

Engels, Frederick, *The Condition of the Working Class in England in 1844*, Florence Kelley Wischnewetzky trans, George Allen & Unwin, London, 1892 (original work, *Die Lage der arbeitenden Klasse in England*, published in Germany, 1845).

Evans, Stewart P. & Skinner, Keith, *The Ultimate Jack the Ripper Sourcebook*, Robinson, London, 2001.

Fanin, Colonel, *The Secret Erotic Paintings: Pictures and Descriptions of Classical Erotic Paintings, Bronzes and Statues*, London, 1871.

Flanders, Judith, *The Invention of Murder*, Harper Press, London, 2011.

Forster, John, '*Rookwood. A Romance.* By William Harrison Ainsworth, Esq', *Examiner*, Sunday, 18 May 1834, p.308.

Forster, John, '*Jack Sheppard. A Romance.* By William Harrison Ainsworth, Esq', *Examiner*, Sunday, 3 November 1839, pp.691–3.

Forster, John, *The Life of Charles Dickens*, Cecil Palmer, London, 1928 (original work published 1872).

Foucault, Michel, *The History of Sexuality: An Introduction*, Robert Hurley, trans, Penguin, London, 1990 (original work, *La Volonté de savoir*, published 1976).

Fryer, Peter, *Forbidden Books of the Victorians*, The Odyssey Press, London, 1969.

Gibson, Ian, *The Erotomaniac: The Secret Life of Henry Spencer Ashbee*, Faber & Faber, London, 2001.

Grierson, Herbert, *Letters of Sir Walter Scott*, 12 vols, Constable, London, 1937.

Harris, Frank, *My Life and Loves*, Grove Press, New York, 1991 (original work published 1927).

Hazlitt, William, 'The Fight', *New Monthly Magazine* IV (14), January 1822, pp.102–12.

Hirsch, Charles, 'Notes and Souvenirs from an old Biblioprick', in *Erotic Fantasies: A Study of the Sexual Imagination*, Phyllis & Eberhard Kronhausen (Noel Burch trans), Grove Press, New York, 1969 (original work published in 1934).

Hollingsworth, Keith, *The Newgate Novel*, Wayne State University Press, Detroit, 1963.

Horne, R.H., *A New Spirit of the Age*, 2 vols, Smith, Elder & Co, London, 1844.

BIBLIOGRAPHY

House, Humphry, *The Dickens World*, Oxford University Press, 1979.

Irwin, Mary Ann, 'White Slavery as Metaphor: Anatomy of a Moral Panic', *The History Journal*, V., 1996, available at: http://www.walnet.org/csis/papers/irwin-wslavery.html#text83 (accessed 15 September 2017).

James, P.D. & Critchley, T.A., *The Maul and the Pear Tree*, Faber & Faber, London, 2010 (original work published 1971).

Jones, Archibald, 'To the Editor of the *Daily News*', *Daily News*, Wednesday, 3 October 1888, available at: http://www.casebook.org/press_reports/daily_news/18881003.html (accessed 24 October 2017).

Jones, Richard, 'Jack the Ripper lived next door', *Jack the Ripper Tour*, 2014, available at: https://www.jack-the-ripper-tour.com/generalnews/jack-the-ripper-lived-next-door/ (accessed 24 October 2017).

Jones, Richard, 'The Murder of Phoebe Hogg by Mary Pearcey', *Jack the Ripper Tour*, 2016, available at: https://www.jack-the-ripper-tour.com/generalnews/murder-of-phoebe-hogg/ (accessed 13 October 2017).

Kendrick, Walter, *The Secret Museum: Pornography in Modern Culture*, University of California Press, Berkley, 1987.

Knight, Stephen, *The Brotherhood: The Secret World of the Freemasons*, Panther, London, 1985.

Laite, Julia, 'No "solving" of the Jack the Ripper case will satisfy our obsession', *Guardian*, Tuesday, 9 September 2014, available at: https://www.theguardian.com/commentisfree/2014/sep/09/solving-jack-the-ripper-case-dna (accessed 15 September 2014).

Leach, Karoline, 'Lewis Carroll', *Casebook: Jack the Ripper*, 1999, available at: http://www.casebook.org/suspects/carroll.html (accessed 26 October 2017).

Lekh, S.K., Langa, A., Begg, P. & Puri, B.K., 'Sketches from the History of Psychiatry. The case of Aaron Kosminski: was he Jack the Ripper?', *Psychiatric Bulletin*, 16 (12), December 1992, pp.786–8.

Levin, John, '1751: 25 George 2 c.37: The Murder Act', *The Statutes Project*, 2017, available at: http://statutes.org.uk/site/the-statutes/eighteenth-century/1751-25-geo2-c37-murder-act/ (accessed 19 May 2017).

Low, Donald A., *The Regency Underworld*, Sutton, London, 1999.

Lytton, Edward George Earle Bulwer-Lytton, *Paul Clifford*, George Routledge & Sons, London, 1863 (original work published 1830).

Marcus, Steven, *The Other Victorians: A Study of Sexuality and Pornography in Mid-Nineteenth-Century England*, Book Club Association, London, 1970.

Mayhew, Henry, *London Labour and the London Poor; a cyclopaedia of the condition and earnings of those that will work, those that cannot work, and those that will not work*, Vol. I., G. Woodfall & Son, London, 1851.

Mayhew, Henry, *London Labour and the London Poor*, Vol. IV, Griffin Bohn & Company, London, 1862.

Moore, Alan & Campbell, Eddie, *From Hell*, Eddie Campbell Comics, Paddington, 1999 (collected edition; original work serialised 1989–96).

Nead, Lynda, *Victorian Babylon: People, Streets and Images in Nineteenth-Century London*, Yale University Press, New Haven, 2000.

Newman, F. W., *The Cure of the Great Social Evil, With Special Reference to Recent Laws Delusively Called the Contagious Diseases' Acts*, Trübner & Co, London, 1869.

Pearsall, Ronald, *The Worm in the Bud*, Penguin, London, 1971.

Reid, J.C., *Bucks and Bruisers: Pierce Egan and Regency England*, Routledge & Kegan Paul, London, 1971.

Reynolds, G.W.M., *The Mysteries of London*, Vol. I., George Vickers, London, 1844.

Richardson, Ruth, *Death, Dissection and the Destitute*, Penguin, London, 1988.

Robinson, Bruce, *They All Love Jack: Busting the Ripper*, Fourth Estate, London, 2016.

Rose, Lionel, *The Massacre of Innocents: Infanticide in Britain 1800–1939*, Routledge & Kegan Paul, London, 1986.

Rumbelow, Donald, *The Complete Jack the Ripper*, Penguin, London, 1988 (original work published 1975).

Ryan, Michael, *Prostitution in London, with a Comparative View of that of Paris and New York*, H. Bailliere, London, 1839.

Select Committee of the House of Lords on the Law Relating to the Protection of Young Girls, *Report from the Select Committee of the House of Lords on the Law Relating to the Protection of Young Girls; Together with the Proceedings of the Committee, Minutes of Evidence, and Appendix*, House of Commons, London, 1881.

Select Committee on Anatomy, *Report and Evidence of the Select Committee on Anatomy*, House of Commons, London, 1828.

Sellon, Edward, *The Ups and Downs of Life*, Wordsworth, London, 1996 (original work published 1867).

Sellon, Edward, *The New Epicurean. The Jack Horntip Collection*, 2017, available at: http://www.horntip.com/html/books_&_MSS/1860s/1865_the_new_epicurean/index.htm (accessed 29 September 2017) (original work published 1865).

'SGO' (Lord Sydney Godolphin Osborne), 'At Last. To the Editor of *The Times*', *The Times*, Tuesday, 18 September 1888, available at: http://www.casebook.org/press_reports/times/18880918.html (accessed 4 November 2017).

Shannon, Richard, *Gladstone: Heroic minister, 1865–1898*, Allen Lane, London, 1999.

Smith, Alexander, *A History of the Lives and Robberies of the Most Notorious Highwaymen, Footpads, Shoplifts, and Cheats*, Routledge, London, 1926 (original work published 1714).

BIBLIOGRAPHY

Smith, P.D., 'They All Love Jack: Busting the Ripper by Bruce Robinson review – a huge establishment cover-up', *Guardian*, Saturday, 3 October 2015, available at: https://www.theguardian.com/books/2015/oct/03/they-all-love-jack-busting-ripper-bruce-robinson-review-withnail-i (accessed 30 March 2018).

Southey, Robert, *Poems*, 2 vols, Bristol, 1799.

Stallybrass, Peter & White, Allon, *The Politics and Poetics of Transgression*, Methuen, London, 1986.

Stead, W.T., 'The Maiden Tribute of the Modern Babylon', 1885, *W.T. Stead Resources Site*, available at: http://www.attackingthedevil.co.uk/pmg/tribute/mt1.php (accessed 14 September 2017).

Stead, W.T., 'Another Murder – And More to Follow?', *Pall Mall Gazette*, Saturday, 8 September 1888, p.1.

Stevenson, Robert Louis, *The Strange Case of Dr Jekyll and Mr Hyde*, Penguin, London, 1979 (original work published 1886).

Stow, John, *A Survey of London*, William. J. Thoms, ed, Whittaker & Co, London, 1848 (original work published 1598).

Straight, Sheryl, 'Edward Sellon: A Family History', *The Erotica Bibliophile*, 2010, available at: https://www.eroticabibliophile.com/author_sellon_about.php (accessed 28 September 2017).

Sugden, Philip, *The Complete History of Jack the Ripper*, Robinson, London, 2002.

Sweet, Matthew, *Inventing the Victorians*, Faber & Faber, London, 2001.

Tait, William, *Magdalenism: An Inquiry into the extent causes and consequences of Prostitution in Edinburgh*, P. Rickard, Edinburgh, 1842.

Tang, Isabel, *Pornography: The Secret History of Civilisation*, Channel 4 Books, London, 1999.

Thackeray, W.M., 'Going to see a man hanged', *Fraser's Magazine*, Vol. 22, No 128, August 1840, pp.150–8.

Thackeray, W.M., *Roundabout Papers*, Smith, Elder & Co, London, 1863.

Thackeray, W.M., *Literary Essays*, Thomas Y. Crowell & Co, New York, 1904.

Thackeray, W.M., *Catherine: A Story*, Caxton, London, 1920 (original work published 1840).

Thackeray, W.M., *Vanity Fair*, Collins, London, 1949 (original work published 1848).

Thomas, Donald, *The Victorian Underworld*, John Murray, London, 1998.

Tobias, J.J., *Prince of Fences: The Life and Crimes of Ikey Solomons*, Vallentine, Mitchell, London, 1974.

Tristan, Flora, *London Journal, 1840*, Dennis Palmer & Giselle Pincetl, trans, Charles River Books, Charlestown, 1980 (original work – *Promenades dans Londres* – published 1840.)

'Verecundia', 'To the Editor of *The Times*', *The Times*, Saturday, 15 September 1849.

Walkowitz, Judith R., *City of Dreadful Delight: Narratives of Sexual Danger in Late-Victorian London*, Virago, London, 1992.

'Walter', *My Secret Life*, Vols I–II, printed privately for subscribers, Amsterdam, 1888.

'Walter', *My Secret Life*, Vols III–XI, 1888, *The Jack Horntip Collection*, available at: http://www.horntip.com/html/books_&_MSS/1880s/1888_my_secret_life/vol_03/index.htm (accessed 2 October 2017).

Ward, Jenny, *Crimebusting: Breakthroughs in Forensic Science*, Blandford, London, 1998.

Whyte, Frederick, *The Life of W.T. Stead*, 2 vols, Jonathan Cape, London, 1925.

Williams, Kevin, *Get Me a Murder a Day! A History of Mass Communication in Britain*, Arnold, London, 1998.

Winslow, L. Forbes, 'To the Editor of *The Times*', *The Times*, Wednesday, 12 September 1888, available at: http://www.casebook.org/press_reports/times/18880912.html (accessed 24 October 2017).

Index

INDEX

INDEX

INDEX